NATURAL
MEDICINE
for
CHILDREN

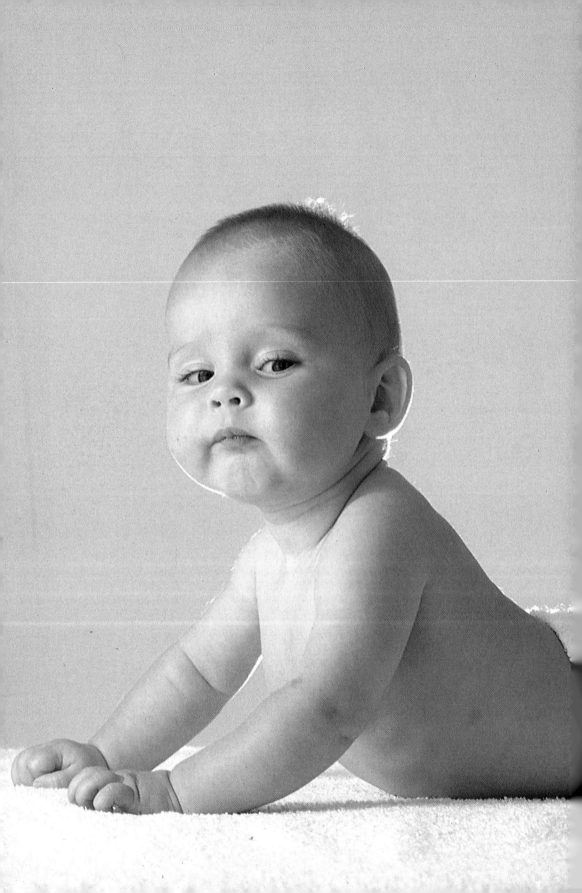

NATURAL MEDICINE
for
CHILDREN

JULIAN SCOTT Ph.D.

**Drug-free health care for children from
birth to age twelve.
A practical, comprehensive guide
to herbs, homeopathy, massage and other
alternative remedies.**

William Morrow & Company, Inc.

A GAIA ORIGINAL

Project editor	Steve Parker
Project designer	Ellen Moorcraft
Illustration	Sheilagh Noble
Homoeopathy consultant	Siam Chow Kwan Yun
Production	Susan Walby Lesley Gilbert
Direction	Joss Pearson Patrick Nugent

Typesetting by Marlin Graphics Ltd, Sidcup, Kent
Reproduction by Technographic Design and Print
Ltd, Saxmundham, Suffolk
Printed and bound in Spain by
Mateu Cromo Artes Gráficas, S.A. Madrid

First U.S. Edition
Published in hardcover by William Morrow and
Company, Inc., 1990

Library of Congress Catalog Card Number: 89-63649
ISBN 0-688-09436-8

10 9 8 7 6 5 4 3 2 1.

Note: Natural medicines are generally safe and effective. But, despite every effort to offer expert and well-tested advice, it is not possible for this book to predict an individual person's reactions to a particular treatment. *Always* refer to the cautions given in Part II under specific herbs, products and therapies before using any of the treatments recommended. If in doubt, consult a qualified doctor, physician or practitioner of natural medicine. Neither the publisher nor the author accept responsibility for any effects that may arise from giving or taking any type of natural medicine, or any other related remedy or form of treatment, included in this book.

This book is dedicated to
Oliver, Nicholas and Lucilla
and to
Merlin and Milano

Julian Scott MA, PhD is an experienced practitioner of natural medicine, specializing in herbal remedies and acupuncture, particularly as applied to the treatment of children. He has studied at the Institute of Traditional Chinese Medicine in Nanjing, and is also interested in the links between diet and disease. He established the Foundation for Traditional Medicine Children's Clinic, where he regularly treats children (and their parents, as necessary).

Specialist consultants
Dr John Latham MA (Oxon) BM, BCh, DObst, RCOG is a family physician in southern England. He has developed an interest in the links between treatments by orthodox medical drugs and by natural medicines.
Susan Scott is a qualified teacher of the Alexander technique, and is experienced in helping children. She has studied the effects of posture, activity and exercise on the health and development of the growing child.
Dr Richard Donze DO is a general practice physician in Philadelphia, USA. He has lectured and written widely about health promotion through lifestyle changes and good nutrition. An advocate of the holistic approach, he is a regular contributor to medical journals, and appears on radio and television.
John Ramsell is Curator of the Bach Centre, near Oxford, England.

CONTENTS

Heel on lower abdomen massage

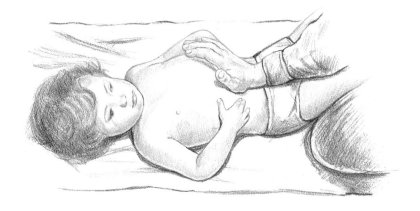

Jingming massage

INTRODUCTION

As parents, we naturally want the best for our children. In particular, we want them to enjoy good health and to recover rapidly when they are ill. This book shows how we can help our children towards better health. It is also intended for the many parents who would like to play an active part in treatment and recuperation when their children become ill.

During the past few decades there has been a growing belief, partly fostered by the orthodox medical establishment, that only a professional, medically-qualified physician can treat illness. This extends even to minor, almost trivial ailments, so that some people feel unable to help themselves – or their children – at all. This book bridges that gap. It gives you, as a parent, the opportunity to take action, by using natural remedies for home treatment when your child has a health problem. It also shows how you can lay the foundations of good health and a strong constitution for your child, by paying attention to diet, exercise and other aspects of daily life.

Natural medicines

Many people feel that giving strong, chemically-made drugs to babies and young children is unnatural. Babies respond so quickly to every passing influence, both their own, and those around them, that a gentle approach seems to be needed. This is where natural medicines can help.

Natural remedies such as herbs have been in use for thousands of years. They have been proven to be safe and effective cures. Even more importantly, they work on the energy level (page 14). They direct your child's enormous energy and vitality towards healing, so that he or she overcomes the problem and, once again, the natural ebullience and enthusiasm of youth can shine through.

This book is not intended as a replacement for orthodox medicine. Rather, it aims to give you a wider understanding of your child, and why he or she becomes ill. It shows that in addition to our modern Western-style medicines there are other, and in many cases better, treatments for various health problems. In most cases these treatments can be combined with orthodox medicine, to produce an even more favourable outcome. A delightful Chinese saying embodies this principle: "Walking on two legs is better than walking on one."

CHINESE MEDICINE

Throughout this book, there are references to various features and sayings from Chinese medicine. This bias towards the East is inevitable for an author trained in Chinese medicine. However, the sayings and attitudes incorporated into the book are not exclusively Chinese, or even Eastern, in their applications. They are Universal Truths. They have their origins in the problems that all peoples of the world face from day to day. And they have their foundations firmly planted in the love that we all feel towards our children.

The causes of illness

One of the basic tenets of Chinese medicine is that there is always a cause for illness. An illness is not seen as something which mysteriously strikes from the outside, from nowhere and for no reason. It is regarded as having clearly identifiable origins. Typically, the Chinese approach is to view the origins in terms of imbalance in the body, and in the body's response to an external stress, such as a cold wind or an emotional upset. Sometimes the external stress may be so violent that even a strong, healthy body is knocked off balance. At other times there is already an inner imbalance, so that even the slightest external stress can bring on illness.

For this reason, in the first part of the book and in the descriptions of individual illnesses, the causes of disease are discussed. There are descriptions of the ways that external events can combine with the body's reactions to them, resulting in ill health. This fuller understanding of illness brings practical results, in the form of effective treatments and the possibility of preventing recurrence.

Disease patterns When a child becomes ill, there are usually a large number of small symptoms associated with the main condition. In orthodox Western medicine the overall picture is described in terms of "syndromes". In natural medicine we refer to "patterns" of disease (page 21).

These patterns often cut across orthodox medicine's syndromes, seeming at times even to contradict them. Nevertheless, the patterns are frequently seen in practice. The reason for this difference is that orthodox medicine concentrates mainly on the physical body and its symptoms; while natural medicine also takes into account the body's energy and emotions, and symptoms on the mental and spiritual levels. These are believed to be just as important as the physical body. Such a wider, holistic view explains many otherwise puzzling symptoms.

How to use this book

Identifying an illness If you are the worried parent of a sick child, and especially when using the book for the first few times, consult the Contents list or Index. Turn straight to the pages in Part III, Treating Childhood Ailments, where the condition that you suspect is described.

Check that your child's symptoms and pattern of illness correspond with the description in the text. This should confirm your diagnosis. If something seems amiss, consult a qualified practitioner for advice.

Choosing a therapy Always read the general remarks in the text and the various treatments advised. For each illness, there are details of three, four or even five different therapies. These alternatives are described because some parents feel more comfortable with one particular therapy. They seem to have an immediate and instinctive knowledge of how to use it. Also, some children respond well to one therapy but not to another. In the first instance, simply start with the therapy that attracts you most. Or you may wish to try the remedies in the order given, or according to the contents of your medicine cupboard. As you gain experience, you may find that your child reacts more favorably to one therapy.

Prescribing When you feel ready to prescribe a remedy, turn to the pages advised in Part II, The Natural Therapies. Here you will find general information on that particular type of treatment. Read this carefully in conjunction with the specific information given for the illness concerned, such as the dosage and how often the remedy may be administered. Always watch your child's reactions to the treatment, and check for and take special note of any cautions or contraindications given for a particular remedy.

Finding out more about remedies You may wish to know the details of an individual remedy, such as the effects of a particular herb, the suitability of a specific tissue salt, or whether a certain massage might help. Consult the Index and turn directly to the relevant pages in Part II, The Natural Therapies. Or scan through the Materia Medica listings to locate a remedy.

Background knowledge Part I, Developing Health, contains a general introduction to the subject of natural medicine, with particular reference to common children's problems. After reading this, you may have further ideas on how to prevent your child from becoming ill, and a clearer understanding of what to do should a problem recur.

Using and changing therapies You should usually give only one therapy at a time – but you may always add massage to whatever therapy you have chosen. Select either homoeopathy, or tissue salts, or herbs, or Bach remedies. For example, when treating a high fever, select either homoeopathic Belladonna or Catmint

(*Nepeta cataria*) herb. Do not give both at the same time. If you find that the remedy you have chosen is not working, you may change to another. You can also change the therapy at different stages in the illness. For example, if you have successfully used homoeopathy during the acute stage of fever, you may use herbs as a tonic to speed recovery.

The massages may be combined with any of the other therapies. Indeed, it often happens that adding massage helps the other remedy to work.

Taking it further

A book such as this cannot describe every illness, all fields of natural medicine, or every one of the many thousands of useful herbs, homoeopathic remedies and massage strokes. If you develop a deeper interest in a specific aspect of home treatment, there are more specialized books available, as described on page 186.

SERIOUS ILLNESS

For many of the ailments described in this book, there is information on what to do should your child's condition become more serious. Parents, above all, know that risks should never be taken with the health and well-being of a baby or child.

If you ever feel worried, for whatever reason, listen to your parental instincts. Consult a practitioner of orthodox or natural medicine as quickly as possible. It is far better to call in professional help early, and catch a potentially serious problem while it is still treatable.

Part 1

DEVELOPING HEALTH

Natural medicine is based upon vitality and life. The descriptions in this book, of health problems and the natural remedies to cure them, are in terms of what vital living beings feel and experience. They involve the subjective sensations of illness and recovery – from discontent to discomfort and pain, and the return through relief and hope to strength, happiness and enhanced health.

Disease is a time of transition, during which all available energy is directed towards overcoming the illness and restoring balance and harmony in the body. This progress through disease towards health is entirely due to the "life-force", and it is the function of natural remedies to direct and enhance this force. Also, as parents we can help our children to focus and direct the life-force, and so speed the transition through imbalance and illness to better health.

Life-force and energy

The idea of vitality or "life-force" has little place in orthodox Western medicine, but it is the key to understanding natural medicine. In different cultures around the world the life-force has various names. In this book we use the word "energy".

Energy is not a material substance, like water or air, but it is equally indispensable for life and its presence distinguishes living things from inanimate matter. Energy is the vitality that stirs in children and makes them want to bounce out of bed at six o'clock in the morning – while lack of it keeps many parents in bed well past this hour.

Energy is the body's controlling force. When a disease occurs, it appears first as a disturbance in the natural flow of energy long before it manifests as physical symptoms. This is why we may feel "out of sorts" for some time before actually being ill. Likewise, the first step in a cure by natural medicine is to restore the flow of energy. When this happens, we start to feel better from within, in our mind and emotions, long before the physical body begins to recover.

In humans, energy vitalizes the physical body, and is the link between body, soul and mind. It permeates the whole being and even extends outside, surrounding the individual with an aura. In Chinese medicine, it is believed that energy originates in the centre of the body and flows into the arms and legs, along pathways close to the nerves. In China, these pathways have been known for thousands of years, and students of traditional Chinese medicine learn about this important aspect of human anatomy and how it functions.

The first part of this book explains how parents can help to lay the foundations of a healthy life for their child, by providing energy and emotional support and by establishing good habits in diet, exercise and activity, and rest, relaxation and sleep. The advice is intended for parents of any age, young or old, and for single-parent families as well as two-parent ones. Whatever their situation, all children have a deep need for the attention, time and love of another. A parent figure is a vital part of any child's life and upbringing.

THE CONCEPT OF ENERGY

The concept of the life-force or "energy" (page 12) is central to understanding how your child stays well for most of the time, but occasionally becomes ill, and can then be cured by natural medicines. Energy may also be passed from one human being to another – and especially between parent and child, with their strong emotional and spiritual bonds.

Energy flow between parent and child

The creation of a new life, when a baby is conceived and then born into the world, is an extraordinary event – the closest most of us get to a miracle. Apart from the amazing physical developments that take place in the womb, there is the mystery of the gift of life itself.

Conception During the act of making love, conditions are set for the creation of a new life. The great passions so aroused seem to create a vortex on the emotional plane, which is so powerful that it draws a new soul into the world. Mystics from many cultures have reported seeing or feeling this vortex, and some of the great painters have attempted to portray it.

The vortex is also joined to the partners and binds them together. If there is no conception, it gradually disperses over the following weeks. But if a new life is

The energy channels originate in the centre of the body, from the heart, lungs and digestive system. They radiate outwards along the limbs and up into the head. This representative diagram shows how the lung channels branch up into the centre of the neck and face, and along the front of the upper arms and forearms, down into the thumbs. The channels are of great use in diagnosis and treatment.

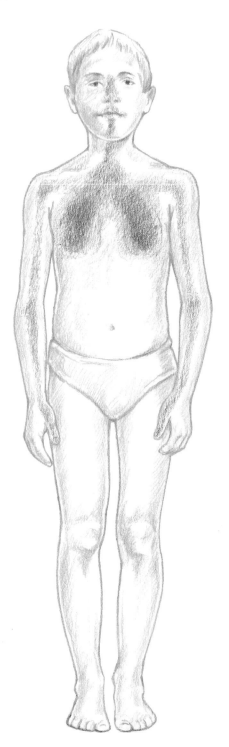

conceived, the partners are bound together as parents for as long as the new child needs their help.

Parental energy supply Throughout pregnancy, birth and the early years, a child needs a constant supply of energy – which the parents provide. Energy is needed for growth and development, and is just as important as food. Although unseen, the energy flows between parents and child in an unbreakable link. Many parents have experienced this flow directly and describe it as an expanding sensation of warmth within the body. With a continued supply of energy, the young child thrives.

In a very young child, the energy channels have not yet fully developed. But with a continued supply of energy, the child thrives and overcomes the various childhood diseases.

As the child becomes older, energy channels develop within his or her own body, and it is no longer necessary for parents to supply this energy. But the emotional link remains, perhaps until puberty or the move away from home. It may be called upon during times of illness and other crises. Some parents detect this "calling" from their child, perhaps as a sense of nausea or a weight in the stomach, when he or she is passing through a crisis such as an accident or illness.

Drawing on the parents

During pregnancy, the expectant mother's energy is diverted towards her developing baby, and is not so readily available for her own use. As a result, many mothers-to-be find that they want to be quiet and calm. They may not have the same desire as before for physical activity or artistic creativity. Some prefer to spend time establishing a good home. This natural instinct allows the baby to receive all the energy he or she needs, with some left over to build up the mother's reserves for the months after birth.

After the birth, a baby has direct access to the mother's (and father's) energy, which he or she needs in order to grow and flourish. As a consequence, many new mothers find they have less energy to do the things they wish. They may even feel there is not enough energy to hold down a job, when the baby demands so much. In other cases, mothers feel they can cope and continue to work outside the home.

Energy problems

Energy blocks In health, energy flows vigorously throughout the body, enabling it to function well. However, the energy channels may be disrupted by illness or by conditions such as over-excitement, so that energy cannot flow to the areas where it is needed. For example, in an over-excited child the energy may become trapped in the stomach so that it cannot flow down to the intestines (page 135). The child then feels a heaviness and pain in the stomach from energy accumulation, and may suffer from diarrhea (page 151) because there is insufficient energy in the intestines to complete digestion.

Energy in disease During illness, a child needs extra energy for the battle back to health. Naturally, we feel worry and concern when a family member is ill – and this can sap our energy reserves. Parents, in particular, are likely to feel strangely and almost unnaturally tired as their child draws on their energy.

15

Squandering energy As adults, we learn to use our energy effectively. We recognize when we are tired, and act accordingly. Babies and young children have not yet learned to economize, and sometimes seem to "squander" their energy. For example, they rush around even when they are extremely tired, seemingly unable to calm down. When this happens, as parents we may be quickly overcome with anger. It may help to remember that the reason for this initially violent emotion is that the child is taking and using the parent's energy, and throwing that away, too.

Energy patterns and emotions

Emotions play an important part in directing the flow of energy. At the basic level, the so-called "positive" emotions such as joy and enthusiasm tend to increase the amount and flow of energy, while "negative" emotions like depression, apathy and fear decrease its quantity and flow.

Energy and emotions in disease When we fall ill and energy flow in the body is disturbed, we are also likely to be overwhelmed by negative emotions which are difficult to throw off. When using natural medicines, it is important to take account of the emotions gripping an ill child. The correct choice of remedy can disperse negative emotions – the pattern of energy flow then changes, and the child soon starts to recover.

Actions also help. When parents nurse their sick child, they often feel instinctively that they want to cuddle and sing softly, be in comfortable and restful surroundings, provide toys and treats, and so on. These actions are aimed at creating a warm, positive atmosphere, which will disperse negative thoughts as well as helping to supplement the child's energy supplies.

Parental emotions and the child

The link between parent and child is very strong, and a baby or child easily picks up a parent's feelings. If you feel grumpy, so too will your child. When tension between parents runs high, the emotional effect on the child can be so strong as to disturb energy flow and cause illness. Many cases of asthma in children (page 104) have been traced back to great tension between the parents. In some instances, parents have been considering a separation, but have not told their children. However, the children have subconsciously detected the tension, which then manifested itself as asthma.

Children may even pick up or "borrow" diseases from their parents. For example, one child with asthma did not respond to any treatments. After some time it was discovered that the mother had a severe lung condition, which she had not revealed. She decided to take treatment herself, and as her condition improved, so did her child's asthma. In the words of an old Chinese saying: "Treat the mother to treat the child."

BUILDING A HEALTHY CONSTITUTION

Before birth

The most important time for building a healthy constitution is before birth. A child's basic constitution and overall level of energy are formed in the early months of pregnancy. The baby in the womb draws nourishment from the mother, and is especially sensitive to the health and energy of the parents.

In Chinese medicine, it is acknowledged that the basic hereditary characteristics are determined at the moment of conception, but that events which happen to the pregnant mother can affect her unborn child. Some of the commoner events are listed below. If you recognize the described pattern in your child, consult the relevant pages, or visit a practitioner of natural medicine. There is often much that can be done.

Fright If a mother undergoes a traumatic experience such as a scare or fright during the last four months of pregnancy, this can be passed on to the baby, who is then born with symptoms of fear (the "fright" pattern, page 84). Such babies are commonly very nervous, have difficulty sleeping, and are frightened when away from their mother. There is often a slight blue coloration between the eyes.

Heat Sometimes a mother becomes especially hot during the later stages of pregnancy – for example, if she carries her baby during a very hot summer, or if she eats too many "heating" foods (page 32) such as curry or game. The heat that she experiences can then cause an imbalance in the baby, who tends to be too hot and red-faced, and also shows a readiness to perspiration.

Toxins A mother who experiences high levels of certain toxins (harmful substances) during pregnancy can pass on the effects to her baby. Such toxins include lead from vehicle exhaust fumes and nicotine from tobacco smoke. Nicotine may cause poor growth in the womb so that the baby has a low birth weight, and also a tendency towards tonsillitis and swollen glands during childhood. In Chinese medicine, oranges are considered particularly bad for pregnant mothers, since eating too many oranges can lead to an over-active baby (page 164).

There are also toxins which are well known to cause developmental problems, such as alcohol and certain drugs and medicines.

Maternal illness If a woman is ill just before conceiving, or at any time during the pregnancy, the imbalance so created can be passed on to her baby. For example, if she contracts hepatitis during pregnancy, her baby may well be born with a poorly-functioning liver and thus have difficulties with digestion (page 23).

Birth problems

The moment when a baby comes into the world is of great importance – and of great mystery. Anything that helps to ease the transition from the womb to the outside world is worthwhile. When problems occur at birth, the baby can be adversely affected. For example, a baby born well before term may have a "weak" energy pattern (page 21).

Likewise, in a difficult or traumatic birth, the baby may have weak energy. In a few cases the baby shows the "fright" pattern (page 84).

17

Transitions during childhood

As a child grows and develops, there are periods when he or she undergoes significant physical, emotional and spiritual changes. These may affect health and make the child prone to illness.

Four to six months This is a time of maximum stress for the digestive system. By this age a baby has used up any energy reserves present at birth, but the energy requirements often continue to be high. He or she starts to lift up the body, spends less of the day sleeping, and is generally more active, as well as putting on weight rapidly. In addition, this is often the time when the first solid foods are taken, the first teeth appear, and the first immunizations may be given.

The common way for this stress to show is in the "liver congestion" pattern of illness (page 23). In strong children the imbalance soon passes, perhaps with loss of appetite for a few days. However, in other children the imbalance can give rise to a significant problem such as eczema, asthma, diarrhea or vomiting.

"Terrible twos" Many toddlers go through an emotionally difficult time around the age of two years. They are starting to feel and develop their own individuality, and they are struggling with speech. They have grasped the idea that speech can be used for communicating ideas, but as yet they have a limited vocabulary and cannot express themselves clearly. This often produces a feeling of frustration and impotence – at the very time when individuality is beginning to emerge. It is little wonder that toddlers are prone to blind rages and temper tantrums. Tonsillitis is related to the expression or suppression of

anger, and it often appears at this age. A toddler's emotions depend heavily on those of other people, and he or she quickly picks up feelings from the parents. We often notice our children becoming irritable when we ourselves feel irritable. Bach flower remedies (page 66) are often helpful in easing this transition, especially remedies such as Holly, Vine and Walnut.

Six to seven years Many children are at their healthiest from the ages of about five to ten years. They have overcome the main problems of early childhood – weakness, childhood infections, extremely rapid growth – but they have not yet encountered the chief difficulties of adulthood, such as competitiveness, pre-adulthood and overwork. But around six to seven years, changes occur which may foreshadow the adult problems.

At this age a child may start to become aware of his or her identity as a distinct person, with distinct opinions – and above all become aware of their emotions. Before this age, the emotions are so entwined that they are not differentiated. After about seven years, a child tends to become aware of distinct and separate feelings, such as anger, doubt and fear, which are now perceived as being different from "self". Once a child achieves this awareness, he or she learns that some emotions are more positive than others. The child starts to disapprove of some emotions, such as anger and rage, and tries to control them.

Also around this age, children start to become competitive. They may want to shine in the classroom, or be the best at a particular sport. So at this time the first stress-related disorders often appear, such as headaches and digestive pains.

Pre-adulthood From around 10 to 14 years, the time of Pre-adulthood, a child enters teenage life and experiences many associated problems. In Chinese medicine this transition is regarded as a "gateway", an opportunity to change health – for better or worse. If it happens during a time of low stress, one's health can take a huge step for the better. On the other hand, if this is a stressful time, problems can be "built-in" and last for many years. It is especially important for girls to take time and relax, with less pressure from schoolwork, during their monthly periods. They may miss a little schoolwork, but by doing so they can avoid many years of difficult and painful menstruation in the future.

There are many "gateways" in life, especially for women: being born, puberty, giving birth, and the menopause. At each gateway there is an opportunity to change one's health for the better – provided the gate opens during a time of happiness and contentment.

Routines and lifestyle

Just as each child has special needs from education, so each has individual requirements to help build health. Many of these are common sense for parents, and many are handed down through families. However, health practitioners of all kinds notice that certain basic causes of ill

19

health seem to appear again and again. These are often related to sleeping and eating, daily routines and other aspects of general lifestyle.

Sleep The amount of sleep children need depends to a certain extent on the latitude at which they live. In temperate parts of Europe and North America, many children need more sleep than those in tropical areas – although various factors alter individual requirements. The table below gives a guide to the amount of sleep a child needs. Children tend to sleep longer at times of rapid growth.

A child who seems to need much more or much less sleep than average may have an internal imbalance – although disease has not yet developed. For the child who sleeps too much, signs to look for are lethargy, obesity, puffiness around the eyes and poor appetite. If a child is getting too little sleep, watch for hyperactivity, underweight and perhaps dark or black rings around the eyes.

AVERAGE SLEEP REQUIREMENTS

Age (years)	Nightly sleep (hours)
up to 3	13
3 to 7	12
7 to 10	11
10 to 14	10

Patterns of regularity Soon after birth, a baby encounters the regular routines of daily life: day and night, eating times, activity and rest. If such patterns are established early, with regular mealtimes and bedtimes, this will help in the future. Some parents may consider a regular routine restrictive, but the requirements of children and adults often differ. Babies and children usually thrive on a degree of order in their lives, provided the rules are relatively flexible – this being quite different from the oppression which masquerades as discipline.

Fresh air and exercise Babies should spend an hour or two outside on most days, if possible; schoolchildren need two or three hours of outdoor activity daily if they are to thrive. Modern trends such as taking children to school by car, exercising in indoor gyms and swimming in indoor pools do not contribute as much to health. There is no substitute for fresh air – without it, the "weak" pattern of illness (opposite) may develop. Without exercise, the "strong" pattern child may develop energy blocks (page 15).

Electromagnetic stress Recent research shows that exposure to strong electromagnetic fields may weaken the nervous system. This research work is still in its early stages, but it is possible that babies and young children are especially prone to so-called "electromagnetic stress". Any high-voltage equipment can be a source, the commonest being cathode-ray screens as found in television sets and computer monitors.

You may notice that, after your child has been exposed to the television screen for more than an hour or so, he or she shows signs of stress such as irritability, restlessness, aggression and physical lethargy. This could be a combination of electromagnetic stress and the over-stimulating, consumer-directed nature of many television programmes.

CHILDHOOD DISEASE PATTERNS

Treatment with natural medicines involves taking into account the whole person: body, mind and spirit. Certain patterns of imbalance are seen very frequently and can give rise to a wide variety of symptoms and emotional states. In children, there are six common disease patterns, which are explained in greater detail in the following pages. In summary, these are:

■ "Strong", when the child usually has plenty of energy.
■ "Weak", when there is a general shortage of energy.
■ "Hot", when the child shows signs of being too hot.
■ "Cold", when there is persistent difficulty in keeping warm.
■ "Liver congestion" pattern, when the child has poor digestion.
■ "Echo" pattern, when the same disease recurs again and again.

In daily life a child may show indistinct signs while healthy, perhaps with mixed features of each. During illness, however, one particular pattern usually becomes clearer and more pronounced.

If you cannot decide which disease pattern your child shows, it may be that he or she has a mild version of the liver congestion pattern, or that the symptoms are confused by medication being taken.

"Strong" and "weak" patterns

In general, a "strong" child who is ill shows violent and pronounced symptoms. You may have the impression of great force encountering a firm obstacle, with a violent struggle resulting. A high fever may occur when the child, although physically weak, is obviously putting great energy into fighting the illness. Similarly, in colic, as the child writhes in pain after

STRONG AND WEAK PATTERNS COMPARED

Strong	Weak
Child usually has a very positive attitude	Child tends to be vacant and dreamy
Strong, high fever (40°C, 104°F)	Weak, low-grade fever (38°C, 101°F)
Seems to battle hard against the disease	Seems to make little effort to get well
Strong, definite pains	Vague, dull aches
Child is strong and sturdy	Child is frail and easily tired
Dominating spirit, tends to rule	Weak spirit, easily ignored by others
Often red cheeks	Often pale faced, with damp, puffy skin
Tends to sleep little	Tends to sleep excessively, though may wake many times in the night
Not too disturbed by small complaints such as scratches	Easily disturbed by small complaints
Quick to recover from injury	Slow to recover from injury

21

eating, you may get the impression that great forces are trying to move something that will not budge. If your child shows this pattern, then during treatment, it is not so important to build up his or her inner strength any further, but to help direct the considerable energy present in the correct way, to combat the particular disease present.

In contrast, the "weak" child does not have enough energy. High fevers are unusual: infection may strike, yet the child does not have the energy to put up a good fight. Similarly, digestive pains are mild, and the child gets a dull ache rather than a severe pain. If your child follows the weak pattern, an important component of treatment is to give medicines or herbs that generally strengthen by increasing energy reserves.

There are parallel aspects on the emotional plane. The strong child demands that something be done, and may fly into a great rage, while the weak pattern child tends to be a "wet blanket" – and is more easily ignored.

"Hot" and "cold" patterns

The theory that illnesses can be either "hot" or "cold" in nature appears in traditional medicines throughout the world. It was a common idea in orthodox Western medicine until the eighteenth century, but the rise of scientific medicine, with its reliance on instruments rather than the subjective experience of the patient, saw the decline of this basic and important concept.

HOT AND COLD PATTERNS COMPARED

Hot	Cold
Child has a red face	Child has a pale face
Active, sleeps little	Lazy, likes plenty of sleep
Throws off bedclothes at night	Sleeps huddled in bedclothes
Aggressive attitude	Tends to be submissive
Feels hot	Feels cold
Likes to wear few clothes	Likes to wear many clothes
Tendency to sweating	Little sweating
Urine is scanty and strong	Copious, clear urination
Constipation, or diarrhea with bad smell	Diarrhea without bad smell
Red tongue, may have a yellow coat	Pale tongue, may have a white coat
Bad breath	Breath not noticeably bad
Voracious appetite, thirsty	Poor appetite, no great thirst
Prefers cooling foods	Prefers heating foods

The idea is simple. In a hot disease, the symptoms are the same as those experienced in hot weather: a feeling of heat, with a flushed complexion, sweating, and so on. A cold disease brings on symptoms which are the same as the features experienced in cold weather: shivering, pale face and dry skin (see the table, below left). These notions remain in our culture today, as everyday expressions such as "hot-tempered", "hot-blooded", "fevered imagination", "warm-hearted", "inflammation" and their opposites.

When treating children with natural medicines, these ideas are important. Some remedies, such as Ginger, are good for the cold pattern conditions and harmful for hot ones. Other remedies, like an ice compress on the back of the neck, help problems such as a nosebleed in hot weather. Similarly, certain foods aid cold conditions, while others are indicated in hot ones (page 34). Indeed, an appropriate change of diet may be enough to cure a long-standing complaint.

"Liver congestion" pattern

The main problem facing a newborn baby is how to digest enough food. During pregnancy, the baby is nourished through the umbilical cord. After birth, all nourishment must immediately be obtained from the digestive system, which was hitherto not working. At this age, food requirements are very high in relation to body weight – a thriving baby's body weight should double during the first six months. Thus, in most babies, the digestive system is working close to maximum capacity as it processes huge quantities of food.

It is not surprising, therefore, that many illnesses in babies are related to a malfunction of the digestive system – the "liver congestion" pattern. There are obvious examples, such as diarrhea vomiting and associated digestive infections caused by viruses and bacteria. But the list of diseases which may be caused by a digestive disturbance also includes apparently unrelated problems like whooping cough, asthma, eczema, glandular conditions and insomnia.

Symptoms of liver congestion In Chinese medicine this pattern is called "blockage". The baby or child feels a sensation of having eaten too much, and wants to get rid of accumulated food – even though there may be diarrhea. The equivalent pattern in adults is brought on by eating too many fatty, greasy meals. In adults the indigestion soon passes, but in children it can continue for month after month. Characteristic symptoms of this pattern are:

■ irregular appetite, sometimes eating a lot but sometimes no appetite at all,
■ swollen abdomen,
■ a sour smell about the child, or the aroma of fermenting apples,
■ irregular bowel movements; constipation or diarrhea with green foul-smelling stools; in mild cases the stools might smell sour,
■ the child behaves badly, is restless and easily angered, and
■ red cheeks, with a little green round the mouth.

In mild cases, before the actual illness has developed, there may be symptoms of sluggish energy circulation. The child feels cold, and is lazy and grumpy, with a poor appetite. These symptoms should disappear when he or she gets some exercise and becomes active, and the energy starts moving.

23

Since a baby's digestive system works so close to maximum capacity, almost any disturbance or imbalance can upset the digestion and bring on the liver congestion pattern of illness.

Over-feeding A particularly common cause of this pattern is over-feeding: so avoid giving too much food. A baby who rejects milk seems to be rejecting the love that goes with it, and we may find it hurtful to prepare food lovingly, only to have it pushed away or ignored. But remember that the child is rejecting only the food, and not the love. In general, in Western-style society, more children are ill through being overfed than by being underfed.

The following points may help you to adjust the amount of food your child eats. For a child under three years old, a whole egg or a whole banana is too much for one meal. Remember to feed your child slowly, allowing time for him or her to savor each mouthful. If he or she goes on demanding food, there may be indigestion; homoeopathy (page 54) may help.

Irregular feeding Partly as a reaction to the rigidity of previous generations, there has been a recent swing towards "demand feeding" – feeding the baby whenever he or she calls for food. This suits many babies, especially very young ones. But some older babies and young children become greedy or turn to food for comfort, and they may then demand to eat almost continuously. As a guideline, try to feed about the same amount of food, at about the same time each day, without giving snacks between meals. If this is not possible, wait at least two hours between feeds. The stomach is an organ that functions on a periodic basis, and it needs

regular rests several times daily in order to work well.

Too much fluid Another possible cause of digestive problems is drinking too much with the meal. Your child should drink only enough to moisten the food being taken. Too much fluid, especially cold water, can dilute the stomach acids and the various digestive juices, and so be a cause of an upset digestion.

Indigestible food When weaning your baby, start with easily digested foods such as baby rice or millet (page 31). "Rough" foods like raw vegetables (including raw carrots), brown bread, muesli, and vegetables that are hard to digest even when

"Wind" or "burp" your baby after feeding.

cooked (such as cabbage and seaweed), should be kept out of the diet until about three years of age. Some babies find even brown rice too rough. Whole foods are good for adults, but with babies some degree of refinement is necessary, because of the delicate and susceptible nature of the growing body.

Insufficient movement This is another cause of liver congestion. After feeding, burp ("wind") your baby properly, to help the food go down the digestive tract. Watch for the tell-tale blue colour above the lips which indicates indigestion. Should your child have a problem of this kind, do not allow him or her to nap directly after the meal, but keep the child awake for at least half an hour. If keeping your child awake after a meal is difficult, try giving a little less food each time.

"Echo" pattern

When babies and children develop an infection or similar illness, the disease usually takes a straightforward course, and most children recover completely. Sometimes, however, the baby or child never quite gets better after the illness, and does not return to his or her original buoyant good health.

In Chinese medicine, this is referred to as an "echo" disease. It is believed that, although the battle against infection has been won, there is still an imbalance left behind – an "echo" of the original infection. For example, when a child catches an infection and develops a productive or "loose" cough (page 96), he or she may then be left with some mucus on the chest which never seems to clear.

The echo disease pattern is a major cause of long-term ill-health. It is often linked to asthma, and is behind many recurring problems like earaches, tonsillitis and chest infections. Untreated, it can stay with a child through puberty and into adulthood, having an adverse effect on health on the physical, emotional and spiritual levels.

Symptoms of the echo pattern General indications of this pattern include:
■ the child's neck glands are usually swollen, even though there is no active infection,
■ he or she catches infections frequently,
■ the child has low energy, or energy prone to sudden drops at odd times during the day,
■ chronic mucus production (phlegm or catarrh), either of the chest or nose, and
■ a negative outlook.

Additionally, the echo pattern usually shows some symptoms of the original disease. For example, in echo whooping cough there may be a chronic barking cough and occasional vomiting; in echo measles there is insomnia, restlessness, irritability, and an intermittent red rash on the skin.

Traditional cultures believe that this illness pattern is caused mainly by attacks from bacteria or viruses. In the twentieth century, another cause has appeared – namely, immunizations. Since the echo pattern can persist into adulthood and old age, many alternative practitioners are opposed to immunization under certain conditions, as explained in detail on page 27.

SEASONAL FACTORS IN DISEASE

The body changes naturally throughout the year. In winter, the colder outside temperature makes the body generate more internal heat by increasing the metabolic rate in order to maintain its inside temperature. There is an inclination to eat more and perhaps run around and engage in physical activity, in order to keep warm. Foods eaten traditionally in winter – stews, meats, heavy puddings, nuts – assist this seasonal adaptation by increasing the body's generation of heat.

In summer the situation is reversed. The body's metabolism slows down and generates less heat. We feel like lying around and avoiding physical activity in order to keep cool. Traditional foods for a hot summer day – salads, vegetables, ice creams, cool drinks – reduce the production of heat in the body.

The problematic times are during the transition between winter and summer, that is, spring and autumn.

Spring and "latent heat"

In early spring the body is still generating enough heat to combat the cold of winter. As the weather warms, the production of body heat should gradually diminish. But a sluggish body takes time to adapt, generating too much heat and causing a predisposition to "hot" diseases (page 22). This is one factor contributing to the epidemics of fevers and sore throats that are so common in spring.

The imbalance caused by excessive heat is often hard to detect in children, because symptoms are mild. Your child may have vague feelings of uneasiness, irritability and restlessness. The problem is termed "latent heat" or "hidden heat" in Chinese medicine. It is as though unwanted heat is

"hiding" in the body, disrupting its energy balance and opening the way for attack by viruses or bacteria.

Although spring fevers are unpleasant, they are usually beneficial. They provide a way for the child's body to expel the latent heat (page 84).

Latent heat, and the resultant spring fevers, can be avoided by a change of diet as spring approaches. Serve less of the thick heavy foods that give comfort and warmth in winter; eat meat only once a week or less; and eat more light foods such as vegetables. (In previous times this practice was built into the religious and social calendar, for example, during fasting for Lent.) It also helps to dress in warm clothes during spring, to encourage sweating, which disperses the body's internal heat.

What happens on a slow scale with the changing seasons, also occurs more rapidly during short-term fluctuations in the weather – and especially unseasonal weather. For example, when the weather suddenly turns hot, a healthy body adapts quickly and generates less heat; but a sluggish body continues to generate heat internally, which again opens the way for disease.

Autumn and "latent cold"

A similar process occurs during autumn, giving rise to "latent cold". This is less common as a cause of disease, because summer is a time of great vitality, and as autumn approaches the body should be at its strongest. For some children, though – especially those unable to benefit from summer sunshine and fresh air – latent cold can bring on autumnal colds and coughs.

INFECTIONS AND IMMUNIZATIONS

The childhood infections

The infectious diseases of measles, mumps, rubella (German measles), chickenpox, diphtheria and whooping cough affect mainly children, and are rarely seen in adults. This is why they are referred to as "childhood infections" or "childhood diseases" (page 122). They fall into two distinct categories: those which, although perhaps severe, can benefit the body, and those which are not beneficial.

Beneficial infections

Measles (page 124) is the archetypal childhood infection. It can be a severe illness, but in Chinese medicine it is seen as eventually bringing benefits to the child, in relation to the process of growing up and expelling poisons from the body. The same events take place, although in a less dramatic way, with mumps, chickenpox and rubella.

For some children these diseases may be extremely unpleasant and difficult to nurse, and in a minority of cases they give rise to severe complications. (About 1 child in 2,000 develops measles encephalitis.) But at the same time, from the Chinese viewpoint, they serve the useful function of ridding the body of accumulated poisons. See page 124 for a detailed discussion of this subject.

Harmful infections

The second group of childhood diseases confers no special benefit on the body. They include polio, diphtheria and whooping cough (pertussis).

Diphtheria (which is fortunately now rare) relates to the problems children may have in expressing themselves, as explained on page 18. Whooping cough is more common and severe today than it has been for some time (page 131).

What is immunization?

The principle of immunization is to give a healthy child a mild or "inactivated" form of an infectious disease, usually as a vaccine composed of killed or disabled germs (bacteria or viruses). The child fights the infection successfully and develops a resistance, or immunity, which is effective when he or she is exposed to the real disease.

There is now a trend to immunize against many childhood infections, in the hope of eradicating them. This poses a dilemma for every parent. In some cases it may be better for a child to face the risk of catching a disease, rather than have the immunization.

The following pages contain general advice on whether an individual child should be immunized for the sake of his or her own health. The discussion as to whether immunization should be given for the sake of the health of other children, when an overall resistance or "herd immunity" builds up in the general population, is a difficult social matter and beyond the scope of this book.

In the US and the UK, immunizations are provided routinely in childhood against diphtheria, tetanus and whooping cough by the DTP "triple vaccine"; against polio; and against measles, mumps and rubella by the MMR triple vaccine. At puberty it is common to immunize against tuberculosis (TB), by the BCG vaccine, and against rubella (German measles) in girls (page 129).

27

Should my child be immunized?

Diphtheria and tetanus Although these two serious illnesses are relatively rare in developed countries, they still occur, and there is great pressure to immunize against them. Experience shows the side-effects of immunization are small, and it can safely be given to healthy children.

Whooping cough (pertussis) Whooping cough is a dreadful disease to nurse, and it can lead to permanent lung damage and even death. But it is slow to develop and responds well to acupuncture, herbs and homoeopathy (as well as to conventional antibiotic drugs). The efficacy of the vaccine is also in question, since some cases of whooping cough occur in previously immunized children. Therefore, if you have a local acupuncturist, herbalist or homoeopath who treats children, you should have time to seek advice and treatment. In these circumstances you might consider not having your child immunized. On the other hand, if there is no real possibility of prompt professional treatment with natural medicines, then it may be better to seek immunization.

Polio (poliomyelitis) The polio virus is widespread, and the course of the disease is so rapid that there is no time to call for treatment. The most popular advice is to immunize against polio.

Measles In developed countries measles has lost much of its severity. In most cases, the advice would be against having this immunization (page 126).

Rubella (German measles) Rubella immunization is routinely offered to young children and also to girls of about 12 to 13 years old. This is not because rubella is a dangerous infection, but because of risks to the unborn baby if the mother contracts rubella during the first three months of pregnancy. Experience has shown there are few dangers in this immunization.

Tuberculosis (TB) Recent research indicates that the BCG immunization may offer little protection against tuberculosis. Many practitioners of natural medicine have seen people suffering from lingering malaise due to this vaccine. The general advice is against giving it.

Contraindications to immunization

A contraindication is a reason why an immunization should not be given. Much depends on the individual case, but in general, immunizations are contraindicated when:
- the child has had convulsions (fits),
- there is a family history of epilepsy,
- the child has a weak immune system and suffers recurrent coughs and colds,
- he or she has already had the disease, or
- there is hyperactivity.

If immunization is carried out in these cases there may be a violent reaction, possibly with convulsions, development of epilepsy, paralysis or brain damage.

It is important to note that if your child is allergic to eggs, a specially-prepared vaccine may be necessary, since many vaccines are made with egg protein.

Preparing a child for immunization

An immunization is a shock to the system. If you decide to immunize, it is worth

REMEDIES TO CLEAR "ECHO" EFFECTS OF IMMUNIZATION	
Echo symptoms resemble	Homoeopathic remedy
Whooping cough Polio Measles	Pertussin 30 Polio 30 Morbillinum 30

preparing by building up your child's health. There are no blanket prescriptions for this, since each child should be considered as an individual. As a guide, ask yourself the following questions:

■ Is there any mucus (phlegm or catarrh)? If so, see page 36.

■ Is there much heat in the body, indicated by restlessness, great activity, insomnia and bad behavior. If so, see page 164.

■ Does the child twitch? If so, see page 90.

■ Is your child having teething trouble? If so, wait until this has passed.

■ Is there anything else in your child's health that concerns you? If you are in doubt as to improving your child's health, consult a natural medicine practitioner.

What can go wrong?

Problems inevitably arise from time to time with immunizations, because the child is given a mild form of a more serious disease. From a day or two after immunization until two weeks later, there may be a reaction as the child fights the infection. Provided the symptoms are not too violent, this is a good sign since it indicates developing immunity. Typical symptoms at this stage are fever, restlessness, bad temper, insomnia, poor appetite, mild diarrhea and a loose, mucous cough.

Treating side-effects Many side-effects of immunization, and particularly those which linger, can be treated by natural medicines. If your child has specific symptoms, such as insomnia or a cough, consult the appropriate page. When you have carried out treatment for a month, conclude it by giving a single dose of the nosode of the immunization that caused the trouble. If your child develops other side-effects, consult a practitioner of natural medicine.

"Echo" pattern after immunization

After the initial stage, some children have lingering "echo" effects (page 25), and in addition:

■Pertussis: A chronic hard cough, which comes and goes for months or even years after the immunization (it often sounds like a mild attack of whooping cough); the child occasionally vomits phlegm; recurrent fevers and earaches which fluctuate each month.

■Polio: A thick, grey mucus builds up over the weeks after immunization, giving rise to a productive cough, a thick, grey nasal discharge and swollen glands.

■Measles: During the month after immunization the child may get a feverish cough, with yellow mucus brought up only with difficulty; swollen glands, insomnia.

BREASTFEEDING AND WEANING

Breastfeeding is the natural and instinctive way to feed a baby, and it is beneficial to mother and child alike. Apart from the feeling of satisfaction it engenders, there are a number of practical advantages. Mother's milk is well adapted to the needs of the child and thus is a perfect food. It contains all the nutrients that the baby needs, as well as antibodies against infections the baby has not yet developed. Above all, it is convenient – there is no problem with sterilizing bottles!

Breastfeeding helps to develop the emotional bonding between mother and baby.

Some mothers experience difficulty in breastfeeding, and many of the difficulties can be helped by natural medicines (page 136).

Weaning a child is the first step towards independence from the mother, and it should be done slowly and with care. Each child is different, but the following general suggestions may help.

When to wean

A baby is usually ready for the first solid foods when he or she starts to push up from a lying position, at about four to six months. This is the first independent movement, and it can be matched by the first step towards the independence of solid foods. Also at this time, the baby's teeth are coming through. A thriving infant's food requirements start to exceed the mother's capacity around this stage. Often too, she begins to feel very tired from the effort of producing so much milk, and the nutritional content of her milk starts to decline.

First foods

A baby's digestion is delicate and easily upset, so the first foods should be introduced in small quantities, one at a time. Particularly suitable are baby rice (finely-ground rice) and millet. In general, avoid foods containing wheat products, since many babies are allergic to the gluten content of wheat at this age (though they usually develop the ability to digest it later on). Some babies are also sensitive to cow's milk (page 37).

Make sure your baby can digest one solid food well before you start the next. It may be more than a month after the first food before the baby is ready for something different, but it is better to let the digestion evolve gradually and gently. Allow at least a week to become accustomed to each new food. Above all, take time when introducing new foods. Do not worry if he or she takes only one food, such as baby rice, at the age of 12 months. Your baby may not yet be able to assimilate other foods.

WEANING DO'S AND DON'TS

- Do wean your baby onto one new food at a time.
- Don't introduce more than one new food each week.
- Do allow at least two hours between meals.
- Don't give foods with a lot of roughage or fiber, such as wholegrain bread.
- Do give gluten-free food during the first year, to avoid milk and wheat products (page 37).

Problems during weaning

There are two main problems to look out for when weaning your baby: the "liver congestion" pattern (page 23), and allergy (page 135). The former can be detected early by changes in the baby's diapers.

Mealtimes after weaning

While a baby is being breastfed, mealtimes and quantities of foods are limited by what is available. Usually, mother and baby fall naturally into a regular feeding pattern, with gaps of two hours or more between. When you wean your baby, or if he or she is bottlefed, these natural restrictions no longer apply. Some babies are by nature greedy and demand more food, more frequently, than is good for them (page 24). It is natural to want to give a baby food when he or she asks for it, but at times this should be resisted, to protect the baby's digestion.

A HEALTHY DIET

The study of diet is a huge subject. In a book of this kind we can only touch on a few of the most important aspects, such as the "hot" and "cold" nature of foods, the effects of meat and sugar, and specific foods that tend to increase mucus.

"Hot" and "cold" foods

In traditional medicine, foods are classified according to their effects on the body – whether they are hot or "heating", or cold and "cooling". Some, like Ginger, are obviously heating. Others, like bananas, are not so obvious (they are cold) – but they have a dramatic effect on cold diseases. Most people instinctively know about hot and cold foods, as seen by the way we vary our diet through the seasons. In winter we naturally lean towards stews with carrots and onions, while a summer's day seems to call for a salad of lettuce and cucumbers. The table on pages 34-35 depicts some of the more common foods according to their heating or cooling effects.

Combining hot and cold foods

Throughout this book there is advice on diet in relation to specific diseases. If your child has a cold illness, warming foods are indicated. Yet this does not necessarily mean you should exclude all cooling foods when treating a cold disease. Rather, it means the balance of meals should be towards warm, and that cold foods should be balanced by something to warm them. For example, mitigate the cold nature of melon by serving it with Ginger, and relieve the coldness of apples by baking or stewing them with cloves. Similarly, the hot nature of beetroot can be tempered by yogurt, as in borscht.

PREPARING FOODS	
Type of preparation	Effect on food
Raw foods	Cooling
Boiling	Slightly cooling to neutral
Frying	Heating
Grilling	Heating
Roasting	Very heating

Meat

Meat is rich in protein, and is in a form near to the "ideal" for absorption into the human body. Although it is suitable for those involved in strenuous physical activity, meat is not normally a good food for children under the age of seven years.

The Chinese say that meat is very "yang", that is, it tends to make people vigorous, active and worldly. It provides a robust and aggressive kind of energy, that quickly translates thought into action. A person leading an active and stressful life, with much travelling and interaction with the physical world, may need to eat meat to assist in this lifestyle. However, some believe that it leads to a material attitude, with a numbing of the senses and a neglect of higher spiritual values; such are the adverse effects of meat.

A knowledge of the energy that meat imparts helps us to understand when it is suitable for children. If your child is vague and dreamy and has difficulty in interacting with the world (such as after a long disease), then meat is an excellent tonic. On the other hand, if he or she is healthy and vigorous, and able to assert individuality, meat should be avoided.

Too much meat Many families eat meat regularly, and it may be inconvenient to provide a special diet for their children. Your child may be able to cope with meat, with no ill effect. However, if your child's digestion is weak, meat more than once each day can cause accumulation of toxins and a build-up of "latent heat" (page 26).

Signs to look out for are:
- boils and skin eruptions,
- irritability,
- aggressive behavior,
- selfishness, and
- a yellow coat to the tongue.

Protein in a meat-free diet

More protein is available in grains, and in beans and other pulses, than is generally realized. For example, whole wheat may contain up to 8 per cent protein, and beans up to 25 per cent (compared with an average of 20 per cent for meat).

Plant protein is sometimes called "second class" because it does not have all the components the body needs for absorption. Less than half the protein in wheat may be absorbed when this food is taken on its own, due to the lack of one amino acid (amino acids are the building-blocks of proteins).

However, second class protein can be converted into first class by the careful combination of foods. For example, baked beans are very high in the amino acid that wheat lacks. By taking baked beans with wheat, in the form of baked beans on toast, and in the proportion of one part of beans to four parts of wheat, much more of the protein in the wheat is absorbed. In fact, many traditional vegetarian dishes, taken as a whole, are higher in protein than the recently traditional diet of meat and vegetables.

Sugar

In China, where sugar is still uncommon and expensive, it is considered to be good for children. Indeed, certain types of sugar are good for children – but in only very small quantities. About two to three grams of natural sugar each day (preferably in the form of fruit) are beneficial, and help a child to grow.

In China, this amount of sugar is rarely available – fresh fruits are very seasonal, while preserved fruit juice is largely unavailable, and refined forms of sugar are expensive.

The situation is reversed in developed countries. Nearly all children have too much sugar. Fruit juice is given regularly as a drink in place of water, honey is used to sweeten foods, and even spicy and savoury foods are sweetened with sugar. High-sugar cakes and cookies are freely available. The average consumption of sugar approaches 200 grams per day! Thus the addition of extra sugar to the diet is indeed excessive and unnecessary. For most parents, the main problem is how to keep sugar out of the diet.

Side-effects of sugar The following are some of the side-effects of too much sugar:
- hyperactivity,
- aggressive behavior,
- excessive mucus,
- insomnia,
- build-up of "latent heat" (page 26),
- tendency to frequent infections, and
- poor tooth development and tooth decay.

Diet and mucus (catarrh or phlegm)

33

In Chinese medicine, mucus is seen as a factor in many diseases. Excessive mucus is thought to originate in faulty digestion,

COLD FOODS	COOL FOODS	NEUTRAL FOODS
Apple Cool effect can be reduced by cooking with cloves **Banana** Very cold, may well cause colic; can relieve constipation or diarrhoea in certain cases **Celery** **Cottage cheese** **Cucumber** Very cold, difficult for many children to digest **Grapefruit** **Lettuce** A rather "windy" food (causes flatulence); in nursing mothers of a hot nature, lettuce increases the supply of milk **Marrow** Helps to reduce heating effect of lamb **Melon** Cool effect reduced by eating with Ginger **Mussels** **Pear** Cool effect reduced by cooking with cloves **Yogurt** Very cold; yogurt and cucumber can help to reduce the heating effect of curry	**Aubergine (eggplant)** **Barley** Barley water is refreshing in fevers **Calf's liver** **Cow's milk** Cool nature is helped by simmering with an onion, which makes it sweet and reduces its phlegm-forming activity **Crab** Some children have an allergic reaction **Cress** Helps to disperse phlegm **Green lentil** **Green tea** A diuretic (fluid reducer); also helps speed the metabolism, and so is a slimming aid; contains caffeine **Lamb's liver** **Lemon** Honey and lemon juice is a refreshing drink in fevers; add a little Ginger in cold-type fever **Mung bean** **Pork** Cook in soya (soy) sauce and Ginger to reduce its cold nature and make it more digestible **Soft cheese** **Pickled (soused) herring** **Soya (soy) milk** **Spinach** **Tofu (bean curd)** Very high in protein and calcium **Tomato (raw)** A cut tomato rubbed on the skin can help relieve sunburn (page 183)	**Broad bean** **Rice** **Coconut** **Corn on the cob (maize)** Too rough to be given to babies; high in phytic acid which makes the iron difficult to absorb; this effect is neutralized by eating with chili peppers **Date** **Egg** Hardboiled eggs are often difficult to digest and are constipating **Grape** Strengthens against anemia **Herring** **Mushroom** Good for anemia **Pea** **Potato** A "wet" food; too much can lead to congestion and heaviness; the "wet" nature can be reduced by baking rather than boiling **Plum** Over-consumption can lead to diarrhea **Runner bean** **Strawberry** Can cause an allergic reaction **Veal** **Wheat** High in gluten, not a suitable food for most babies **White cabbage**

WARM FOODS

Blackberry (cooked) High in iron
Carrot Cooked carrots are a suitable first food for babies
Chocolate Strengthening in cold, damp weather; too much leads to mucous congestion; avoid if prone to headaches and migraine
Chicken A tonic in cases of weakness, especially after childbirth
Cocoa Same as chocolate
Coffee Helps stimulate the mind in moderation; useful in sunstroke; excess may harm the liver or heart
Fig Helps relieve constipation
Goat's milk Better than cow's milk if there is a tendency to mucous congestion
Greens (brassicas)
Mint tea Promotes perspiration in fevers
Oats Strengthens the nervous system; helps stabilize the sugar balance
Onion Helps to reduce mucus (phlegm or catarrh); over-consumption can increase the amount of sleep needed
Orange Avoid in pregnancy and during migraine; the peel of bitter oranges (as in marmalade) can help to reduce mucus; excess increases the amount of mucus
Parsnip
Peanut Roast peanuts can cause a lot of mucus or pus; avoid in chronic cough or eczema; can cause an allergic rash
Pig's liver
Pumpkin
Radish Helps to reduce mucous congestion
Red bean Causes colic if undercooked; always cook with cloves
Sesame seed High in calcium
Indian tea Excess can lead to stomach problems, intestinal upset and sore back
Tomato (cooked)
Turnip Tends to cause wind (gas); more digestible if seasoned with nutmeg; helps to promote milk flow in nursing mothers
Venison Not suitable for children

HOT FOODS

Almond Bitter almonds are good for the lungs
Beet (including beetroot)
Brown lentil
Brussel sprout Can cause wind (gas)
Cayenne pepper Not suitable for children
Cinnamon Useful addition to a tea to promote perspiration during colds; can cause palpitations and insomnia
Clove Especially useful for dispersing flatulence in the stomach; should be added to all bean dishes to promote digestibility
Eel Often served in jelly, to reduce its heating nature
Garlic Powerful in reducing mucus (catarrh or phlegm) and preventing colds; excess can lead to sore, red eyes
Ginger Tonic for a weak digestion; too much can burn the stomach
Lamb Some people (especially in the East) are allergic to lamb
Peach
Pepper (black)

either from the "liver congestion" pattern (page 23) or from difficulty in digesting certain foods. Also, when a child is healthy, he or she can cope with a wide range of foods which tend to cause mucus. But if your child is tired or ill, pay greater attention to providing foods that diminish the production of mucus (see table).

Eating habits and mucous congestion Some eating habits seem to encourage the production of mucus. They include eating too much, eating a heavy meal late at night, and eating snacks between meals. The converse is true: moderate amounts, eating the main meal early in the day, and avoiding snacks between meals, all tend to reduce mucus production.

Natural remedies to reduce mucous Certain remedies affect the general level of mucus in the system. Consult the Materia Medica listings (pages 42-71) for further information.
Useful herbs include Golden seal (*Hydrastis canadensis*), Barberry (*Berberis vulgaris*), Quinine (*Cinchona officinale*) and Elecampane (*Inula helenium*). Suitable tissue salts are Nat. mur. and Kali mur.

FOODS THAT AFFECT MUCUS PRODUCTION

Foods that tend to increase mucus greatly
Cow's milk, cream, butter, cheeses, roast peanuts, too many oranges (more than one a week for children, or equivalent juice), bananas, excessive sugar.

Foods that tend to increase mucus slightly
Rich foods in general, too many fatty foods, too much meat, fried foods, too much salt or sugar.

Foods that tend to reduce mucus slightly
Parsley, celery, green tea, jasmine tea, pickles, lemon.

Foods that tend to reduce mucus greatly
Garlic, onions, watercress, horseradish, mustard, umeboshi plums (Japanese salt-pickled plums).

Caution: when you give your child one of these remedies, lung mucus may temporarily increase. Such remedies should be given under supervision if the child has asthma or breathing difficulties.

FOODS SUITABLE FOR A MILK-FREE DIET

All fruits (but not topped with milk or cream)
Raisins, dates, dried fruits
All vegetables (provided they are cooked without butter or milk)
Goat's milk, soya (soy) milk, milk substitutes (often available by prescription)
Meat, fish, eggs, liver, kidney, poultry
Vegetable margarine, lard, cooking and salad oils

All cereals, rice, semolina, sago, macaroni, spaghetti
Most breakfast cereals, muesli, oats and similar products
"Milk-free" bread, cakes and cookies
Honey, jam, jelly
Herbs, spices, yeast and beef extracts, salt, pepper, vinegar
Plain dark chocolate, clear fruit ices
Baked beans and similar products
Fruit juices or squash, tea, coffee, cocoa

The milk-free diet

Some babies and children are allergic to cow's milk. Others benefit from a milk-free diet in various ways, and milk and its products are to be avoided as part of the treatment for some diseases.

All the nutrients in cow's milk, including its proteins, are found in other foods. Provide a variety of these foods every day and your child can enjoy a well-balanced, healthy diet free of cow's milk. Consult the table below to find which food can replace each nutrient in cow's milk.

MAIN NUTRIENTS IN COW'S MILK AND ITS PRODUCTS

Nutrient	Function	Other foods containing nutrient
Vitamin A	Bone and tooth development, night vision and health of skin	Eggs, liver, beans, peas, lentils, vegetable margarine, tomatoes, carrots, apricots, green peppers, parsley, broccoli, pistachio nuts, dark-green leafy vegetables
Vitamin B2 (riboflavin)	Function of nerves	Wholegrain cereals and bread, yeast, kidney and liver
Vitamin D	Formation and maintenance of bones and teeth	Vegetable margarine and effect of sunlight on skin
Calcium	Formation and maintenance of bones, teeth and nerves	Sardines, canned salmon, fish, shellfish, soya (soy) and blackeyed beans, soya (soy) milk, millet, almonds, brazil nuts, sesame and sunflower seeds, pistachio nuts, figs, oranges, lemons, tahini (sesame seed/paste)
Proteins	Building and repair of body tissues, antibodies to fight infection	Soya (soy) milk, milk replacement formula, meat, fish, eggs, liver, kidney, poultry, beans, lentils, wholegrain cereals, rice and pastas, nuts and seeds
Fats	Supply energy and help the body to absorb vitamins A and D	Vegetable margarine and pure vegetable oils, oily fish (such as sardines), meat, olives, avocados, nuts, seeds

37

Part II

THE NATURAL THERAPIES

Natural therapies have been used for centuries. However, in recent times, people in the West have largely lost sight of nature's cures, due to the rise of orthodox medicine and its preoccupation with physical symptoms, its batteries of synthetic drugs, and its increasing reliance on tests and surgery.

The natural therapies outlined in the following pages represent a generally simple, safe and effective approach, especially to the common and less serious ailments of childhood. As you begin to prescribe and use natural medicines for your child, you will become more aware of his or her condition – not only in the physical body, but also on the emotional, spiritual and mental levels. You will be able to recognize the therapies with which you feel most at ease, and identify which are most effective for your own child's developing constitution.

CAUTIONS

In general the various homoeopathic remedies, tissue salts and massages are safe for babies and children. Some herbal remedies may have adverse effects in certain situations, as indicated in the Materia Medica listings.

Always check that the remedy you wish to use is suitable for your child, in your particular case. If there is any doubt, or if you do not have the details of a remedy at hand, do not administer it. Consult a qualified practitioner of natural medicine for advice.

Organization and use

This part of the book contains details of many dozens of herbal preparations, homoeopathic remedies, tissue salts, Bach flower remedies and therapeutic massages. The introductory pages to each of these therapies give basic background knowledge.

The herbs, homoeopathic remedies and tissue salts are listed alphabetically by their internationally-recognized names (scientific botanical names in the case of herbs). Bach remedies are listed in the order described by their discoverer, Dr Edward Bach. Massages are ordered "from top to toe", beginning with the head and face, then the chest and back, followed by the arms and hands, and finally the legs and feet.

This part of the book may be used in two ways. First, as a back-up to the third part, Treating Childhood Ailments, as explained on page 80; and second, to help you prescribe your own remedies. For example, your child may develop an ailment not described in Part III. Or you may find that a particular herb or other remedy is strikingly effective for your child, and you wish to know more about its wider application. In such cases, refer directly to the Materia Medica pages where the remedy is described in detail.

Nature's cures are gentle and soothing. They work with the body, rather than against it, and encourage an awareness of the natural world in your child.

HERBAL MEDICINE

Herbs and other plants have been used for healing since the earliest times, in all civilizations and cultures. Today, about half of the drugs used in orthodox Western medicine were first derived from plants.

Herbal medicine works on many levels. The most obvious is the physical effect, when a relatively large amount is taken. In quantity, some herbs nourish in much the same way as foods. Indeed, there is no clear dividing line between a food and a medicine – for example, carrots and lettuce have a significant medicinal effect as well as providing nourishment. In the past, some people "ate" herbs in the same quantities as we eat other foods today.

More recently, herbs have been used medicinally in much smaller amounts, yet have been just as effective. This is because even quite small quantities of a properly-prepared plant extract contain the life force – the energy (page 12) or "vibration" – of the plant itself. This significant fact is one of the main advantages of herbal medicine (along with other natural therapies). The remedies are prepared in a way that retains as much of the plant's energy as possible, which acts to increase and direct the body's own energy.

By contrast, orthodox medicine tends to focus primarily on the physical symptoms of the body. Also, its remedies are prepared by technological processes such as sterilization and purification, which destroy the life force and energy, leaving only the material substance.

Herbal medicine works on an energetic level, which recommends its use for babies and children. Their bodies are small and frail compared to adults, but their energy levels are much greater by far. As a result the natural medicines, and particularly the herbal remedies, have striking and rapid effects.

Obtaining or collecting herbs

Dried herbs and the various preparations made from them, such as tinctures, are readily available from health food stores, pharmacies and other commercial suppliers (page 187). If you are unable to locate a source, a local practitioner of natural medicine should be able to help.

Many of the herbs mentioned here are easily grown in gardens or found in the wild, and dried and prepared in the home. If you gather your own herbs, bear in mind the following:

■ If collecting from the wild, observe wildlife laws and obtain permission from the owner to collect the plants.

■ Take a knowledgeable person or a good wildflower book, to be absolutely sure you have identified the herb correctly.

■ Pick only fresh and healthy plants, untouched by pesticides and other chemicals, as you would expect your food to be.

Types of herbal preparations

Information on preparation of individual herbs, such as which part(s) of the plant should be used, is given in the Materia Medica (pages 44-53).

Infusion (tea) An infusion is made by pouring hot (usually boiling) water over the part of the herb required, to make a herb tea. This method is preferred to decoction (see below) for herbs containing volatile oils, which are the substances that give aroma, taste and medicinal value to the herb, and which the hot water dissolves out of the herb. Usually, an infusion is made with one heaped 5mls teaspoon of dried herb to a standard-sized teacup (about 250mls, or 8fl ozs) of water. Stir the herb in, leave it for a few minutes, then strain the liquid infusion to drink when cooler. Some herbs such as Chamomile (*Anthemis nobilis*) are available in tea-bags. Infusion is unsuitable for roots, which take longer to release their consti-tuents.

Decoction A decoction is a preparation in which the herb is simmered in water for 10-30 minutes, in a non-metallic pan (non-stick, enamel, or glass). The recom-mended amounts are three heaped 5mls teaspoonfuls of powdered root to 500mls (about one pint) of water. The mixture is then strained to obtain the decoction. The adult dose is about one wineglassful (around 100mls, or 3fl ozs). This method is suitable for roots and the few herbs containing more insoluble compounds.

Tincture This is an extract made by macer-ating (soaking) the herb in an alcohol/water mixture (see below). Usually a tincture is 1:5, that is, 1 part of herb to 5 parts of the alcohol/water mixture. This is known as the "mother tincture".

The alcohol content of the alcohol/water mixture is generally 25 per cent, the alcohol being necessary to preserve or stabilize the extract. In some areas, the alcohol (ethyl alcohol) required is avail-able at pharmacies or similar suppliers. If not, it is possible to use a spirit such as brandy, or iso-propyl alcohol. It takes about one week to prepare a tincture from leaves, and some three weeks for roots, which may be an inconveniently long time. However, tinctures last for many years without going bad.

Standard dosages

If there are no specific instructions for dosages in the following pages, or under

SAFE DOSES AND UNUSUAL REACTIONS

As mentioned, typical doses of herbs given today are much smaller than in the past, because we have learned how to extract the plant's energy. This means the exact amount of herb used is less important, compared to the dosages of orthodox medical drugs.

Provided the instructions are fol-lowed, and cautions for each herb are observed, the dose levels given in this book should be safe. However, in rare cases a child may be sensitive or allergic to a particular herb. If your child shows any unusual reactions after taking a herb, stop the treatment and contact a practitioner of natural medicine for advice.

the ailment in question in Part III of the book, use the following general guidelines (see also the guidelines concerning how to use this book, page 10).

Dried herbs The standard dose for an adult is one heaped 5mls teaspoon of leaves, or one level 5mls teaspoon of roots.

For children, the standard dose is one-quarter to one-half of the adult dose. For babies, it is one 5mls teaspoon of infusion or decoction.

Unless directed otherwise, give one dose three times daily for chronic conditions, and one dose every two to four hours for acute conditions. The herbs may be taken dry and washed down with water, or drunk as an infusion or decoction.

Infusion or decoction For children, prepare the herb as for an adult, but unless stated otherwise, give one-quarter to one-half of

41

the liquid for children. Administer only one 5mls teaspoon of the liquid for babies.

Tincture The normal adult dose is 10 drops of mother tinture of each herb, three times daily. So for a compound prescription of four herbs, the dose will be a total of 40 drops, three times daily.

Use an approved dropper bottle to measure the drops. This should give a single drop volume of about 0.04mls, that is, about 25 drops per milliliter. The standard dose for children is much smaller. Two to four drops are usually enough, given three times daily. For babies, one drop is sufficient, three times daily. However for acute conditions in children, herbs may be given in appropriate dosages as often as every two hours.

Always give tinctures in water, never neat Add the drops to a cup containing about 50-

100mls of water, stir, and allow the child to sip it. Given neat, the high alcohol content of an undiluted tincture can burn the delicate skin inside the mouth.

Other ways of administering herbs

If your baby or child resists taking herbal preparations by mouth, they can be given in other ways. The tincture may be rubbed into the skin of the abdomen, at three times the normal dose. This method is especially suitable for babies whose problems originate in the digestive system. Or the preparation (tincture, decoction, infusion) may be put into the bath water, at 10-20 times the normal dose for a bathtubful of water. These methods work because the skin of a baby or young child is somewhat porous, and allows some of the preparation to pass through and be absorbed into the body.

Page	Common name	Scientific name
49	Horehound	*Marrubium vulgaris*
46	Horsetails	*Equisetum arvensis*
48	Hyssop	*Hyssopus officinale*
47	Licorice	*Glycyrrhiza glabra*
52	Lime	*Tilia europaea*
49	Lobelia	*Lobelia inflata*
45	Marigold	*Calendula officinalis*
44	Marshmallow	*Althea officinalis*
46	Meadowsweet	*Filipendula ulmaria*
53	Mistletoe	*Viscum album*
49	Motherwort	*Leonurus cardiaca*
44	Pasque flower	*Anemone pulsatilla*
50	Passion flower	*Passiflora incarnata*
50	Plantain	*Plantago major*
50	Poke root	*Phytolacca decandra*
53	Prickly ash	*Xanthoxylum americanum*
	Queen of the Meadow	*see* Meadowsweet
52	Ragwort	*Senecio jacobaea*
50	Ribwort	*Plantago lanceolata*
	Rudbeckia	*see* Echinacea
51	Sage	*Salvia officinalis*
48	St John's Wort	*Hypericum perfoliatum*
	Sweet flag	*see* Sweet sedge
44	Sweet sedge	*Acorus calamus*
52	Thyme	*Thymus vulgaris*
50	Tormentil	*Potentilla tormentilla*
52	Valerian	*Valeriana officinalis*
	White horehound	*see* Horehound
51	Wild cherry	*Prunus serotina*
44	Yarrow	*Achillea millefolium*

Each herbal remedy has an "aura" – a kind of vibration or energy that characterizes its properties. The aura of Fennel, shown here, has a spiky nature on the leaves that relates to its ability to move the digestion. The flower's halo is smooth and comforting.

HERBAL MATERIA MEDICA

This list of herbs has been specifically selected with children in mind, and to describe characteristics of the herbs advised for each ailment. The "portrait" of each herb is of necessity abbreviated, and readers who become interested in herbal medicine are advised to consult more specialized books (page 186).

The herbs listed here have wide applications and are frequently mentioned in the text of this book. A few herbs, of more limited use, are occasionally advised for specific ailments, but they have been omitted from this list for reasons of space. In such cases, refer to specialized publications.

Herbs may be used for adults, too. Some specifically treat problems which affect adults, such as high blood pressure.

Achillea millefolium
Yarrow

Parts used Plant.
Actions Helps to bring out perspiration in fevers. Drying, stimulating, warming.
Indications Encourages perspiration in "chilly" fevers. A great tonic that may be taken at all stages in fevers, and for several days afterwards, to restore appetite and strength. Useful in measles before eruption of spots, to stop bleeding (as in nosebleeds), for night cramps, and for boils and spots. A herb with many and varied uses, it

is often combined with Hawthorn (*Crataegus oxycantha*) in equal amounts as a general tonic. In spring it can help to dispel "latent heat" (page 26).
Dose To bring down a fever, one-quarter of a 5mls teaspoon of tincture in warm or hot water every 2 hours for children over 5 years. This produces a gentle warming and stimulating effect.
Contraindications None.

Acorus calamus
Sweet sedge (Sweet flag)

Parts used Roots.
Actions Tonic for the stomach, reduces digestive gas or wind, promotes flow of bile, diuretic.
Indications Used mainly for digestive disturbances, indigestion and colic with flatulence. Assists digestion of rich foods. Very effective when taken with Wormwood (*Artemisia absinthum*) and Woodruff (*Asperula odorata*) in equal amounts, as a travel (motion) sickness mixture, but it is very bitter. It acts as a diuretic by circulating stagnant fluids which have accumulated in the digestive system.
Contraindications None.
Cautions Prohibited by the United States Food and Drug Administration.

Althea officinalis
Marshmallow

Parts used Leaves.
Actions Cooling and generally soothing.

Indications Used to soothe inflammations, especially urinary and respiratory. Hence it is used for cystitis, urethritis and nephritis; also bronchitis, and pleurisy when combined with other herbs for the chest. It may be applied externally as a poultice for inflammations and arthritis, and as a mouthwash for mouth ulcers and sore or inflamed gums.
Dose Requires larger than normal quantities to be effective. Give 1 heaped 5mls teaspoon of dried herb, or one-quarter of a 5mls teaspoon of tincture, in each dose. Half this amount under 3 years, double over 8 years.
Contraindications None.
Cautions Do not use any iron utensils with this herb, since iron interferes with its action.

Anemone pulsatilla
Pasque flower

Parts used Leaves.
Actions Tonic for the nerves, relaxes spasms, reduces mucus (phlegm), clears rashes, promotes perspiration in fevers.
Indications Specific for feverish coughs. The tincture reduces inflammation in the lungs (as in the hot type of cough) and intestines (as in the hot type of diarrhea. It soothes spasmodic coughs, and is of particular use when the child is emotional and tearful.

Also brings out rashes in measles and other eruptive diseases, to hasten the course of the illness. In spring it can

expel "latent heat" (page 26) and so avert a seasonal fever.
Contraindications None (but see Cautions).
Cautions The fresh plant is poisonous in large doses. A safe dosage for adults is 2-3 drops of tincture, for children 1 drop.

For babies put 1 drop in a teacup of water and give half the water.

Anthemis nobilis
Chamomile (common)

Parts used Flowers.
Actions Calms the stomach, soothes pain, calms the mind, relaxes spasms in the muscles and digestive system.
Indications One of the most widely used herbs for calming and soothing. Recommended when the child is "over-heated", especially with rage, and thus is good for the strong type of child, red-faced and screaming.

Chamomile is the first remedy to try for sleeping problems and general over-excitement. It also calms spasms, so can be used for colic, and helps in teething, though German chamomile (*Matricaria chamomilla*) is more effective. People who drink coffee often dislike or become sensitive to its distinctive taste.
Dose Make the tea to a pale straw color, and sweeten with honey as desired. For babies, a 5mls teaspooon of the tea is enough; for children, give one-half to 1 teacup of tea.
Contraindications None.

Arctium lappa
Burdock

Parts used Roots.
Actions Increases the flow of bile, diuretic, clears "liver congestion" (page 23), nourishes the skin, promotes perspiration in fevers.
Indications The main remedy for many skin complaints, eczema, acne and boils. It can improve poor skin following chickenpox, and generally helps the skin by promoting bile flow from the liver, so aiding digestion and clearing "liver congestion". As a diuretic it strengthens the whole of the lower abdomen, so it can aid (with other herbs) diaper rash and bed wetting.
Dose Quite a large dose is needed. Give about one-quarter of a 5mls teaspoon of powdered root as a decoction, as a single dose. Half this amount under 18 months, double over 5 years.
Contraindications None.

Arnica montana
Arnica

Parts used Petals.
Actions Heals bruises and swellings, especially those due to injury (page 179).
Indications Use as a tincture, applied on a compress to bruises and swellings. Give 2-3 drops of tincture, diluted and taken internally, for the same purpose, and also to reduce internal bruising and bleeding.
Contraindications Do not apply tincture when the skin is broken or sensitive.
Cautions Repeated application may cause skin rash or irritation. Take internally only in very diluted form. Large doses are an irritant to the digestive system, and may bring on heart palpitations.

Barosma betulina (also known as *Agathosma betulina*)
Buchu

Parts used Leaves.
Actions Diuretic, promotes perspiration in fevers, aids digestion, heals the urinary tract, mild stimulant.
Indications Reduces inflammation in the urinary tract and so is powerful when used for urinary infections and inflammation of the urinary tract. May be combined with Horsetails (*Equisetum arvensis*) and Cleavers (*Galium aparine*) in equal amounts.

A secondary use is as a gargle for sore throats and tonsillitis. This herb has a distinctive smell which some people find unpleasant.
Contraindications None.
Cautions Do not use if there are signs of kidney infection, irritation or damage or any history of kidney disease.

Calendula officinalis
Marigold

Parts used Petals.
Actions Cools and soothes the skin, has various antiseptic properties.
Indications Used mainly externally as a cream or

HERBAL MATERIA MEDICA

ointment for skin complaints. (The decoction may be used in a bath.) It cools and soothes inflammations of the skin, sores, ulcers, eczema and warts. In many cases it is more effective than cortisone "steroid" creams, with no harmful side-effects. As an antiseptic, the ointment or tea may be applied to cuts.
Contraindications None.
Cautions Never use a tincture for eye problems, since the alcohol content causes severe stinging.

Chionanthus virginica
Fringe tree

Parts used Bark of roots.
Actions Assists digestive function of the liver, mildly diuretic, tonifying.
Indications One of the most important remedies for sluggish digestion, especially for difficulty in digesting fats. May be used for poor appetite with irritability. Good for children under stress where this affects digestion and for chronic diarrhea.
Contraindications Since it promotes the flow of bile and has a laxative effect, do not give during acute diarrhea. Small doses may be given in chronic diarrhea.

Crataegus oxycantha
Hawthorn

Parts used Flesh around the berries.
Actions Strengthens the heart, calms, diuretic, relaxes muscular and digestive

spasms, general tonic.
Indications In children, effective for insomnia due to over-excitement, over-stimulation or weakness. In babies, commercially-available hawthorn extract or "slices", known as "Chinese hawflakes" (the equivalent of 1 berry), given after feeding assists in milk digestion and helps to prevent the "liver congestion" pattern of illness (page 23).
Contraindications None.

Echinacea purpurea
Echinacea (Rudbeckia, Cone flower)

Parts used Roots.
Actions Reduces phlegm, purifies the blood, antiseptic and antibiotic.
Indications Conditions where the body produces pus, such as boils and ulcers. Useful as an assistant herb in skin eruptions, measles and chickenpox. A very powerful herb, it benefits low energy, mucous conditions, and low resistance to bacterial infection.
Dose 50mgs of the root or one-quarter of a 5mls teaspoon of the tincture in water for each dose. Half this amount under 3 years, double over 8 years.
Contraindications None.
Cautions None, when taken in reasonable doses (as above). Tests by the United States Food and Drug Administration show that massive doses can be harmful to experimental animals, but

there is no evidence that these results can be applied to small doses for humans.

Equisetum arvensis
Horsetails (Bottlebrush)

Parts used Plant.
Actions Diuretic, stops bleeding, drying, cooling, reduces blood pressure.
Indications Mainly kidney and bladder trouble such as swollen legs, water retention, urine retention, nephritis, cystitis, inflammation and ulcers in the urinary tract. A secondary use is to stop bleeding such as nosebleeds and menstrual bleeding.
Contraindications None for children. Adults with high blood pressure should start with a small dose.

Filipendula ulmaria
Meadowsweet (Queen of the meadow)

Parts used Plant.
Actions Drying, cooling, soothes the stomach.
Indications A very cooling herb, recommended for diarrhea, fevers and stomach problems, especially those of a "hot" nature. Its drying action in diarrhea makes it the one of the most effective herbs for this complaint in children.
Contraindications None.

Foeniculum vulgaris
Fennel

Parts used Seeds.
Actions Aids digestion, relieves flatulence, soothes

colic, increases milk supply in nursing mothers.

Indications The prime herbal remedy for babies, because it gently assists digestion and calms colic – although it will not clear "liver congestion" (page 23) on its own.

Dose Can be given in larger quantities, for example as a tea, 1 level 5mls teaspoon of dried herb to 250mls of water, sweetened with 1 level 5mls teaspoon of honey.

Contraindications None.

Gentiana lutea
Great yellow gentian

Parts used Roots.

Actions Tonic, promotes flow of bile, cools fevers, helps expel intestinal worms.

Indications A great strengthener. It is a tonic for all weak conditions, especially after illness when appetite is poor. Specific for vomiting and useful in all forms of indigestion, especially "liverish" types, overeating, or difficulty in digesting rich foods. It may cure mild attacks of "liver congestion" (page 23) but is better combined with Black root (Leptandra virginica). It has been used for jaundice. A herb with a very bitter taste, which may limit its use.

Contraindications None.

Geranium maculatum
Cranesbill (American)

Parts used Plant.

Actions Drying, tonifying, slows or stops bleeding.

Indications Diarrhea, dysentery and similar conditions. Also used to stop bleeding of all types. Its astringent effect makes it useful in incontinence and bed wetting. All the geraniums have similar indications, and Herb Robert (G. robertiana) may be substituted.

Dose Administer at twice the standard dose.

Contraindications None.

Glycyrrhiza glabra
Licorice

Parts used Roots.

Actions Pectoral (chest stimulant), general tonic, tonic for the digestion.

Indications In Western medicine, licorice is mainly used for mucus (phlegm) in the lungs, and is an ingredient in many cough syrups. In Chinese medicine it is regarded as the "King of Herbs". On its own, it acts to loosen phlegm and clear impurities from the blood, healing complaints like boils and chronic sore throats. It also soothes stomach ulcers and relieves constipation. When combined with other herbs, it has the effect of energizing them. For example, Coltsfoot (Tussilago farfara) directs licorice's energy to the lungs, for respiratory complaints.

Contraindications Do not use during pregnancy, high blood pressure or kidney disease.

Cautions Large doses over a long period (more than 10 times the recommended dose)

can lead to raised blood pressure and possibly adverse effects similar to strong steroid drugs.

Humulus lupulus
Hops

Parts used Flowers.

Actions Calms nerves, soothes pain, encourages sleep, diuretic.

Indications The calming action soothes inflamed nerves, nervous pain and irritation, and insomnia. Even the vapor is helpful, and a hop-filled pillow may help with sleeping problems.

Contraindications Do not use when there is bed wetting, great lethargy or depression. Overuse may increase the amount of sleep required.

Cautions The flowers may cause skin irritation in some people.

Hydrastis canadensis
Golden seal

Parts used Roots.

Actions General tonic, clears mucus (phlegm) from the body, mild laxative.

Indications An important and effective digestive tonic. It improves digestion and the movement of food through the intestines. The herb of choice for long-term conditions characterized by too much mucus; it may be taken over long periods. Combine with herbs for the chest, such as Coltsfoot (Tussilago farfara) for chronic coughs. A dilute tea made from Golden seal

47

HERBAL MATERIA MEDICA

can be used as a soothing eyewash.
Contraindications Avoid in pregnancy, because it stimulates the uterus (womb).
Cautions At first it increases the amount of mucus being expelled, so start with small doses.

Hypericum perfoliatum
St John's Wort

Parts used Flowers and leaves.
Actions Relaxes and strengthens the nerves, reduces pain from injury, heals deep wounds, relaxes breathing, drying.
Indications The primary use for children is as an external application, prepared as an oil or ointment. It is valuable for stopping pain and healing bruises, since it is the herb that acts most quickly on the nervous system. The oil is preferred, but provided the skin is not broken, the tincture may be used (see Cautions). The oil helps to heal deep wounds and those where pus has formed. The diluted tincture is used for dry coughs, and as a general relaxant.
Contraindications If the person taking this herb is very tired it can provoke greater lethargy or depression.
Cautions Do not use the tincture on broken skin, since the alcohol content will cause pain. Over-consumption can lead to over-sensitivity to sunlight. Rated as unsafe by the United States Food and Drug Administration.

Hyssopus officinale
Hyssop

Parts used Plant.
Actions Soothes coughs, lung tonic, strengthens the stomach, reduces digestive gas or wind, drying, promotes perspiration in fevers.
Indications Primarily to heal lung ailments, being useful for all lung problems, both chronic phlegm (mucus) and acute infection. It is added to many cough mixtures. It is a tonic and promotes perspiration, so it may be given at all stages in influenza. A secondary use is for colic and flatulence.
Contraindications None.
Cautions The essential oil of hyssop is very strong and should only be used in small quantities for children.

Inula helenium
Elecampane

Parts used Roots.
Actions Clears mucus (phlegm) from the chest, diuretic, tonic, antiseptic, increases the flow of digestive bile.
Indications An excellent herb for all lung conditions with phlegm, both acute and chronic, such as coughs, bronchitis, asthma and emphysema. It also helps skin infections and any condition where pus is generated. Other minor uses are as a diuretic, to brighten the eyes, to increase the flow of bile, and for pain in the flanks. The common factor in all these complaints involves cleansing

the liver. In babies this herb is especially recommended for coughs which accompany "liver congestion" (page 23).
Contraindications Not to be used in large quantities by anyone who is anemic.

Iris versicolor
Blue flag

Parts used Dried roots.
Actions Decongestant, especially for the glandular system, softens thick mucus (phlegm), diuretic, stimulating.
Indications Primarily used to treat "echo" diseases (page 25) when there is an accumulation of hard phlegm, as in swollen glands. When first given, the softening effect on the phlegm often causes a productive cough. In small doses it moves the bowels gently. Beneficial in many skin conditions.
Contraindications Not to be used in inflammatory conditions.
Cautions Use only the dried root, and only in small doses. Large amounts may cause diarrhea.

Juglans cinerea
Butternut

Parts used Bark of roots.
Actions Moves the bowels, reduces mucus (phlegm), clears "liver congestion" (page 23), expels worms.
Indications Habitual constipation, especially when there is also a skin disease. It eliminates phlegm from the liver and intestines and is

good for the "liver congestion" form of constipation. Small doses are laxative and strengthen the bowel muscles. It is a close relative of Walnut, which is used as a Bach remedy (page 70).
Contraindications Not to be taken when there are loose stools or diarrhea.
Cautions Large doses (several times more than the recommended amount) are strongly purgative and are therefore unsuitable for children.

Leonurus cardiaca
Motherwort

Parts used Plant.
Actions Calming and tonifying to the nervous system, good for menstrual problems, relaxes spasms and cramps, aids perspiration in fevers, general tonic.
Indications The Latin name reflects its strong tonifying action on the heart. Especially good for heart "flutters" (palpitations) that arise from nervousness and emotional distress. The common name reflects its use as a tonic for female problems.
   This herb is particularly helpful for soothing nervous irritability and inducing a sense of calm. It is used in fevers, as a tonic and to calm a panic-stricken child; it has a special use in warding off feverish fits; and it relieves certain types of insomnia.
Contraindications None.
Cautions Do not take during pregnancy.

Leptandra virginica
Black root

Parts used Dried roots.
Actions Clears "liver congestion" (page 23), induces diarrhea (in large doses), tonic, promotes perspiration.
Indications The main use is to clear thick mucus (phlegm) from the intestines and liver. Persistent phlegm throughout the system tends to clog it up, and this herb will stimulate the most clogged system. Hence, for children, it is specific for "liver congestion". In small doses it moves the phlegm along the intestines, causing loose stools at first. However it can safely be used for chronic diarrhea in small doses, and can be continued in other conditions for prolonged periods, as a tonic.
Contraindications None if the dried root is used. The fresh root contains possibly harmful substances.
Cautions In the first week of treatment, renewed bowel movements may cause flatulence and restlessness at night. Large doses are purgative and unsuitable for children.

Lobelia inflata
Lobelia

Parts used Plant.
Actions General relaxant, encourages perspiration in fevers, clears mucus (phlegm) from the chest, lowers blood pressure. See Cautions, below.
Indications One of the widest acting relaxants, it also has a

strong effect on the lungs; so it is frequently used for asthma, as an expectorant to help loosen and expel phlegm. Recommended for all harsh coughs, including croup and whooping cough; also shock, trauma, high blood pressure and nervous tension.
Contraindications Do not administer during nervous prostration, low blood pressure or paralysis.
Cautions ★This herb is restricted in some countries, and must be used under the supervision of a practitioner. In small quantities it may cause a temporary tight sensation in the throat, as well as slight nausea, but this soon passes. In large quantities it is an emetic.

Marrubium vulgaris
Horehound (White horehound)

Parts used Plant.
Actions Loosens and clears mucus (phlegm) particularly from the chest, tonic, mild diuretic.
Indications Good for all lung complaints, especially when there is copious moist phlegm being coughed up. Other conditions are croup and ulceration of the lungs.
Contraindications None.

Matricaria chamomilla
German chamomile

Parts used Flowers.
Actions Very similar in action to the common Chamomile

49

HERBAL MATERIA MEDICA

(*Anthemis nobilis*), but slightly more sedative and calming. Used specifically for teething problems and to prevent fits.
Contraindications None.

Nepetia cataria
Catmint (Catnip)

Parts used Plant.
Actions Promotes perspiration in fevers, relaxes spasms and cramps, calms nerves, clears flatulence, general tonic.
Indications Primarily a children's herb, especially for headaches, nervousness, cramping pains and insomnia. In fevers it produces perspiration without raising the temperature further, and so is indicated for feverish fits and scarlet fever.
Dose When treating fits, give larger quantities than standard. For a baby, up to 1 heaped 5mls teaspoon of dried herb as an infusion for each teacup, increasing to 4-6 teaspoons when treating fevers in adults. If a baby will not take the herb, rub diluted tincture into the abdomen (5 times standard dose) or sponge the body with the tea.
Contraindications None.
Cautions The active ingredient is volatile, so this herb should be taken as a diluted tincture or infusion, never boiled.

Passiflora incarnata
Passion flower

Parts used Dried plant.
Actions Nervous system relaxant, general sedative,

relaxes muscle spasms and muscular cramps.
Indications Helpful for insomnia and after stimulating events such as parties. Also for neuralgia, migraines due to over-excitement, delirium, hysteria, epilepsy and fits in children. Readily available in pill form at many health food stores. In small doses, it can safely be given over a long period of time, with no side-effects or withdrawal symptoms.
Contraindications None.
Cautions In large doses (more than 8 5mls teaspoons daily) over a long period, it can cause migraine.

Phytolacca decandra
Poke root

Parts used Dried roots.
Actions Decongestant, especially for the glandular system, softens thick or knotted mucus (phlegm).
Indications With Blue flag (*Iris versicolor*), this is the main herb for "echo" diseases (page 25) when phlegm has become thick. It has a special effect on the throat and aids tonsillitis. It speeds up fat metabolism and is one of the few herbs that can help overweight children. Treats irregular appetite and soothes indigestion accompanied by good appetite. It softens phlegm, so the glands may swell and mucous discharges increase for a week or two after treatment starts. It is cleansing so spots and boils

often appear when it is first taken. Specific for mumps.
Contraindications Can aggravate bed wetting.
Cautions The fresh herb is poisonous; use only when dried. In large doses, induces diarrhea and/or vomiting.

Plantago major
Plantain (also *Plantago lanceolata*, Ribwort)

Parts used Leaves.
Actions Cooling, diuretic.
Indications A cooling herb taken internally for "hot" conditions, especially inflammation in the urinary tract or lungs. In children it aids earaches (otitis media), when the tincture is diluted with an equal volume of warm water and dropped into the ear at hourly intervals. This often causes the child to perspire.
Dose For urinary or lung problems, use in larger quantities – for children, the dose is one-half of a 5mls teaspoon of dried herb, as a tea, every 2 hours.
Contraindications None.

Potentilla tormentilla
Tormentil

Parts used Whole plant, including roots.
Actions Astringent (drying), cleansing.
Indications One of the strongest yet safest astringents, which benefits all forms of diarrhea and other discharges such as nosebleeds. Also recommended for cleansing,

skin eruptions and boils, and as a gargle to soothe sore and ulcerated throats.
Contraindications None.
Cautions Large doses may lead to vomiting.

Prunus serotina
Wild cherry

Parts used Bark (the leaves are poisonous).
Actions Chest stimulant, sedative, drying, general tonic.
Indications Primarily for relieving spasmodic coughs, particularly croup and whooping cough. Its digestive action is weak, so for whooping cough it should be combined with Black root (*Leptandra virginica*). It has a secondary use in first aid, in the acute stage of asthma, when it can often bring relief. Best in syrup form, which has an agreeable taste.
Contraindications None.

Rhamnus purshiana
Cascara (Californian buckthorn)

Parts used Bark.
Actions Laxative, tonic to the intestines.
Indications Employed in some hospitals as a laxative and purgative. It affects the stomach, liver, bile ducts and intestines.
Dose Small doses (5-20 drops of tincture daily) over a long period aid bowel movements and act as a gentle laxative. Adjust the dose to suit your child; usually it can be gradually reduced with time.

Contraindications None.
Cautions Large doses (10 times standard) are a violent purgative.

Salvia officinalis
Sage

Parts used Leaves.
Actions Drying, tonifying, relieves flatulence, helps heal wounds, antiseptic, and a tonic for the nerves.
Indications A wonderful herb, readily obtainable in most areas. Works well against diarrhea, weakness and exhaustion, and makes an effective gargle for sore throats. It helps to stop bleeding from deep cuts and wounds – sprinkle powdered

Sage's aura is smooth and regular, and this herb is a great calmer and regulator, especially of the digestive system.

sage over a cut and a durable, flexible scab soon forms. Its black color looks unsightly, but it heals very effectively.
Dose For diarrhea, one-half of a 5mls teaspoon of herb is infused for 10 minutes in a teacup, strained and given to a baby in a bottle. As a tea for weakness and exhaustion, make in the usual way but infuse for 20 minutes, so the bitter essences can draw out.
Contraindications None.
Cautions Do not use the essential oil form in children.

Sambucus nigra
Elder

Parts used Flowers and berries (internally), leaves (externally).
Actions and indications The flowers promote perspiration in the early stages of influenza, especially when combined with Peppermint (*Mentha piperita*). The berries make a good tonic wine and cough syrup; for the latter they are preserved by heating with sugar to form a syrup. The leaves are used in Green ointment (page 184).
Contraindications None.
Cautions None for the flowers or berries. Do not give the leaves, roots or bark internally.

Sanguinaria canadensis
Bloodroot

Parts used Roots.
Actions Calms harsh coughs.
Indications Chiefly asthma, whooping cough, bronchitis

HERBAL MATERIA MEDICA

and croup. It calms convulsive coughs and relaxes the chest.
Dose Up to 5 drops of tincture, diluted as usual.
Contraindications None.
Cautions In larger doses it is likely to cause vomiting and diarrhea. Use small doses only. Classified by the United States Food and Drug Administration as unsafe in certain circumstances.

Senecio jacobaea
Ragwort

Parts used Plant.
Actions Aids perspiration in fevers, clears mucus (phlegm) from the chest.
Indications Its special effects on the mucous membranes help in infections where there is inflammation and phlegm. Excellent for catarrhal coughs and influenza, and specific for acute tonsillitis.
Contraindications None.
Cautions Ragwort is known as poisonous to cattle. Used correctly, however, it is not so to humans.

Taraxacum officinale
Dandelion

Parts used Roots.
Actions Increases bile secretion, diuretic, mild laxative and slight stimulant.
Indications Used mostly to treat liver disorders. It can aid weak digestion, especially when there is difficulty in digesting fat, and mild "liver congestion" (page 23). Helps to reduce adolescent acne, and also reduces cholesterol in the blood. Its action is more pronounced when it is combined with other herbs, and in fact it is often used to strengthen other remedies. Its mild stimulating effect, especially when roasted (as dandelion coffee), can energize lethargic children. Blanched dandelion shoots and the leaves are sometimes eaten as a vegetable or in green salad.
Contraindications None.

Thymus vulgaris
Thyme

Parts used Leaves.
Actions Calms convulsive coughs, relieves spasms and cramps, acts as an antiseptic and general tonic, reduces flatulence.
Indications Thyme is usually combined with other herbs, and is helpful in healing whooping cough, phlegm accumulation and sore throats. From this plant comes thymol, an important ingredient in commercial cough tablets and gargles. Also assists digestion and relieves colic. This common and well-known herb is readily available from food stores and supermarkets in many regions.
Dose For children, make a simple infusion of one-half to 1 level 5mls teaspoon of dried herb to a teacup of water, sweetened with honey. For babies or toddlers, administer thyme in the water at bath time (page 132).
Contraindications None.

Tilia europaea
Lime flowers

Parts used Flowers.
Actions Calms nerves, promotes perspiration in fevers, soothes the stomach.
Indications All-purpose calming herb, made into a tea that is popular in some parts of Europe. It calms and strengthen the nerves and settles the stomach, so it can be used to treat insomnia and irritability, especially in sensitive children. Also recommended to calm general nervousness, and specifically nervous stomachs. Its action in promoting perspiration in fevers makes it suitable for the "hot" type of fever.
Contraindications None.

Tussilago farfara
Coltsfoot

Parts used Plant.
Actions Clears chest mucus (phlegm), soothing.
Indications *Tussilago* means "cough-dispeller" and it is the herb of choice for lung complaints. It can safely be given when the child is weak, since it soothes the bronchi (main airways). Often used in combination with Horehound (*Marrubium vulgaris*) and Licorice (*Glycyrrhiza glabra*).
Contraindications None.

Valeriana officinalis
Valerian

Parts used Roots.
Actions Calms the nerves, relieves flatulence, relaxes

spasms and cramps in the muscles and digestion.
Indications This herb has a great reputation as a relaxant, and the tincture is readily available at health food stores or pharmacies in many areas. It relaxes without tiring; in fact, in many users the relaxation quickly gives way to a feeling of new vigor and clarity of thought. Used for nervous tension, insomnia, spasms, cramps and fits, including feverish fits in babies. It aids digestion and often relieves flatulence when other herbs have failed.
Contraindications None.
Cautions Safe in medicinal doses, but consult a practitioner before use. When taken in large doses (more than 100 grams daily), Valerian can cause muscular pain, heaviness in the head, stupor and heart palpitations.

Viscum album
Mistletoe

Parts used Leaves (the berries are highly poisonous).
Actions Relaxes spasms and cramps, strengthens the nervous system and heart, tonifying, diuretic, reduces high blood pressure.
Indications Sacred since antiquity, this is a herb with many uses. For children's ailments its chief indication is for fits and epilepsy, for which it is specific. It reduces inflammation in the nerves and gently calms and strengthens. Also advised as a

diuretic to lower the blood pressure and strengthen the heart. Stems uterine bleeding and promotes milk production in nursing mothers.
Contraindications None.
Cautions Use only under supervision. Large doses (more than 25 grams daily) can raise blood pressure, cause internal haemorrhage and weaken the heart. American Mistletoe is classified as unsafe by the United States Food and Drug Administration.

Xanthoxylum americanum
Prickly ash

Parts used Bark of roots.
Actions Digestive stimulant, general tonic, promotes perspiration in fevers.
Indications Mainly as a stimulant to the digestive system, producing a sense of warmth in the stomach. It is used for poor or weak digestion with swollen abdomen, flatulence, pale face and lethargy. A secondary use is to stimulate the circulation, thus relieving cold hands and feet. It can help to warm up a feverish but "chilly" child, and is effective in the later stages of an ailment when the child lacks adequate strength to overcome the last of the illness.
Contraindications None.

Zea mays
Corn silk

Parts used Flowers – the "silk" or "beard" (pistils).

Actions Diuretic, soothes urinary tract inflammation, antiseptic.
Indications Corn silk is a mild tonic for the urinary system and is ideally suited to children. Good for urinary complaints such as cystitis, urethritis and diaper rash.
Contraindications None.

Zingiber officinale
Ginger

Parts used Fresh roots.
Actions Stimulates the digestion, reduces flatulence, pleasingly aromatic and clears mucus (phlegm) from the chest.
Indications Cold and weak conditions in children (and the elderly), especially when the digestion is weak. It is very warm and soothing. It stimulates the flow of digestive juices, relieves menstrual pain and congestion due to cold, when applied externally as a compress over the abdomen (as the fresh root), or taken internally with molasses. The simplest way to give Ginger is to add a little of the fresh root to food. Simmer it in the milk for bottlefed babies, or grate a little into the baby food for weaned babies.
Contraindications Do not use if there is inflammation, as it can be burning.
Cautions If taken in large doses over long periods (10 times standard), it can cause inflammation and weakness.

53

HOMOEOPATHY AND TISSUE SALTS

Homoeopathy uses the energy or "vibrations" of remedies rather than their material substances or essences. It is based on the general law that a substance which is poisonous in large doses can cure in very small doses. This is summed up by the time-honored phrase: "Like cures like." This means the symptom pattern cured by homoeopathic (very low) quantities of a substance is similar to the symptom pattern produced by poisonous (larger) quantities of the same substance.

Tissue salts As commonly used today, tissue salts are a limited selection of homoeopathic remedies. Originally conceived as mineral supplements, they were sometimes given in large quantities to treat disease due to mineral deficiency. However, most manufacturers today prepare tissue salts in very dilute form, as for homoeopathic remedies. The tissue salts are listed separately on pages 64-65.

Availability Both homoeopathic and tissue salt remedies are widely available, prepared and ready for home use, from suppliers of natural medicines. If you have trouble locating a supply, ask a local homoeopathic physician, natural medicine practitioner or at a health food store.

Preparation and potency

The mother tincture (for herbs), or the mother solution (for animal or mineral substances), is usually prepared in alcohol. It is then diluted successively in water by a factor of 10 each time. For example, 10mls of mother solution is added to 90mls of water. After one dilution from the mother solution, by this factor of 10, the resulting solution is called a 1X potency. The 1X potency

diluted by a factor of 10 becomes a 2X potency, and then 3X, 4X and so on.

At each dilution, or "potentiation", the liquid is "sucussed". This means the flask containing the liquid is subjected to very strong agitation, by banging or shaking hard, to spread the energy and vibrations through the flask and fluid.

Scales of potency In Britain, the commonly used scale of potency is the X scale, as described above. In continental Europe, the C scale may be used, where potentiation is by a factor of 100. Some practitioners use the M scale, at a factor of 1,000.

Throughout this book we advise the use of 6X potencies. These are generally considered to be the safest. Give the wrong remedy at 6X potency – and nothing happens. Higher potencies are stronger, deeper-acting and work over a long period, and can produce unwanted results when used by the inexperienced.

Presentation Remedies are usually sold in the form of tablets, pills or capsules. These are made of a simple, harmless carrier substance such as lactose, which has been sucussed with the liquid remedy at the relevant potency, to absorb it. Another form is a sachet or envelope of powder or granules, again usually lactose. In some areas liquid remedies are available.

Methods of prescribing

In classical homoeopathy, remedies are selected on the basis of matching symptoms in the remedy (at high dose) to symptoms in the patient. For example, a healthy person who takes large doses of herbal Pasque flower (*Anemone pulsatilla*) experiences a burning sensation in the throat, thick yellow nasal discharge, a feverish "hot" cough, diarrhea with a burning sensation, and a tendency to tears. So a patient who shows this pattern of symptoms would be helped by the homoeopathic remedy Pulsatilla.

Priority of symptoms There is much discussion among homoeopaths about which symptoms are most significant. There is no general rule, but many adopt the principle: "From above to below". This means you consider the mental symptoms first, then emotional, and then physical. That principle is adopted here, and any departures are noted.

Constitutional prescribing Each child is an individual and has distinctive likes, behavior and preoccupations. In some children these personal characteristics are so marked that they can be used for constitutional prescribing.

For example, imagine a tall, thin, pale child who lacks energy and is quiet and withdrawn. Illness strikes at the weakest part, so this low-energy child is likely to develop diseases of the "weak" and "cold" patterns (page 21). Different illnesses, which show as different physical symptoms, all exaggerate this child's constitutional tendency towards a "cold", apathetic and listless reaction.

You may find that you choose a remedy for your child on the basis of his or her immediate symptoms, such as a cough or digestive upset – but again and again, the remedy turns out to be the same one. This is a sign that your child has a definite "constitutional type", and that he or she requires the corresponding "constitutional remedy", whatever the illness.

It is possible to prescribe a constitutional remedy for prevention. As a parent, you may feel your child is becoming ill, although you do not yet know the problem. At this stage, an illness can often be prevented by administering one dose of the constitutional remedy for your child.

Dosages and administration

Throughout this book, 6X potencies should be used unless stated otherwise.

In acute (sudden) diseases, give one dose (one pill or powder sachet) of the remedy every half hour for the first six doses, then hourly for the next six doses, then three times daily. (If the remedy is in liquid form, follow the instructions.)

You may continue to give the remedy for up to two weeks. But after this time, or in a chronic (long-term) condition, consult a homoeopathic practitioner.

Remedies should not normally be given within 15-20 minutes of food and drink. Allow the remedy to dissolve under the tongue. For best results, it should not be washed down with water.

Caution Avoid all coffee and peppermint, including peppermint toothpaste, since these nullify many remedies.

GETTING STARTED: HOMOEOPATHY OR TISSUE SALTS?

Homoeopathy as a system of medicine has many advantages. The remedies are easy to administer, especially to children. They are often readily available, and suit a very wide range of people and ailments. They can treat initial symptoms before these develop into full-blown disease (but see also page 65).

HOMOEOPATHY MATERIA MEDICA

This section aims to give a "symptom picture" for each commonly used remedy. The remedies are listed here in the alphabetical order of their international scientific names. There are many more remedies in the full homoeopathic range, but space here is limited. For further information, consult specialized books (page 186).

To select a remedy, simply match its character and pattern to the pattern of symptoms (mental-emotional-physical) shown by your child. The closer the match, the stronger the results should be.

The 12 tissue salt remedies are listed on pages 64-65.

Cautions

By their nature, remedies that can cure in very dilute (homoeopathic) form, may be poisonous and cause illness in large quantities. Use only the correctly-prepared homoeopathic remedies.

Seek medical advice for any symptoms or conditions that persist or become serious, or if you have any worries.

Aconite

Actions Acute, sudden, immediate, intense. For a fast reaction when the body has experienced a sudden, severe disturbance or emotional fright and is unable to react in time (compare Belladonna). *Indications* First-stage remedy for "cold" type fevers. Colds due to sudden change in

temperature or strong wind. Sudden fright or shock. *Symptom picture* Onset: symptoms occur within a few hours; they develop rapidly and are very marked.

Mental outlook: child is fearful, restless and agitated. Face shows great anxiety and possibly terror.

Sleep: sleepless, with fear and agitation increasing during the night.

Fevers-chills: high fever but no perspiration. Chills and fear of cold, yet the child wants to throw off coverings and open the window.

Head: headache with violent bursting pains; sneezing and nasal discharge or stuffed-up nose; eyes are red, dry and stinging.

Chest: throat is red, dry and stinging; child has an intense thirst for cold water.

Skin: dry with the high fever; symptoms are relieved by perspiration.

Child is helped by: open window, drinks of cold water.

Avoid: warm and stuffy atmosphere. Worse at night.

Arnica
Arnica montana

Actions Reduces swelling of blood vessels, inflammation of muscles and nerves, shock and tension. Aids relaxation and peaceful sleep.
Indications Accidental injuries, shocks, falls, surgery, fractures. Previous injuries where the effect of trauma remains, with physical or mental-emotional symptoms.

Prolonged physical effort or mental strain (includes whooping cough).
Symptom picture Mental outlook: initially shock numbs the system, the child is dazed and quiet and may say nothing is wrong.

Head: face has a pale, greyish color in severe cases. In later stages, if there is fever, the face becomes red.

Sleep: initially restless with disturbing dreams as a means of working out the effects of the shock. Difficulty sleeping due to physical exhaustion. After, sleep is peacefully restored.

Chest: in whooping cough, the child is exhausted, tense and frightened of the next coughing attack.

Child is helped by: rest, lying down.

Avoid: touch, pressure, any type of motion.

Ars. alb.
Arsenicum album

Actions Combats anxiety, lack of energy. The anxiety arises from insecurity – often manifested as a fear of being abandoned. Regulates the digestion.
Indications Constitutionally, the child tends to be thin, fastidious and tidy, worries and overworks, is often precocious, intelligent and an "achiever". Being thin, a large proportion of heat is easily lost through the body surface, so the overall picture is "chilly" (page 22). Suitable for general symptoms such as

pains relieved by warmth; periodic recurrence of the same symptom without a full recovery. Specific for diarrhea from food poisoning.

Symptom picture Mental outlook: see Indications.

Head: intense congestive headache from too much study or worry, or during a fever. Pale face that flushes with excitement, although the extremities are always cold. Nose and throat are sensitive to cold. Watery nasal discharge.

Digestion: easily upset by external cold and cold-type foods (page 34), resulting in diarrhea. Fatigue after each bowel movement that is further weakened by cold, clammy perspiration.

Sleep: terrified of the dark, fears intensify at night.

Child is helped by: bed rest, being covered warmly with head kept elevated and cool, hot drinks, company.

Avoid: cold, tension, too much change.

Belladonna

Actions Acute, full, strong, rapid. The symptoms reflect the external provoking condition, which is strong, extreme and penetrating. There are characteristic intense feelings of heat, redness, throbbing and burning. Compare Aconite.

Indications The first stage of fevers due to staying too long in extreme cold or icy draughts, or over-exposure to

sun or heat. Also indicated in whooping cough.

Symptom picture Onset: immediate, within a few hours, full-blown by the next day. Strong reactions and strong symptoms with a fever that develops quickly and comes down sharply too.

Mental outlook: irritable, acutely sensitive, does not want to be disturbed. May become furious.

Fevers-chills: fever develops rapidly, profuse perspiration during the fever or after its peak. Since this draws body heat to the surface, there is a sense of inner coldness.

Head: a hot "congestive" headache with throbbing pain, which may be relieved by gently pressing the head to reduce the throbbing. Eyes feel hot and burning, eyelids are swollen, and pupils are dilated (hence sensitivity to bright light). Middle ear is infected (otitis media), great sensitivity to noises. The parotid glands are swollen, as in mumps. Nose is swollen and red, but little discharge. Throat is red, congested, swollen and burning, swallowing is painful and difficult. There is a great thirst for cold drinks.

Chest: dry, painful cough because the heat of the fever dries body fluids, resulting in little phlegm.

Digestion: distended abdomen with a hot, cutting pain across the navel.

Sleep: jumps up and "starts" on falling asleep, is greatly

agitated during sleep, and may have nightmares.

Skin: red, hot and dry until "boiling point" is reached and the perspiration breaks through. Heat radiates strongly from the skin.

Child is helped by: dim and quiet surroundings, being warmly covered, lying semi-erect with head elevated.

Avoid: alteration in noises, lights, temperature, draughts.

Bryonia

Actions Complaints characterized by energy obstruction. In Chinese medicine, it is said that pain is caused when energy tries to flow through an internal blockage (page 15), so this remedy is characterized by pain which is aggravated by movement. Associated inflammatory indications.

Indications See Actions. Also lung conditions such as bronchitis, whooping cough, chest pains.

Symptom picture Mental outlook: irritable, dislikes being picked up.

Head: a bursting headache, worse on movement. Red eyes, hot and sore.

Chest: any chest pains are worsened by coughing. The child may yawn frequently.

Digestion: thirsty, likes milk, sleepy after feeding.

Skin: hot and painful, with prickling sensations.

Child is helped by: perspiration; some localized symptoms improve with dry warmth.

57

HOMOEOPATHY MATERIA MEDICA

Avoid: sitting up, being handled or moved around too much, and warm damp weather or surroudings.

Calc. carb.
Calcium carbonicum

Actions Calcium is essential for bone and teeth formation, muscles and tendons, and nerve and brain function. Hence this remedy combats tendencies for a physically loose or "floppy" body and slow movements.
Indications A child whose constitution is "fat, fair, chilly, flabby, damp". The pattern arises from the poor intake and use of calcium. The "softness" of bones and muscles means the child has difficulty in "standing on his own two feet" and needs to feel supported and protected. Teeth are late in coming through, and the child may be late in standing and walking. He or she may have difficulty in "connecting" with new people and prefer familiar faces. Often indicated in "echo" diseases (page 25).
Symptom picture Mental outlook: rather fragile, becomes nervous and clingy from repeated falls or other mild injuries.
Sleep: sensitive to the dark, often has nightmares.
Chest: tendency to swollen glands and tonsillitis. Accumulations of thick mucus (phlegm) cleared by coughing.
Fevers-chills: physical effort is tiring and quickly leads to overheating and profuse perspiration. As a result, the child may catch colds and chills easily.
Digestion: transforming food into energy is relatively slow and inefficient, hence the low metabolic rate and a tendency to feel chilly and gain weight. Difficulty in digesting milk, although the child likes to drink it. Production of phlegm (see Sulfur) which may appear nasally or be coughed up. Tendency towards "cold" indigestion and liver congestion (page 23). There is constipation due to slow digestion, but the child feels better in this state.
Limbs: generally weak muscle tone. Although the child appears round, chubby and bursting with health, the excess weight is unnecessary fat and not muscle.

Calc. fluor.
Calc. phos.
Calc. sulph.

See page 64.

Carbo veg.
Carbonicum vegetabilis

Actions Combats deficient energy, or slow or stagnating energy flow (page 14).
Indications After an infectious illness or food poisoning. In newborn babies it may occur after a difficult or long birth. Many symptoms are similar to those of Silica, but in Silica there is a recognizable "will" inside the child struggling to get out, while in Carbo veg. the child seems exhausted.
Symptom picture Mental outlook: irresolute, short of energy, soon tires.
Head: pale dull face, often dribbling at the mouth, frequent sneezing.
Chest: shallow breathing, weak ineffective cough.
Digestion: weak and watery. Poor appetite, choosy over food. Stools tend to be watery or loose.
Skin: cold and moist to the touch, profuse perspiration.
Sleep: wants to sleep a lot in the day. May wake frequently at night, take a small drink and then go back to sleep.
Fevers-chills: feels cold and numb inside.

Chamomilla

Actions Relieves tense, nervous pain; acts on the liver, where pent-up emotions accumulate (page 23). Characteristic of this condition is a "one-sided flush" noticeable on the face, which is linked to the effects of uneven circulation.
Indications Teething, particularly during periods when the child is not just "irritable" but truly in pain. The remedy should be given frequently, as often as every half hour, during the acute stage, and 3 times daily when the symptoms are mild. Also indicated after exposure to cold or winds.
Symptom picture Mental outlook: sensitive and irritable, wants to be carried since this provides comfort.

Calc. carb.-Ferr. phos.

The turbulent aura of Chamomilla's centre, and its spiky exterior, closely relate to the mental condition of a child who can be helped by this homoeopathic remedy.

Head: head is hot, with clammy perspiration on the forehead and scalp. Face is red and flushed, generally with one side more intense. There may be acute earache, dribbly mouth and tender gums.

Chest: tickling, a dry irritable cough during the day which may accompany teething. Mucus (phlegm) in the lungs; when lying down, this rattles in the chest.

Digestion: flatulence and colic; child screams from acute pain. There may be diarrhea with yellow or green or loose, slimy stools.

Limbs: whole body becomes hot and agitated; the child throws off bed covers.

Nervous system: this is the remedy to administer to avoid fits (convulsions) that some children get when teething.

Child is helped by: cool air, cool drinks or soothing gum applications, being carried.

Avoid: heat, anger, wind and extremes of cold.

China

Actions Combats fluid loss, especially of blood, diarrhea or excessive sweat. The body may release fluids but internally fluids do not reach the places where they are needed. This can lead to "liver congestion" (page 23).

Indications Conditions where fluids are or have been lost from the body (diarrhea, sweat, blood, discharges).

Symptom picture Mental outlook: the physical lack of lubrication is matched emotionally. The child is "prickly", resentful and tries to upset others.

Face: may have red cheeks characteristic of liver congestion.

Chest: dry or harsh cough, which may be triggered by laughter or anger.

Digestion: weak, food tends to lodge, swollen abdomen, loose foul-smelling stools.

Sleep: drowsy in periods through the daytime, especially after eating.

Fevers-chills: shivering and cold to the touch, alternating with heat and fevers. Profuse perspiration, even if no fever.

Ferr. phos.
Ferrum phosphate

See also page 64.

Actions Iron (ferrum) corrects the tendency to show anemia-like characteristics of pallor, weakness, poor circulation of blood to the extremities and a degree of breathlessness. Phosphorus helps to strengthen weak nerves.

Indications During the first stage of any fever, as a strengthener. Also useful in the first stage of all mucous and inflammatory fevers, throat and respiratory infections, after throat or nose operations, and to control bleeding and relieve soreness.

Symptom picture Head: red cheeks (rather than the whole face) which are sore and hot. Acute earache. Symptoms of the first stage of a head cold, or predisposition to colds. Nosebleeds. Red, swollen tonsils or throat.

Chest: dry cough.

Digestion: weak, so the child has trouble with rich or hard-to-digest foods, is choosy over food, and may vomit undigested food.

Sleep: restless, with anxious dreams and sweats. Wakes in the night.

Fevers-chills: chilly around or just after midday.

Child is helped by: rest, cold applications to the skin.

59

HOMOEOPATHY MATERIA MEDICA

Avoid: touch, being jolted or moved about suddenly, other sudden changes.

Gelsemium

Actions Counteracts "dampness" in all its forms, physical and mental (see Sulfur. In Chinese medicine, "dampness" is impure, cloying, obstructing and slowing. Energy flow and breathing are most affected, leading to heavy, muddled thinking, and vice versa. Dampness is "heavy" and sinks, and can be drawn from the body in urine.

Indications When dampness affects the body's ability to fight disease, especially in colds and coughs, and eruptive infections like measles. Also for nervous, tense behavior, due to anticipation ("exam nerves"). Overconsumption of mucus-encouraging foods (page 36).

Symptom picture Onset: symptoms develop gradually over a few days, are vague rather than clearly-defined.

Mental outlook: child feels listless, timid, dulled memory and lack of concentration. As the illness progresses he or she may be weak, and dizzy when trying to stand.

Head: face is flushed and congested. A heavy, dull headache, either across the forehead or down the back of the head and neck, typically relieved by urination. Drooping, heavy eyelids; eyes are glassy and vision is blurred. Severe sneezing.

Chest: Sore, puffy throat, swallowing gives a feeling of pressure up into the ears. Violent spasmodic cough and slow weary breathing.

Digestion: no thirst, despite the sweating; diarrhea.

Skin: hot and sticky. In measles, Gelsemium helps to clear the damp blockage and allow the rash to develop (page 124).

Urination: profuse, clear.

Limbs: weak and trembling during the fever, possibly with numbness; cold hands and feet.

Sleep: agitated, from the fever or mental overwork.

Fevers-chills: chills pass up and down the back in waves, then a mild fever develops, with sticky perspiration.

Child is helped by: lying down with head slightly raised, gentle warming.

Avoid: mucus-encouraging foods, too much mental stress and exertion.

Kali mur.
Kali phos.
Kali sulph.
Mag. phos.

See pages 64 and 65.

Merc. sol.
Mercurius solubilis

Actions Deep-acting remedy for the whole constitution. There is an accumulation of "damp heat" (see Sulfur, page 62), and exhaustion, especially of the mind and general nervous system.

Indications Recurrent fevers, even when repeatedly treated by antibiotics. When the breath, excretions and body odors smell foul. Any tendency to form pus which is thin, green, putrid or streaked with blood.

Symptom picture Mental outlook (constitutional, not fever stage): when well, the child may be bright and have a sharp, probing mind. When off color, the opposite occurs and the mental responses are slow, dull and lethargic.

Head: dizziness when lying on the back, a "heavy" head as though bandaged. Oily sweat on the head. Pale, dirty-looking, puffy face with spots. Thick yellow discharge from the ears, earache. Sore nose, excessive saliva, but the child is still thirsty. Tongue has a thick, dirty coat. Bad breath, tooth decay. Throat is sore, especially on the right side; pain shoots up to the ears on swallowing.

Digestion: loose, usually painful stools.

Chest: cough with yellow phlegm, the child feels a need for air.

Limbs: weak, clumsy. Growing pains in the legs; clammy perspiration on legs at night.

Skin: almost constantly moist with perspiration.

Fevers-chills: persistent fevers which never clear, alternating heat and chills, night sweats.

Avoid: wet damp weather, warm surroundings and other conditions which induce perspiration.

Nat. mur.
Sodium chloride, common salt

See also page 65.

Actions Deep-acting and wide-ranging remedy. Releases blocked emotional energy, such as grief, fear or anger, helps the circulation of fluids.

Indications Catching a cold, complaints due to sluggish or blocked energy.

Symptom picture Mental outlook: a "wet blanket" with a negative outlook, bursts into tears, wants to be alone.

Head: symptoms of a head cold, runny nose and watering, dull eyes. Ears full of secretions and the child may be hard of hearing or hear crackling noises in the ear upon swallowing. Pale, dull face.

Chest: watery cough, tears flow when coughing. Heavy feeling in the chest.

Digestion: likes salty food, but is worse for it. Watery vomit. Thirsty, but does not like drinking. Loose stools.

Sleep: sleeps a lot in the day, but restless at night.

Skin: itchy, red rash.

Nat. phos.
Nat. sulph.

See page 65.

Nux vomica

Actions One of the great "constitutional" remedies, but more applicable to adults than children (and so is given limited space here). Counteracts the effects of frustration or suppressed anger and an "overheated" liver. (In Chinese medicine the two are closely related.) This results in an energy build-up which eventually needs an outlet.

Indications Nausea and vomiting. The effect of too much mental work, especially if there is lack of exercise.

Symptom picture Mental outlook: irritable, short-tempered, especially from heat after too much sunshine.

Head: headache aggravated by concentration and coffee. Red face, sore red eyes, itchy nose with discharge, sore inflamed mouth.

Chest: irritating dry cough.

Digestion: nausea, vomiting. Travel (motion) sickness. Abdominal aches and colic which give strong, "blocked" pains.

Limbs: weakness, dragging feet, stumbles easily.

Sleep: difficulty in going to sleep, mind too lively. Wide awake in the early hours.

Avoid: rich food, eating while concentrating on something else (such as television).

Administration Often more effective after doses of Sulfur.

Pulsatilla

Actions Wide-acting, can be used for many conditions. In Chinese medicine, advised for those with weak (rather than congested) liver energy. Changeable moods and sensitivity when ill; on the physical level, a strong body and a sunny outlook.

Indications Acute infectious diseases and chronic problems, especially when the child has become emotional and tired, and easily bursts into tears. Tendencies to sluggish digestion, accumulations of greenish phlegm. Also for measles.

Symptom picture General: symptoms are changeable and often contradictory.

Mental outlook: variable but generally timid, gentle, wants support and sympathy, responds to affection.

Pulsatilla has three distinct auras. In the centre is an intense energy concentration; around this is a less concentrated "cushion"; and surrounding the flower itself is a more flexible area.

HOMOEOPATHY MATERIA MEDICA

Head: In Chinese medicine the eyes relate to the liver. Watering eyes, itching and burning, yellow discharge, sensitivity to light. Yellow sticky nasal discharge. Earache with mucus, possibly a bad-smelling ear discharge; difficult hearing (due to secretions in the middle ear).

Digestion: avoids fat greasy foods, hot foods (both hot temperature and hot energy), feels ill after greasy foods (compare Sulfur). Vomiting from emotional upset or excitement. Flatulence, heartburn. Dull aches in the abdomen. Likes ice cream and fruit, but is not thirsty even though the mouth is dry. Diarrhea from cold and cold-energy (page 34) foods and drinks.

Chest: dry cough in the evening and at night, sits up in bed to get relief. Loose cough in the morning, brings up thick greenish phlegm.

Urine: cystitis because poisons in the system have to be passed out in urine.

Rhus tox
Rhus toxicosis

Actions When "dampness" causes the accumulation of toxins (see Gelsemium). The dampness can come from damp weather, getting very wet and cold, or poor digestion of rich food. The toxins affect muscle function, and appear on the skin as red spots.
Indications Muscular strains and sprains when first moving but better with further

movement. Getting wet. Septic conditions. Chickenpox and related infective and eruptive skin conditions.
Symptom picture Mental outlook: may be restless and have a negative outlook.

Head: feels heavy due to fluid build-up. Damp eruptions on scalp, stiff neck. Red, discharging eyes. Tongue is coated except for a red tip, bitter taste in mouth, thirsty. Sore throat with swollen and painful glands.

Chest: dry teasing cough all night with sore muscles.

Silica

See also page 65.
Actions Wide-acting, suitable for lack of energy and stamina, resulting in extreme inertia and poor resistance to disease – but also a stubborn streak. Suitable for a child who has to use his or her strong will to force the rather weak body into action.
Indications Wide range of conditions; mainly digestive, with malabsorption and consequent malnutrition. The child may be a slow developer. Often the first remedy in "echo" diseases (page 25). Has a definite expulsive effect (such as on splinters and thorns). First stage of colds.
Symptom picture Child appears pale, sickly, shivery; and is sometimes damp, thin, tired-looking.

Mental outlook: timid, fears failure, can only cope with little tasks. Withdrawn and hesitant. Easily tired.

Head: sweaty, feels better with head wrapped up; in chronic headache, worse when anxious. Eyes have recurring styes, sensation of grit. Chronic earache. Gums bleed, teeth sensitive to cold air. Sore runny nose, frequent sneezing. Recurrent tonsillitis, enlarged and tender glands.

Chest: violent cough, worse when lying down; coughs up thick lumpy phlegm.

Digestion: nausea, vomiting, abdominal pains. Likes frequent but small meals, prefers cold foods and drinks. Constipation, stools may appear but then recede again into body due to lack of energy to expel them.

Back: weak spine, sensitive to draughts and chills.

Limbs: cracked, pitted nails. Icy-cold and sweaty or moist feet.

Skin: Every scratch tends to becomes septic. Ill effects of immunization.

Child is helped by: warmth, rest. Better in summer.

Avoid: wet weather, cold air, mental or physical effort.

Sulfur

Actions Perhaps the widest range of applications on all levels – mental, emotional, physical, constitutional – as well as at different stages of illness, acute or chronic. Works from the body's center to the outside, cleansing and reactivating. Symptoms are characterized by burning, congestion, eruptions, itching and redness. In Chinese medicine, this is explained in terms of "damp heat" which has many different origins: prolonged damp weather; too much rich and spicy foods or greasy, fatty foods; feverish illness which leads to phlegm (see Gelsemium); and a constitutional tendency. The "damp" affects digestion and impedes the normal flow of energy, thus slowing and stagnating. Mentally, Sulfur is linked with digesting thoughts and memories and the stimulation of ideas. The "heat" spreads outwards, and the orifices are affected, being the "exit" sites of the body.

Constitution "Salt-of-the-earth" type, or "child of the universe". The child is not stifled by rules and order but has an inner sense of freedom and happiness. For example, strict hygiene does not come naturally, and the child may even become selfish and slovenly (contrast Ars. alb.). Moods range from the desire to roam freely, or if restricted, to fury like a volcano about to erupt.

Indications Beginning of chronic conditions, especially those with "latent heat" (page 26), effects of suppressive medications. End of acute conditions, to eliminate damp heat and prevent recurrence. Latter stages of fevers, flu and lingering colds.

Symptom picture Head: pain of headache. Sensation of a band around the forehead; or the scalp feels loose as if the head were about to burst. Cradle cap. Chronic yellow nasal discharge, red sore nostrils. Eyes are red; itching and burning eyelids are crusty and gummed in the morning. Lips are bright red. Tongue is coated and in acute conditions there is a red tip and red stripes along the sides. Dry mouth with thirst for cold water. Chronic throat inflammations, swollen glands, offensive breath.

Digestion: in babies, a tendency to digestive upsets from milk. In children, usually a large appetite with well-defined tastes, prefers highly spiced foods, sweets, fatty meat, red meat (compare Pulsatilla). Sluggish after meals. Characteristic mid-morning hunger with accompanying feelings of weakness and faintness if a snack is not available. Enlarged abdomen is a prominent feature, even if the child's build is thin. Flatulence, acidity and tendency to jaundice, colic; diarrhea that produces anal redness and itching. Liable to diaper rash.

Chest: dislikes stuffy atmospheres. Needs fresh air but sensitive to draughts. Repeated attacks of bronchitis or asthma, oppression and burning in the chest. Rattling of phlegm (mucus) in the chest, especially when lying down; when coughed up it is thick, yellow, or greenish. Struggles for breath in the middle of the night, which may force the child to sit up.

Urination: frequent by day, bed wetting at night. Mucus and pus in the urine, with urgency, and a red and sore urinary orifice.

Fevers-chills: waves of heat with occasional shivering; offensive perspiration, often on only one part of the body. Recurrent fevers.

Sleep: wakes up singing or in fits of laughter, or has nightmares if upset.

Limbs: has hot feet at night, sticks feet out of bed. During the day, hot head and cold extremities.

Skin: eruptions, itching, cradle cap, urticaria, soreness in skin creases, diaper rash, boils, acne, wounds that are slow to heal. Characteristic aggravation from washing or bathing.

Child is helped by: cool dry surroundings, loose clothing; opportunity to expand on mental, emotional and physical levels.

Avoid: rich diet, red meat, dairy foods, fried foods, sugar, fats, overeating, lack of exercise, bathing or immersion in water.

TISSUE SALTS MATERIA MEDICA

For general information on the 12 tissue salt remedies, their use and their relationship to homoeopathy, see page 54. The remedies are listed here in the alphabetical order of their international scientific names.

Calc. fluor.
Calcium fluoride

Actions Concerned with elasticity or tone of muscles. *Indications* Children who have no energy or "bounce". Tends to soften hard accumulations, so may be effective (with other remedies) in "echo" diseases (page 25) with hard swollen glands. Calcium is present in the enamel of the teeth, so this remedy is indicated for poorly formed teeth and for gum inflammation.

Child is helped by: massage and warmth.

Calc. phos.
Calcium phosphate

Actions Strengthens bones and teeth; constitutional development. This mineral is abundant in bones. With poor absorption, there is a weak constitution and perhaps rickets and other problems. Its significance as a remedy is wider, covering many of the transitions during development and maturity which relate to a strong constitution. *Indications* Convalescence after disease, delayed development, weak bone structure, late

appearance of teeth, diarrhea during teething, slow at school, late appearance of periods, anaemia and difficult and/or painful first periods.

Calc. sulph.
Calcium sulphate

Actions Reduces pus formation, controls continuous discharges of pus (and so complements Silica). *Indications* All pimples and boils which discharge, also pus from the ear or nose, or pus in the stools. Cough that brings up phlegm mixed with pus, or tonsillitis with copious pus in the throat.

Ferr. phos.
Ferrum phosphate

See also page 59.
Actions Combats weakness, fevers, injuries. Iron is strengthening, especially for the blood, and phosphorus is warming and strengthening for the nerves. Together they release the body's energy to fight the problem. *Indications* All types of weakness, inability to get things done. Fevers, especially in the early stage, and low-grade inflammations such as boils, ulcers, pimples and swelling around wounds. Teething, nosebleeds.

Kali mur.
Potassium chloride

Actions Acts on the over-production of mucus (phlegm).

Indications Various thick white discharges, as from the nose or ears. Productive cough, indigestion, vomiting phlegm, loose slimy stools, vaginal discharge. The child often feels worse after eating rich or fatty food. Also for blisters and burns, and can often strengthen the digestion against worms.

Kali phos.
Potassium phosphate

Actions Essential for nerve function. *Indications* Nervous exhaustion. Typical symptoms are being jumpy and irritable. Nervous headaches, tantrums alternating with weariness and depression. Insomnia from over-stimulation, weariness from too much schoolwork. In babies, fevers which persist and cause over-sensitivity and fear. Nerve-type pains such as tingling, itching and creeping sensations.

Child is helped by: rest and comforting warmth.

Avoid: too much mental and physical effort.

Kali sulph.
Potassium sulphate

Actions Against yellow discharges, which in Chinese medicine are a sign of "damp heat" (see homoeopathic Sulphur, page 63). *Indications* Fevers and infectious diseases where there is heat and yellowish

TISSUE SALTS MATERIA MEDICA

discharge, as from the ear, yellow slimy deposits on the tongue, skin complaints with yellow discharge, dandruff. Yellow vaginal discharge. In the early stages, before disease has developed, the underlying condition is indicated by a desire for fresh air and dislike of warm, stuffy places.

Mag. phos.
Magnesium phosphate

Actions Relieves muscular spasms and cramps and other muscle aches.
Indications Leg cramps (such as growing pains), muscular twitches, sciatica, hiccups, abdominal cramps (as in the "cold" type of insomnia), menstrual cramps. A sharp or shooting pain is characteristically helped by this remedy.
  Child is helped by: heat, bending double.
  Avoid: cold.

Nat. mur.
Sodium chloride, common salt

See also page 61.
Actions Corrects the baby's water balance.
Indications Watery discharges such as dripping nose (as in a cold), dribbling from the mouth, watery vomit, loose stools, frequent urination. Also in situations where water collects, as in a puffy, damp, swollen face, or fluid in the abdomen or legs. On the skin, it shows as nettle rash. Characterized by a rather

negative outlook; the child is often grumpy and uncooperative.

Nat. phos.
Sodium phosphate

Actions Balances acid indigestion and "liver congestion" (page 23). In babies and young children the main dietary fat is in milk, and the main organ concerned with digesting food is the liver.
Indications Acid-type indigestion, difficulty in digesting fatty foods, colic from rich foods, insomnia from indigestion, diarrhea with green stools. Desire for sweets, sore tip to the tongue, creamy-yellow coating on tongue.

Nat. sulph.
Sodium sulphate

Actions A purifier against green discharges when the body seems infected and ridden with pus.
Indications Green nasal discharge, coughing up green phlegm, coated tongue, flatulence, boils, pimples and other eruptive conditions.

Silica
Quartz

See also page 62.
Actions Purifies, stimulates the body to throw out poison. One of the deepest-acting tissue salts, with many wide-ranging uses.
Indications Spots and boils.

Coughs with pus. Specific for sore throats and tonsillitis. When imbalance leads to pus formation, body fats are not used properly, giving the characteristic indication of cracking fingernails and sweaty, smelly feet. The constitution of a "Silica child" (page 55) is sensitive and easily influenced by other people and outside events, feels cold, and reacts badly to any change in the weather.

Combination tissue salts

Combination B: Calc. phos., Kali phos., Ferr. phos.
Combination E: Calc. phos., Mag. phos., Nat. phos., Nat. sulph.
Combination H: Mag. phos., Nat. mur., Silica.
Combination J: Ferr. phos., Kali mur., Nat. mur.
Combination Q: Ferr. phos., Kali mur., Kali sulph., Nat. mur.
Combination R: Calc. fluor., Calc. phos., Ferr. phos., Mag. phos., Silica.

Getting started

Because homoeopathy has such a wide choice of remedies (page 55), it can be bewildering at first. If you are starting to treat your family at home, the 12 tissue salts are an excellent first set of remedies. They have a relatively mild action, compared to homoeopathic remedies. As you gain more experience, you may wish to obtain stronger homoeopathic remedies.

65

BACH REMEDIES

Of all natural treatments, the Bach flower remedies are the simplest to use, the most widely applicable, and the most positive in their attitude to health. At first sight their very simplicity is disconcerting, but those who try them can confirm their effectiveness and speed of action.

The philosophy underlying the Bach remedies is a positive attitude towards health. The choice of remedy is made from the child's mental and emotional state, rather than from the physical symptoms of illness. Some states of mind are considered neither good nor bad, but simply inappropriate to a particular situation, causing the person to suffer.

For example, the indications for Holly include the opposites of anger and generosity. Normally we would regard anger as "bad" and generosity as "good". The state of mind behind these feelings is neither good nor bad, but shows a difficulty in balancing opposites, and is a natural result of a genuinely warm personality.

How to prescribe the remedies

Always try to assess your child's state of mind, and pay little attention to the physical symptoms. This can be difficult if the child is suffering, but it is essential for success. Usually, the negative aspects will strike you first. This is a good way to start, and usually leads to the correct remedy; but try also to compare the positive aspects, which may be more characteristic of the child when he or she is well.

How many remedies? For children, it is rarely necessary to give more than four remedies at once. You may use up to seven in one prescription, but for such a number it is wise to look again and see if you can form a clearer picture.

The response to Bach remedies differs between acute and chronic illnesses. In the former, changes are similar to those for other therapies. In a fever, for example, the child soon feels better and starts to perspire. With a long-term disease, or an imbalance which has not yet developed into illness, the child may become more aware of his or her thoughts and feelings.

Dosage

The remedies are usually bought as concentrated "stock" solutions in labelled bottles, but they are used in a very diluted form. Follow the instructions supplied. Otherwise, almost fill a small (about 20-30mls) dropper bottle with spring water or boiled tap water, and add two or three drops of the stock remedy. When administering the remedy, place two to four drops of the diluted form directly under the tongue, or add two to four drops to food or drink, four times daily. If your baby is breastfeeding, moisten the baby's lips with the remedy.

Classification of Bach remedies

Dr Edward Bach, the originator of the Bach system, divided the 38 remedies into seven groups, according to the predominant mental and emotional symptoms. The remedies are listed on the following pages in Bach's original groupings:
- Group 1 for fear.
- Group 2 for uncertainty.
- Group 3 for disinterest.
- Group 4 for loneliness.
- Group 5 for over-sensitivity to ideas and influences.
- Group 6 for despondency and despair.
- Group 7 for being too involved in the welfare of others.

INDICATIONS FOR BACH REMEDIES

These descriptions of the indications are brief, for reasons of space and simplicity. Should you wish to learn more, see page 186. The groupings of the remedies follow Dr Bach's original system and are given opposite.

Rock rose (group 1)

Keywords Terrified, panic-stricken.

For a baby or child who is over-sensitive. Babies and children are more sensitive than adults, and they easily over-react to events (real or imagined) and quickly become panicked or terrified. The heart pounds and the eyes stare wildly. On the positive side, the child is sensitive, responsible, and very courageous. Useful for panic on waking from a nightmare, for fevers (especially if they persist), and for avoiding feverish fits.

Mimulus (group 1)

Keywords Fears known things (compare Aspen), courageous.

The child is afraid of something identifiable, such as a particular person, travel, or exams. On the positive side, he or she shows great courage – although this may overrule "sensible" fear and lead to risk-taking in truly dangerous situations. The child may be sensitive and blush easily; he or she appears extrovert, but usually needs to spend much time alone.

Cherry plum (group 1)

Keywords Fears that the mind may give way.

The child is mentally distressed and feels his or her mind is being torn apart. He or she is easily startled and bursts into tears, yet may be suddenly violent or cruel – while being afraid of the violence of such emotions. On the positive side, the child has great self-control and the will to overcome emotions.

Aspen (group 1)

Keywords Afraid of imaginary things; fear without real or actual cause.

The child is afraid: of the dark, "monsters in the corner" or other things unknown. Often he or she has a vivid imagination and great sensitivity. On the positive side, the child may have psychic abilities, which may lead to extraordinary and possibly dangerous behavior.

Red chestnut (group 1)

Keywords Excessively protective of the family and those near-and-dear.

The child fears that something dreadful will happen to loved ones around. For example, he or she may grow anxious when a parent leaves the house. On the positive side, the child has great faith in the abilities of family and friends, and believes them to be the best in their field.

Useful for weaning (when it should be taken by the mother) and possibly asthma.

Cerato (group 2)

Keywords Self-doubt, worries, needs guidance.

For the child who dislikes being alone and continually seeks advice from others, even though the answer can be found within. Yet, on the positive side, he or she possesses inner certainty and, having found a truth, wants to pass it on. Often this child is found teaching and helping younger children.

Scleranthus (group 2)

Keywords Indecisive, "grasshopper" mentality, mood swings.

The child first wants one thing, then another, then returns to the first, and may even be paralyzed by indecision. There might be difficulty in starting a project or beginning homework. He or she is very passionate, and experiences the problems that occur when the passions rule the mind. On the positive side, the child has the ability to take prompt action and make lightning decisions.

Useful for travel sickness.

Gentian (group 2)

Keywords Easily discouraged and depressed.

The child is full of energy for a project at first, but is easily discouraged by

INDICATIONS FOR BACH REMEDIES

setbacks. When something goes wrong, he or she wants to give up or hide (compare Elm) and often cries if made to continue, even seeming to enjoy the depression brought on by setbacks. On the positive side, the child is enthusiastic and inspiring.

Gorse (group 2)

Keywords Despairing, gloomy.

The child tends to suffer from deep depression (especially when ill), feeling that everything is hopeless, and there is no way out (compare Mustard). On the positive side, when well, he or she may radiate a quiet and confident optimism.

Hornbeam (group 2)

Keywords Puts things off, lacks strength to face ordeals.

For the child with perpetual "Monday morning feeling", who does not want to start the day. He or she is basically well, but seems tired and discouraged due to a lack of energy. On the positive side, the child has an inner confidence, and loves variety.

Wild oat (group 2)

Keywords Uncertain, unsettled, dissatisfied.

The child does not know which way to go or what to do, and is generally insecure. Useful when trying to make decisions such as which school subjects to take up, and to help the child to accept and enjoy living in the present. Wild oat (or Holly) may be given as a last resort to clarify a vague picture.

Clematis (group 3)

Keywords Vacant, daydreaming, inattentive.

The child lives in "a world of its own", and so appears vacant and inattentive, often with glazed eyes (compare Honeysuckle). Too much reading or television may reinforce this imaginary existence. However, on the positive side, some daydreaming is helpful.

Useful after a long illness, to help return to the real world.

The aura of the honeysuckle flower shows vibrations from the stamens that shoot forwards with vigor, those from the pistils point backwards, as though in apology and regret.

Honeysuckle (group 3)

Keywords Lives in the past, wistful, homesick.

The child is preoccupied with the past and relives former events or happier times. Similar to that of Clematis, except in Clematis the child lives in an imaginary world, while in Honeysuckle this world is real but in the past. On the positive side, he or she may be a good record-keeper and enjoy collecting. Useful for children who spend time away from home.

Wild rose (group 2)

Keywords Apathetic, resigned.

The child lacks interest in people or surroundings, has no enthusiasm, and feels there is little point in doing anything – a "wet blanket". This problem is often seen after illness or "echo" diseases (page 25). On the positive side, when the child is well, he or she is full of enthusiasm and energy.

Olive (group 3)

Keywords Extremely exhausted, listless.

The child is exhausted after a long period of overwork, illness or lack of sleep, with lack of enthusiasm. He or she may continue daily activities "on autopilot", with no real attention or energy. On the positive side, the child can bear stress and discomfort without apparent effects.

White chestnut (group 3)

Keywords Obsessive, repetitious thoughts, lacks concentration.

The child has trouble clearing his or her mind of worries, mental argument and unwanted thoughts, and the same ideas keep going round and round. He or she appears preoccupied as a result. In White Chestnut, the child recognizes the repetitive thoughts and wants to stop, but cannot. On the positive side, the child may at times have a very clear mind. Useful for insomnia.

Mustard (group 3)

Keyword Depression without a known cause.

The child is depressed for no apparent reason (compare Gorse), and he or she may not recognize that constructive action is needed to lift it. On the positive side, the child radiates calmness and serenity. Useful to help the child recognize a problem and make a decision to do something about it.

Chestnut bud (group 3)

Keywords Unable to learn from personal mistakes.

The "I've-always-done-it-this-way" child, who is unable to learn from his or her faults – although quick to point out the mistakes of others. This may cause a mental block and slow progress at school. On the positive side, in some

areas he or she is a quick learner. Useful for breaking habits and altering repetitive behavior patterns – for example, when parent and child repeatedly argue.

Water violet (group 4)

Keywords Aloof, disdainful.

The child is withdrawn, appearing aloof and arrogant through being unable to communicate well, and with weak emotional energy, but often very intelligent. He or she is probably rather "cool" and pale. On the positive side, the child can play or work quietly for hours, without outside guidance.

Impatiens (group 4)

Keywords Impatient, restless, independent.

The child quickly gets bored with an activity and is unable to sit still. He or she is also mentally restless, although often quick and intelligent. On the positive side, he or she also has great sympathy and understanding, and is very (perhaps too) independent. Useful for insomnia and fevers, when the mind cannot slow down.

Heather (group 4)

Keywords Self-preoccupation, very talkative.

The child overconcentrates on his or her own self, and often is obsessed that his or her ailments and problems seem much worse and much

more important that those of others. In both health and illness, the child tends to drain the energy of those around. On the positive side, he or she is able to see the best in a person or situation, and has an optimistic outlook. Useful for colds and at other times of low energy.

Agrimony (group 5)

Keywords Outwardly cheerful and carefree, but inwardly worried and restless.

The child puts a brave face on things, cheerful on the outside, but inner feelings are different – anger, or depression. He or she may appear ineffective because of difficulty in coming to terms with these inner feelings. Physically this often results in throat problems and gall bladder problems. On the positive side, he or she plays down suffering when ill, and is one of "nature's pacifiers".

Centaury (group 5)

Keywords Timid, easily manipulated.

The child wishes to help those around – so much so, that he or she may behave like a "doormat"', seemingly lacking in willpower. Yet inside, he or she dislikes being told what to do. The child who needs this remedy often has a pale face, and easily gets minor illnesses. On the positive side, he or she can be gentle, kind, and occasionally decisive, saying "no".

INDICATIONS FOR BACH REMEDIES

Walnut (group 5)

Keywords Over-sensitive, especially to life transitions.

The remedy for letting things flow smoothly, in a child who otherwise clings to established patterns and habits. Useful when making transitions in life, such as teething, new school or house, or puberty. Also useful for constipation. In addition, the remedy protects from harmful outside influences, for example, by helping the child to expel unwanted thoughts planted by external sources. On the positive side, the child is strong-willed and unaffected by the opinions of other people.

Holly (group 5)

Keywords Angry and hateful, yet generous.

The child is angry, suspicious, vengeful and jealous – all rather anti-social activities. Yet on the positive side there is love, warmth and generosity, freely given without thought of return.

Holly (or Wild oat) may be given as a last resort to clarify a confused picture.

Larch (group 6)

Keywords Lacks self-confidence.

The child is convinced of being a failure, and therefore often does not even try. He or she may be artistic rather than numerate, responding to encouragement and developing talent through painting. On the positive side, the child is aware of personal limitations, and so is able to define and complete a task. Useful for children who are too much in awe of their teacher or who are bullied.

Pine (group 6)

Keywords Regretful, guilty.

For the child who dwells on something in the past that he or she is ashamed of and does not want to remember. As a result, he or she may work too hard and be too apologetic. The remedy helps the child to come to terms with hidden guilt and "freshen up" the past. On the positive side, he or she is a patient helper of those less fortunate, and has sound judgement.

Elm (group 6)

Keywords Becomes temporarily discouraged and overwhelmed by setbacks.

The child puts all energies into one grand project, but feels weak and tired at the thought of not being able to cope with any setback. On the positive side, he or she soon weathers the disappointment and comes back with renewed vigor (compare Gentian). Also he or she may be a natural leader.

Sweet chestnut (group 6)

Keywords Anguish, distress.

For times during an illness when the emotional agony or strain seems too much to bear and the child does not know which way to turn. On the positive side, when the child is well, he or she is generally calm and emotionally stable.

Star of Bethlehem (group 6)

Keyword Shock.

For a child who suffers any sudden shock, either physical or mental, including before or during birth. The shock temporarily detaches the mind from the body, so that the baby or child appears dazed, or cannot be consoled and goes on screaming. Physically, if the shock has been present for some time, it can allow toxins to build up, which are manifested as boils or pimples when the remedy is given. This remedy is usually used in a specific situation rather than for a particular personality. However on the positive side, often not seen clearly, the child adapts easily to different circumstances. Useful for resolving delayed shock, which may show as a blue coloration on the bridge of the nose and as insomnia.

Willow (group 6)

Keywords Resentful, bitter.

The child is a grumbler and complainer, bears grudges, is jealous and finds it difficult to forgive and forget. Often he or she is a "cold" type (page 22). On the positive side, the child has optimism and faith, and accepts responsibility for his or her own fate.

Oak (group 6)

Keywords Responsible, also strong and courageous.

Like the oak tree itself, the child obstinately bears a (mental) burden until he or she suddenly cracks. Problems may occur after an illness, or be induced by too much pressure or being over-conscientious at school. The child often has dark lines under the eyes. On the positive side, he or she has great perseverance and emotional strength.

Crab apple (group 6)

Keywords Feels unclean or "dirty" for no obvious reason.

The child has a highly developed sense of cleanliness, and as a result feels "unclean" in some way – perhaps being unable to live up to impossibly high personal standards. Physically there may be boils and discharges. On the positive side, the child may in reality have good hygiene, be broad-minded, and graciously accept the faults of others. Useful for toilet training.

Chicory (group 7)

Keywords Critical, possessive.

The child is a "nagger" and attention-seeker, who always wants something – but it is never quite right. He or she needs people around to show appreciation, but can be tiring company. On the positive side, the child has great persistence and coolly pursues a goal to its end. He or she is able to put up with hardship and discomfort when necessary, and is often a "cold" type (page 22) when ill.

Vervain (group 7)

Keywords Intense, single-minded, hyperactive.

The child is often highly strung, over-persistent and unable to stop an activity even after being told to many times. He or she may even seem to enjoy the repetition. On the positive side, he or she can concentrate well, and pursue a task to completion with great purpose. Useful for a child who cannot sleep.

Vine (group 7)

Keywords Dominating, cruel.

The child is a "Little Emperor", who is greedy for power and enjoys dominating those around. He or she may even show signs of cruelty and aggression, and enjoy seeing others suffer. The remedy is often indicated during the "terrible twos" phase (page 18) and in strong-willed children. On the positive side, this type of child may make a great leader or teacher, and inspire great confidence – after learning to respect the feelings of others.

Beech (group 7)

Keywords Intolerant, likes excessive order and discipline, makes personal sacrifices to extremely high goals.

The child often has a clearly developed moral sense of right and wrong. He or she expects others to conform to this, and is highly critical when they do not. Typically fussy over details, he or she likes everything in its right place. These feelings often give rise to anger and tantrums. On the positive side, he or she has an intuitive understanding of human frailty and bears no grudges.

Rock water (group 7)

Keywords Rigid outlook, inflexible, single-minded.

The child is rather taut and "tight", and acts according to fixed ideas. He or she holds clear, strong opinions and resists change, even if this stubbornness leads to personal discomfort. There may be glandular problems. On the positive side, the child has high ideals, and if shown to be wrong, he or she is prepared for a change of mind.

The Rescue remedy

This is a combination of Star of Bethlehem, Rock Rose, Impatiens, Cherry plum and Clematis. It is useful in first aid for accidents, injuries and shocks, and when a child is very ill. It can also act as a preventative, for instance, before an operation. It is available commercially as a cream and may be applied to particularly painful or injured areas.

MASSAGES

Hollow of back massage

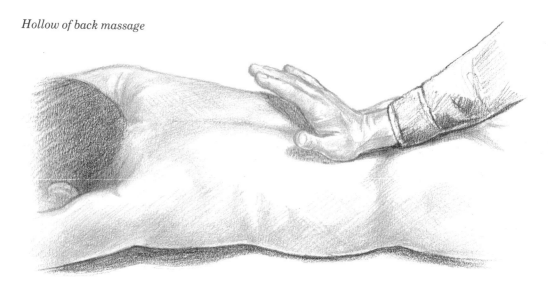

Massage is one of the oldest and most instinctive forms of healing. The Chinese have developed massage techniques to a high art, because of their discovery of the energy channels (page 14). They use it for treating many conditions, and it is an established therapy at their state hospitals. Massage is especially favored for children, because it can be so gentle, and because the physical contact benefits both child and parent.

Many people in the West are unfamiliar with the techniques of massage. For this reason, simpler and more effective strokes have been included here. They are completely safe (provided they are not done too vigorously), suitable for babies and children, and can be combined with other therapies, including orthodox medicine.

Advice on how to massage

■ Calm yourself and your child as much as possible before starting. This is often difficult with an ill, restless or irritable child, but it is worth making the effort. Spend a little time doing slow breathing or a similar relaxation technique.

■ Choose calm and peaceful surroundings, without bright lights, loud music or other distractions.

■ Lubricate the area to be massaged with a little oil. Almost any oil is suitable, and olive oil is a good general choice.

■ Do the massage gently but firmly, being responsive and aware of your child's reaction. Speak calmly and gently. If the child becomes agitated, stop and relax, then start again.

■ While massaging, imagine a healing force coming from your hands and fingertips to benefit your child. Do not let your wrists become stiff – keep them flexible, so that the healing energy can flow through.

■ Imagine that the massage strokes direct the child's energy to where healing is needed. For example, try to draw hot energy away from the head in the Spinal stroke massage, or imagine stimulating the bowels in the Down sacrum stroke.

INDIVIDUAL MASSAGE TECHNIQUES

All the massage strokes included in this book are listed here. They are in "top-to-toe" order, beginning with the head and face, then chest and back, arms and hands, and finally legs and feet. Most of the techniques are described in detail in this section. For certain massages, which apply specifically to a particular ailment, you will be referred from this list to the pages where those massages are described in more detail. All techniques are listed in the main Index.

Up forehead

Hold the child's head facing you, with both hands (see illustration). Stroke upwards with alternate thumbs, from

the bridge of the nose to the hair line. 50 times.
Indications Fevers, headaches.

Across forehead

Hold the child's head facing you, with both hands (see Up Forehead). Using your thumbs, gently stroke across the forehead, outwards from the center. Repeat 50 times.
Indications Fevers, headaches.

Fengchi (Draught hollow, Back of head or Headache)

Massage the points in the hollows just below and to the sides of the lower rear lump on the skull (see illustration), with both thumbs, or thumb and index finger. The points are just outside the ridges of

muscle that hold up the neck; they are often tender. Vibrate for 1-2 minutes or rotate gently 50 times. Older children can self-massage for eye strain or headache.
Indications Headaches, eye strain, fevers.

Nose-upper lip

See Fits, page 91.
Indications To bring back consciousness during fits (seizures), epilepsy or fainting.

Around eyes and Jingming (Bright eyes or Clear sight)

See Red and sore eyes, page 117, and illustration, page 7.
Indications Red or sore eyes, short (near) sight.

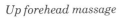

Up forehead massage

Fengchi massage

INDIVIDUAL MASSAGE TECHNIQUES

Chest

Sit the child on your knee, facing you, and hold him or her firmly under the arms. Use your thumbs to massage the chest between the nipples, gently stroking away from the midline towards each nipple. 3-4 minutes.
Indications Coughs, asthma.

Shoulder

See Asthma, page 106.
Indications Severe asthma attack.

Scapular

Sit the child on your knee, facing away from you, and hold him or her firmly under the arms. With your thumbs, massage the back between the shoulder blades (see illustration). Stroke firmly, from near the top of the back to between the bases of the shoulder blades (scapulae). 50-100 times.
Indications Coughs, asthma, wheezing, general lethargy and weakness.

Scapular massage

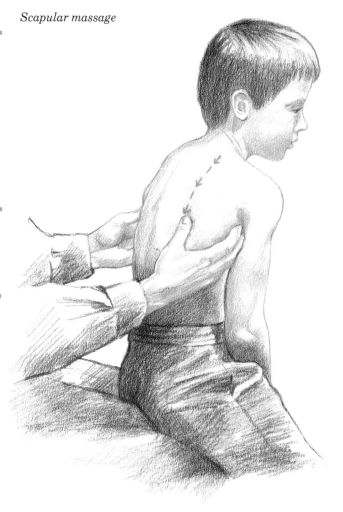

Rotating abdomen (Around abdomen)

Let the child lie comfortably, chest up. Gently massage the abdomen in a clockwise direction, using two or three fingers (see illustration on page 139). For some ailments, the counter-clockwise direction is more effective, as described on the relevant pages. Repeat 50-100 times.

Indications "Liver congestion" illnesses (page 23), constipation, colic and abdominal pain, insomnia caused by abdominal pain, weak digestion.

Heel on upper abdomen

Use the heel of your hand to massage the upper part of the abdomen (see Heel on lower abdomen), between the base of

the rib cage and the navel, gently pushing about 50 times over 2-3 minutes.
Indications Indigestion, weak digestion, insomnia due to weak digestion, lack of appetite.

Heel on lower abdomen

Use the heel of your hand to massage the lower part of the abdomen, below the navel (see

Chest and abdomen

illustration on page 6), gently pushing about 50 times over 2-3 minutes.
Indications As for Heel on upper abdomen, also general weakness, bed wetting, urinary problems.

Zhongwan (Smooth digestion, Stomach passage or Belly)

Let the child lie down comfortably, chest up. Gently massage the point midway between the navel and the lower tip of the breastbone (sternum) using your index and middle fingers (see illustration). Gently rotate about 200 times keeping your wrist and hand flexible.
Indications Liver congestion (page 23), indigestion, poor appetite, general digestive problems and weakness.

Guanyuan (Constitution or Intestines point)

As for Zhongwan, but massage the point midway between the navel and the top of the pubic bone.
Indications General weakness, urinary problems.

Tiantu (Windpipe, Wind tunnel)

Sit the child upright, or hold a baby almost vertical and support the head. From behind, massage the hollow at the base of the front of the neck and the top of the chest with your index finger (see illustration). Vibrate gently but firmly 200 times.
Indications Coughs, asthma.

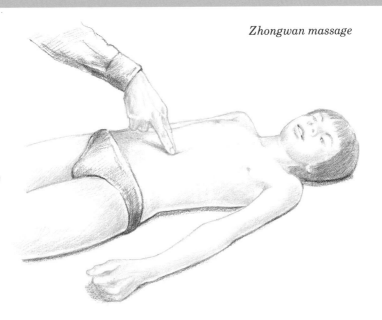

Zhongwan massage

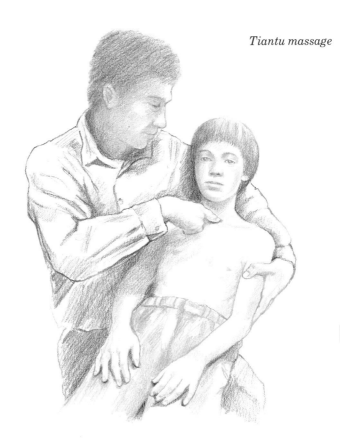

Tiantu massage

75

INDIVIDUAL MASSAGE TECHNIQUES

Back pinch-pull (Back stimulation or Roll up)

Note: This massage is for babies only. It can be tried on older children but it is usually less effective, being most suitable for babies up to the age of about 9 months.

Lie the baby face down. With the thumb and forefinger of each hand, gently grasp a fold of flesh on either side of the lower back (see illustration on page 168). Gently roll it along, with your thumb going downwards and finger moving upwards, so that the fold of flesh travels up the back rather like a wave. When you reach the shoulder area, start again. Repeat 20-50 times over 2-3 minutes.
Indications Weakness.

Spinal stroke

See Fevers, page 87.
Indications Fevers, sore eyes, headaches.

Down sacrum

See the description of the Up sacrum stroke in Acute diarrhea, page 155. Using the heel of your hand, massage firmly down the sacrum to the tip of the "tail" just above the buttocks. Repeat 50-100 times.
Indications Constipation.

Up sacrum

See the description in Acute diarrhea, page 155.
Indications Diarrhea.

Elbow to little finger massage

Shenshu (Cure the kidneys)

Stretching apart your index and middle fingers, massage either side of the spine, level with the top of the hip bone and just below the waist line. Vibrate gently for 1-2 minutes. In older children you may not be able to stretch your fingers wide enough, so do one side at a time.
Indications Urinary problems, general kidney problems and urinary tract weakness.

Hollow of back

Lie the child on his or her chest. Massage the hollow at the base of the back gently but firmly, using the heel of your hand (see illustration on page 72). 50-100 times.
Indications Urinary problems, general weakness, bed wetting.

Elbow to little finger

Sit the child comfortably in front of you. Hold the child's hand in your left hand (if you are right-handed) and gently stroke down the forearm from the inside of the elbow to the little finger, using your index and middle fingers (see illustration). 30-50 times, repeat on other side.
Indications Fevers, hot head, panics. Especially effective in children under 3 years old.

Thumb to elbow

Hold the child's hand in your left hand (if you are right-handed) and gently stroke up the forearm from the base of the thumb to the inside of the elbow, using your index and middle fingers (see Elbow to little finger). 30-50 times, repeat on other side.

Back and arms

Indications Weak digestion, chills, diarrhea. Especially effective in children under 3 years old.

Sanjiao channel (Ears and eyes)

Sit the child comfortably in front of you. Hold the child's hand in your left hand (if you are right-handed) and gently massage down the outside of the forearm, from the elbow to the back of the hand, along a line midway between the two long bones (see illustration on page 121). 30-50 times, repeat on other side if that is also affected.
Indications Earaches, red or sore eyes.

Thenar eminence (Mound of thumb)

Hold the child's thumb in your left hand (if you are right-handed) and gently stroke the mound-like joint at the base of the thumb, which is known as the thenar eminence. Stroke upwards towards the wrist 200-300 times, repeat on the other hand.
Indications Indigestion, diarrhea, respiratory problems. Especially effective in children under 3 years old.

Forefinger

Hold the child's hand in your left hand (if you are right-handed) and stroke the back of the forefinger (index finger) towards the wrist (see illustration). 200-300 times, repeat on other side.
Indications Indigestion, diarrhea. Especially effective in children under 3 years old.

Dewpond

Hold the child's hand palm-upwards in your left hand (if you are right-handed). Moisten the palm with cool cream or water. Massage from the tip of the little finger, in a curved movement around the "heel" of the palm to the thumb's base (see illustration). 50 times, repeat on other palm.
Indications Fevers, panics, heat type of insomnia.

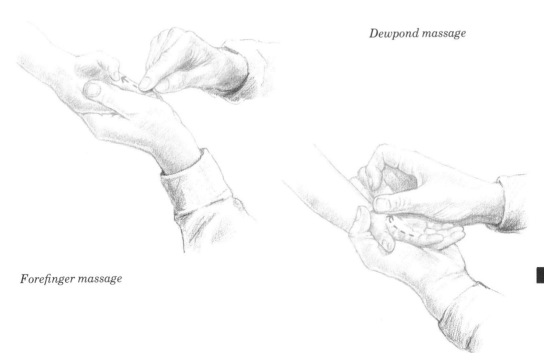

Dewpond massage

Forefinger massage

INDIVIDUAL MASSAGE TECHNIQUES

Stomach channel massage

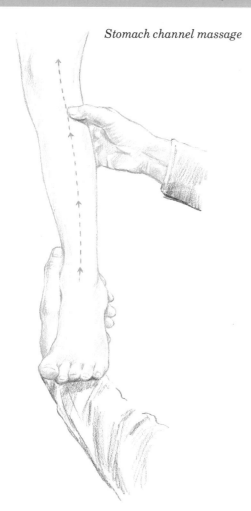

Zusanli massage

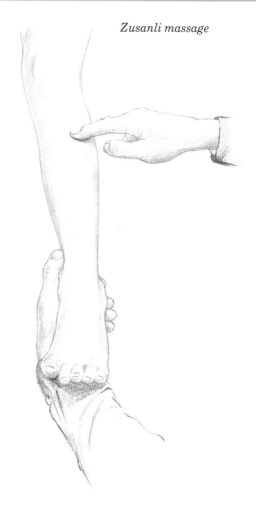

Ten kings

Using a matchstick or the tip of a pencil, massage the ten points at the flesh over the base of each fingernail on each hand. It is usually enough to press each point firmly 1-2 times. Press on each finger in turn, working along one hand and then the other.
Indications Fright type of insomnia, delayed shock.

Lifeline

See the description in Sleeping problems, page 165.
Indications Insomnia, night terrors and panics.

Hegu (End of crease)

See Teething, page 159. This point may also be treated with an overnight poultice of ground cloves.

Indications Indigestion, teething, insomnia from teething, short (near) sight.

Fingerprints

Hold the child's wrist in your left hand (if you are right-handed), with the finger to be massaged supported by your right hand, leaving your right thumb free to do the massage. Push upwards on the print

Hands, legs and feet

area towards the fingertip. Press about 100 times, then repeat on other hand.
Indications For indigestion or chronic mucus (phlegm) massage prints of thumb, index finger and middle finger.

Neiguan (Internal organs, Rebellious stomach)

See Motion sickness, page 147.
Indications Nausea, vomiting, travel (motion) sickness.

Stomach channel

Hold the child's leg in your left hand (if you are right-handed) and massage up the front of the shin, on the muscle one finger's breadth to the outside of the shin bone (see illustration opposite). 1-3 minutes, repeat on other side.
Indications Indigestion, vomiting, diarrhea, general weakness.

Zusanli (Stomach point or Three-mile walk)

See also Stomach channel, above. The point is on the channel, in the curve of the bone just under the knee. Use your index finger to massage here for 1-2 minutes. Repeat on other side.
Indications Indigestion, vomiting, diarrhea, general weakness.

Bladder channel

This channel runs down the back of the leg, where the seam of a stocking would run. For cystitis or similar inflammation or infection of the bladder, massage downwards from the hollow at the back of the knee to the Achilles tendon above the heel, to draw the inflammation away.

If the bladder is weak but there is no infection, massage along the same line but upwards, to bring energy to the bladder. Continue for 2-3 minutes, repeat on other side.
Indications Urinary problems, bed wetting.

Hollow of heel

With your thumb and index finger, pinch the hollow just below the calf and above the back of the heel, inside the Achilles tendon. Vibrate vigorously for 1-5 minutes with a rotating and squeezing action (but not too roughly). Repeat on other side. If the child is held by another person, both heels can be massaged at the same time.
Indications Fits (seizures or convulsions), hot head.

Yongquan (Bubbling spring or Middle of foot)

Let the child lie on his or her back, on the floor or on the bed beside you. Find the point on the sole of the foot, on the midline, one-third of the way from toes to heel (see illustration). Grasp the child's foot with your left hand (if you are right-handed) and massage the point with your thumb for 1-2 minutes. Repeat on other foot.
Indications Fevers, hot head, red or sore eyes, vomiting, diarrhea.

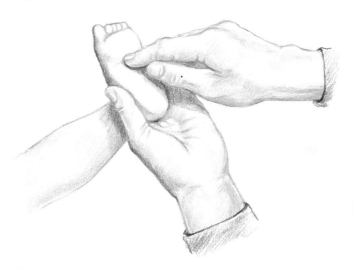

Yongquan massage

Part III

TREATING CHILDHOOD AILMENTS

Home treatment by natural medicines is perfectly feasible for a wide range of childhood illnesses. Yet for many people, using natural medicines represents a step into the unknown. They are used to visiting the doctor, having a diagnosis made, obtaining a bottle of pills from the pharmacist, and taking them as directed. However, those who make the effort soon

CAUTIONS

Natural medicines can treat a wide range of childhood ailments. However, many parents have not had the chance to develop expertise in their use. In some cases, they have "handed over" the health care of themselves and their children to the medical profession. In fact, in the recent past, orthodox Western-style medical practice has almost encouraged this relinquishing of responsibility.

Times are changing, but slowly. Therefore, in some cases the advice of a qualified physician is required:
• to confirm a confusing, obscure or unclear diagnosis,
• to check that complications are not setting in,
• to assess any sudden or unexplained deterioration in your child's general condition, and
• to deal with any life-threatening emergency as it arises.

come to understand how natural medicines work, and how their powers can be recognized and harnessed.

Because you are taking on some of the responsibility for your child's condition, you are more likely to become involved and develop a greater understanding of your child's physical and emotional temperament. You become "tuned in" to detect the early signs your child sends out, as he or she begins to succumb to illness. You monitor your child's progress through disease more closely, keeping in touch and giving comfort, and sharing in the relief and happiness of recovery.

Organization and use

This part of the book is divided into four main sections. Each section groups together ailments with common origins, as explained in the section introductions. Use of the material is explained on page 10, How to use this book, and a full listing of all ailments covered is found in the Contents on pages 6-7. Or you may refer to the Index for more information.

It is also possible to select a treatment from the lists of remedies in the second part of the book. In addition, remember that the massages can be used in combination with any therapy, natural or orthodox.

"Getting to know you." Illness is a trying time, but it is also an ideal opportunity to develop closer bonds.

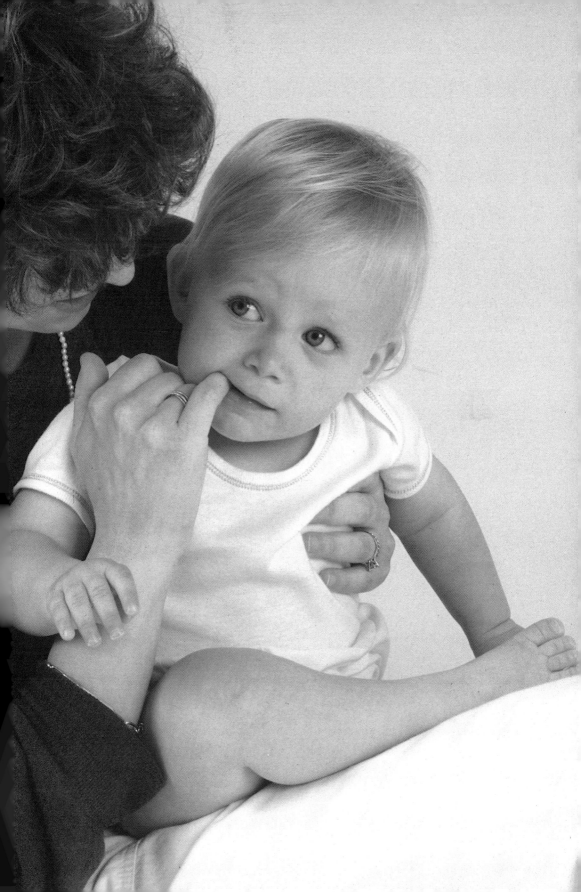

Respiration and Mucous Membranes

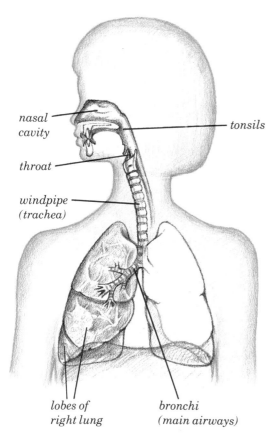

nasal cavity

tonsils

throat

windpipe (trachea)

lobes of right lung

bronchi (main airways)

This diagram shows the main parts of the respiratory system, from the nose and nasal cavities down into the lungs.

The ailments grouped in this section affect the body's mucous membranes. These include the linings of the nose, sinuses, mouth, throat, windpipe (trachea) and lungs. The delicate coverings of the eyes and the linings of certain parts of the inner ears are also covered by similar mucus-producing membranes.

The small amounts of mucus protect these surfaces, keeping them moist and trapping dust and dirt. But because these parts are exposed to air, they are susceptible to airborne infection spread by viruses, bacteria and other microbes. Natural medicines are very often surprisingly quick and effective in treating these ailments. They stimulate the body to fight the infecting agent. In natural medicine, it is believed that a healthy body is capable of combatting, controlling and repelling viruses or bacteria, and that symptoms of infection only occur as a result of an internal bodily imbalance.

The purpose of treatment is to determine the nature of the imbalance and to direct energy to the affected parts. Once the energy arrives there, the body's immune system will do its work. This is one reason why massage, with its conscious directing of energy, is so effective in treating children's ailments, especially in the early stages.

The use of antibiotics

Sometimes an infection attacks so strongly that a child's body does not have the strength to fight back without help. In these circumstances, antibiotics can often be of great help. However, they always have side-effects (see opposite).

If your child suffers a severe illness, antibiotics may kill the infecting agents, but they do not restore balance in the body. As a consequence, your child's condition is the same after the illness as it was before. The imbalance remains, and therefore infection may occur again. With natural medicines, the internal balance can be restored.

If, in spite of your efforts with natural medicines, your physician advises treatment by antibiotics, do not be discouraged. After checking with the physician, carry on treatment with natural therapies, using them in addition to the orthodox medical drugs. And above all, continue with natural medicines after your child seems to have recovered. This will help to restore his or her energy balance and prevent illness from recurring.

Side-effects of antibiotics

Antibiotic drugs kill or disable bacteria, and they are useful only for bacterial infections. In some circumstances their timely use avoids serious damage to the body, or even saves a life.

However, the effects of antibiotics on the body are strong and long-lasting. In general, they should be used only as a last resort, when health is threatened and other treatments have failed. Their side-effects include the following problems.

Diarrhea Digestion is carried out in the intestines with the assistance of many beneficial types of bacteria. When antibiotics are taken they affect all bacteria, whether beneficial or not. As a result, digestion is disturbed and incomplete, leading to diarrhea.

When the course of antibiotics is finished, the diarrhea should subside. But in some children it never goes away completely, especially if a child has taken several courses of drugs. When the digestion is disturbed in this way, the "liver congestion" (page 23) pattern of illness may develop.

There are two aspects to treatment. First, act to restore the internal balance of your child's body by treating the diarrhea itself (page 151).

In addition, help to restore the natural intestinal bacteria. This can be done by giving your child a small amount of safe, live (unpasteurized) yogurt, especially one containing *Acidophilus* culture. Only a small amount is needed – one level 5mls teaspoon for an older child, reducing to one-quarter of this for a younger child. If there is allergy to dairy products, give doses of goat's yogurt in the same way.

Skin rash Some children come out in a severe rash a few days after starting a course of antibiotics. Should this happen, inform your medical physician at once, and enquire about stopping the drug.

Surprisingly, the skin rash is not always as harmful as it appears. The reaction may be due to the body expelling "latent heat" (page 26). This will be the case if your child's mood improves after the rash comes out. If the rash persists for more than a week after stopping the drugs, consult a practitioner of natural medicine as soon as possible.

Phlegm (mucus or catarrh) When an infection is treated with antibiotics, it is common for phlegm to be left behind. In many children this clears up naturally. But in others, the phlegm provides a breeding ground for bacteria, and the child soon succumbs to another infection – which necessitates more antibiotics. To break this cycle treat the phlegm itself, by natural medicines and by diet (see, for example, page 36).

Thrush Antibiotics are effective against bacteria, but not against fungal infections. So they may encourage the secondary infection of thrush (whitish *Candida* fungus), in the mouth or vagina. This can be treated by further medicines, but a more effective way is to replace the bacteria in the system, as described above. Herbs may be given to reduce accumulated phlegm in the body, which also encourages fungal infection.

FEVERS

Fevers are a common condition of childhood, and so feared by some parents (and practitioners) that quite disproportionate measures are taken to avoid them. This fear is often misplaced. For many children (and adults) an occasional fever is beneficial, because it is a way of clearing any accumulated "latent heat" (page 26).

For a small minority of children, fevers can be serious, since there may be a risk of fits (page 90). It is important to know and look out for the danger signs (see panel).

The following pages cover the symptoms and treatments of straightforward fevers – those which occur chiefly on their own, uncomplicated by other significant problems. For fevers that accompany other illnesses such as earache, measles or tonsillitis, consult the relevant pages.

Symptoms and types of fevers

Usually, the first signs of a fever are behavioral. Your child becomes irritable, grumpy and often very "clingy", not wanting to allow you out of sight. The body's heat balance becomes disturbed (page 22), so that the child feels either too cold or too hot, and the appetite is reduced.

Typically, the face then becomes red and the forehead is hot to the touch. Body temperature is a useful guide to a fever's severity. In babies and young children the onset may be rapid, with the transition from good health to a high fever taking only a few hours. In the course of a straightforward fever, the temperature remains high (up to 39°C, 102°F) for a few days. Then, after a period of sweating, it falls and the child quickly recovers. Fevers of this kind are extremely common in childhood, and although they are worrisome to parents, they do not usually present any threat to health.

DANGER SIGNS

Obtain expert help as quickly as possible if your child:
■ becomes very hot, with body temperature above 40°C, 104°F,
■ becomes vague and confused, or loses consciousness,
■ seems hot on one side of the body yet cold on the other, or
■ starts to twitch.

There are various types of fevers, with characteristic signs in addition to the raised temperature. Recognizing the type of fever is the key to choosing the most effective treatment.

"Hot" and "cold" fevers

In a "hot" type or stage of fever, your child complains of being too hot, has a red face, sweats and throws off bedclothes. In a "cold" type or stage of a fever, he or she shivers and complains of feeling cold, even though body temperature is raised. In some cases he or she swings between the two stages, although usually either "hot" or "cold" predominates.

There are additional patterns which may occur in any type of fever. In the "phlegm" fever, seen particularly in babies, there is usually a thick, yellow nasal discharge, and a cough. In a "fright" fever, the baby or young child is alarmed by the sensations that the fever gives. This shows as great distress, crying and clinging desperately to the parent.

In some cases a fever may overload a baby's digestive system and give rise to the "liver congestion" (page 23) pattern of fever.

Causes and factors

At the basic physical level, fevers are a response to bacterial or viral infection, and indicate an increased activity of the body's immune defense systems.

External stress Children are relatively unaware of how hot or cold they are. They may sit in the sun and become overheated, or swim for too long and become chilled.

Internal factors In natural medicine, fevers are seen more as a symptom of healing than a disease, and are a way of redressing an imbalance that has already built up in the body. The nature of this imbalance is usually one of stored "latent heat" (page 26). Perhaps surprisingly, in these cases the fever tends to be beneficial to the body, by providing the opportunity to expel latent heat. It is characteristic of this type of fever that afterwards the child – though tired – feels much better inside.

Emotional factors Emotions can give rise to fevers in two ways. In babies and young children the relationship between mind, emotions and body is very direct, so any disturbing thought or emotion can soon provoke a fever.

For example, if your child flies into a rage or has a sudden fright, a "fright" type of fever may soon develop. Similarly, hidden or suppressed emotions, as after a scolding or bereavement, are translated into excess latent heat (see table).

Older children have more control over their bodies, so it is less likely that sudden emotions will provoke fevers. But negative emotions, such as depression or dislike of school, may slow the response of the immune system.

Developmental factors As explained on page 18, a fever may occur at a time of transition, such as the "terrible twos", or at seven years old, when individuality begins to emerge.

SOURCES OF EXCESS HEAT IN FEVERS

Cause	Pattern
Latent heat (heat accumulated in winter but not naturally dissipated in spring)	Epidemic fevers in springtime
Slow adaptation to weather changes	Likely to occur a few days after the weather suddenly turns hot
Too many "hot" foods (page 34)	Tends to be a gradual build-up; during the fever the tongue often has a thick, dirty-yellow coat, and there are spots and mouth ulcers
"Echo" disease (page 25)	Repeated attacks of fevers, always with the same pattern, sometimes as frequently as once a month

85

A raised body temperature and increased perspiration can make your child feel uncomfortable and "sticky". Sponge gently with plain lukewarm water, especially around the face, and on the hands and feet.

General care

Fevers are treated by expulsion through perspiration (sweating), and occasionally through purging. If your child has a fever but is not perspiring, try to stimulate perspiration by using natural medicines. Purges are strikingly effective in certain fevers; you should find that the fever comes down more quickly, and there are fewer side-effects when using a mild herbal purge than with antibiotic drugs.

In a "fright" fever, the fright is a significant symptom and may delay the healing process. Calm and stroke your child so that these feelings subside.

Other measures include putting your child to bed, keeping him or her warm (but never too hot) and keeping out draughts. Avoid giving a bath. If your child is "sticky" and dirty, gentle sponging is best for washing.

Diet Keep food to a minimum, so that your child's energy is not used to digest food, but is free to fight the infection, and also to prevent "liver congestion". Fevers can be considerably prolonged by giving too much to eat, especially rich and "hot"-type foods (page 32).

Even when the fever comes down and the appetite returns, it may be advisable for your child to avoid food for another 12 hours, unless there are signs of great weakness. However, a drink of honey and lemon in warm water may be given at all times during fevers.

Temperature If your child's temperature goes over 40°C, 104°F, cool him or her by whatever means are available. For example, put cold water bottles under each armpit; sponge the face, arms and legs with cool water; or use a fan.

Recovery

When the temperature begins to fall, your child will probably be exhausted, and need to build up strength again. In short fevers, of less than 24 hours, normal diet can soon be resumed, with extra helpings of food if requested.

After longer fevers, you should take certain precautions. Start foods again very gradually. Babies can begin with

RESPIRATION AND MUCOUS MEMBRANES

very dilute sugared water and then watered milk or dilute fruit juice. Older children might begin with a small portion of porridge or a light soup and a small piece of toast. Even though your child may feel hungry, it is better to start with small amounts of food and see how he or she copes. For great weakness, after the first 24 hours of recovery give beef tea or the juice from a stew. And always allow your baby or child to have plenty of rest. Babies naturally sleep for as long as they need. Older children may have to be persuaded to take additional rest in the afternoon. As an approximate guide, children should be kept at home (or at least, away from school) after a fever for as many days as the fever itself lasted.

TREATMENT FOR "HOT" FEVERS

Herbs

Note: See page 40 for dosages and cautions for herbs.
- The basic remedy is Catmint (*Nepeta cataria*), which cools as well as helping to cure the condition. If the fever is very high (40°C, 104°F or more) and there is constipation give Catmint and also a laxative such as Sennokot, available from pharmacies (dose as given on the packet).
- As an alternative to Catmint – Cascara (*Rhamnus purshiana*), 1 dose of 20 drops (half dose under 2 years, double over 5 years).
- For phlegm, fright or liver congestion types of hot fevers, or if there are digestive cramps, add extra herbs as described under cold fevers (page 88), to the basic Catmint remedy for hot fevers.

Homoeopathy

Note: See page 54 for dosages and cautions for homoeopathic remedies.

- If the child has a red face, dilated pupils and possibly hallucinations – Belladonna (note: see page 57).
- If there is some yellow color in the face, signs of phlegm (mucus or catarrh) and cough – Merc. sol.

Other therapies

- See next page, under treatments for "cold" fevers.

Massage

Note: See page 72 for information on massages.
- To help draw heat away from the head and promote perspiration – Spinal stroke (see illustration). Repeat the stroke 100 times over about 5 minutes.
- To promote perspiration – Elbow to little finger, 50 times on each arm, every 2 hours.
- To aid recovery for a child – Zusanli, Rotating abdomen.
- To aid recovery in babies – Back pinch-pull.

continued on next page

Continued on next page

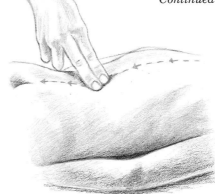

Spinal stroke massage

TREATMENT FOR "COLD" FEVERS

Herbs

Note: See page 40 for dosages and cautions for herbs.

Herbs are one of the oldest methods of treating fevers, and still one of the best.
- The basic children's remedy for a cold fever – Elderflower (*Sambucus nigra*) combined with Peppermint (*Mentha piperata*). Prepare as on page 41, or obtain a bottle of Syrup of Elderflower and Peppermint from a health store.
- Another common remedy is the herb Yarrow (*Achillea millefolium*), although some children may not like its bitter taste. It is especially good for older children (and adults) because it is a tonic as well as acting as a febrifuge (fever-fighter).
- Lime flowers (*Tilea europaea*) may be used in the same way as Yarrow, and are calming to the nerves.

The temperature should soon begin to fall; then give the above herbs every 4 hours. When the temperature is normal, give the herbs 3 times daily for 3 days as a tonic to assist recuperation.
- For "phlegm" cold fevers – add Hyssop (*Hyssopus officinale*), Coltsfoot (*Tussilago farfara*) or Elecampane (*Inula helenium*) to the basic remedy as above, to help the chest.
- For "fright" cold fevers –

add Motherwort (*Leonurus cardiaca*) or Passion flower (*Passiflora incarnata*) to the basic remedy for a cold fever, as above.
- For "liver congestion" cold fevers – add Black root (*Leptandra virginica*) to the basic remedy as above.
- For digestive cramps – add fresh Ginger root (*Zingiber officinale*) to the basic remedy as above.
- For any fever, to aid recovery when the child is pale, weak and has poor or no appetite – Gentian and Ginger, before meals. For younger children, tincture of Oats (*Avena sativa*) and Alfalfa (*Medicago sativa*).
- For any fever, if there is a lot of phlegm (mucus) afterwards – Golden seal (*Hydrastis canadensis*) and Elecampane before meals. Additionally give the child a bath with 10-20 drops of Eucalyptus oil in the water.

Homoeopathy

Note: See page 54 for dosages and cautions for homoeopathic remedies.

Give the remedy every 30 minutes at first. If it works, the first change will be improvement of mood. Some symptoms may worsen, especially sweating, as with herbal remedies.
- If there is a high fever, not much phlegm (mucus), and

the child is restless and anxious – Aconite.
- If the child feels heavy and lethargic, looks dazed and there are signs of phlegm – Gelsemium.
- If the child is pale and listless and the fever has not yet developed – Gelsemium.
- For "phlegm" cold fevers – Gelsemium if the mucus is pale, Merc. sol. if it is yellow.
- For "fright" cold fevers – Aconite.
- For any fever, if the high temperature and sweating persist for more than 24 hours, this indicates heat is being generated from "liver congestion" – give Sulfur 30X, 2-3 times daily.
- For any fever, to aid recovery – Calc. carb. (also for "echo" illnesses).
- For any fever, if there is a lot of phlegm afterwards – Sulfur, before meals.

Tissue salts

Note: See page 64 for information on tissue salts.
- For any fever – Ferr. phos.
- For cold fevers, especially if there is constipation – add Kali mur. to Ferr. phos.
- For "phlegm" cold fevers – Nat. mur. if the mucus is thin, Kali mur. if it is thick.
- For any fever, to promote perspiration – Kali sulph.
- For any fever, to reduce excessive perspiration – Calc. phos. or Kali phos.

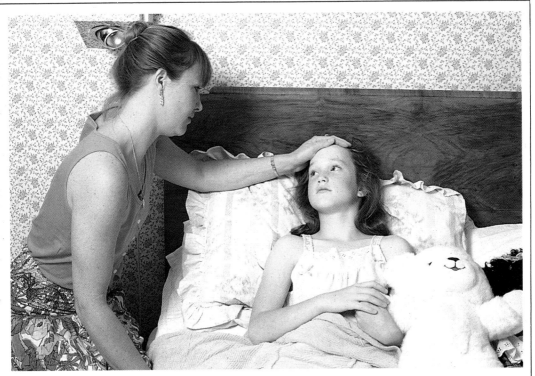

• For any fever, to aid recovery when the child is pale, weak and has poor or no appetite – Combination B.
• For any fever, if there is a lot of phlegm afterwards – Combination J.

Bach remedies

Note: See page 66 for information on Bach remedies.

There is no specific Bach remedy for fevers, but the Rescue remedy especially is a great help in the "fright" type of fever. Keep a glass of water containing 1-2 drops of Rescue remedy near the sick bed. Other remedies include Impatiens, Chicory, Holly, Hornbeam, and during recuperation, Clematis.

Acupuncture

Acupuncture is particularly effective in feverish conditions, and usually the fever starts to come down within a few hours.

Healing

The most basic healing occurs when you "will" your child to recover, as you send out

Allow your child to recover at his or her own rate. Rushing matters could encourage the fever to return.

strong thoughts and visualize your child getting better. In persistent fevers, healing – either absent ("remote") or by laying on of hands – can be a turning point in the disease.

Massage

See page 87.

FITS (FEBRILE OR INFANTILE CONVULSIONS)

There are several different types of fits (also called convulsions, infantile convulsions or seizures). Febrile fits are due to malfunction of the brain which may occur during a very high fever (page 84), a severe attack of middle ear inflammation (otitis media) or when teething. (The fits of epilepsy are of a different type.)

The activity of the brain, like other organs in the body, increases with temperature. In some children, when the temperature of the brain rises, the delicate coordination between its nerve cells is disrupted and the cells spontaneously start to "fire" uncontrolled signals through the nervous system to the whole body. These give rise to the characteristic convulsive movements of a febrile fit.

In Chinese medicine, fits are considered more likely to occur if there is a lot of phlegm (mucus or catarrh) in the system, because this affects brain activity. Fits are also more likely to occur when your child is frightened. A sudden fear can easily disturb the brain function in a baby, and fright is a common additional symptom in certain types of fevers.

Symptoms

Since a febrile fit occurs during a fever, your child will probably already be obviously hot with a raised temperature and possibly perspiring, with a red face and restless, distressed behavior.

As the fit starts, the eyes may swivel up in their sockets and the face turns pale. The hands or feet generally start to twitch, the movements quickly becoming more marked and spreading to the whole body. The arms and legs move around in violent jerks, out of control, while the back arches and the face contorts. The child usually loses consciousness.

There is, however, great variation. Some children have very mild attacks, with the eyes turning up and the body stiffening for only a few seconds. Less mild attacks include the twitching movements which gradually fade, stopping after a minute or so. In a severe attack, convulsive movements continue until the child's whole body goes rigid. This state may continue for several minutes before the muscles gradually relax and the child regains consciousness. After such a fit the child is usually exhausted and dazed for several hours, and may fall into a deep sleep or become confused.

Risks

Febrile fits are common among children. About 1 child in 25 has a fit at some time. Although fits may be frightening to behold, and seem to attack the very essence of the child, they are not usually dangerous unless they last a long time (more than about 10 minutes), or occur frequently (more than once every few days). In such cases the oxygen supply to the brain might be cut off for too long, and there could be permanent brain damage.

In very rare cases meningitis can be the cause of the raised temperature. Typical

IMPORTANT ACTIONS

● Always call a doctor if a child has a first fit, of any type. It could be a first fit of the epileptic type. For assessment, consult practitioners of both orthodox and natural medicine.
● If further attacks occur, orthodox medical drugs can help to control the symptoms and prevent brain damage.

symptoms are a high fever, restlessness, sharp bird-like cries from pain in the head, a stiff jaw, and feeling hot in one part of the body but cold in another. If your child shows these symptoms, summon emergency medical help. In the meantime give homoeopathic Apis mel. every 15 minutes.

Prevention

To prevent "latent heat" (page 26) from developing into a high temperature, make sure that your child's digestion is functioning well and there is no accumulation of undigested food as happens in the "liver congestion" (page 23) pattern of illness. In addition, avoid mucus-producing foods (page 36) and also heating foods (page 34). This includes avoiding all meat for a time, especially red meat.

If a fever develops, take steps to control your child's body temperature (page 86).

Another aspect of prevention is to avoid fright. During a fever, it is especially important to keep your child calm. Avoid sudden or loud noises, and be on hand to give soothing comfort.

TREATMENT FOR FITS

Herbs

Note: See page 40 for dosages and cautions for herbs.
• For prevention during a fever – Catmint (*Nepeta cataria*) and Rue (*Ruta graveolens*) as a tea.
• Other herbs which may help – Valerian (*Valeriana officinalis*) and Motherwort (*Leonurus cardiaca*), given as above.

Homoeopathy

Note: See page 54 for dosages and cautions for homoeopathic remedies.
• For prevention during a fever – Belladonna or Merc. sol. according to the indications.
• If the fits are brought on by teething – Chamomilla.
• If the fits are brought on by a fall – Cicuta.

• If the fits occur during whooping cough – Cuprum metallicum.
• If the fits occur during measles – Stramonium.
• If you have already given these remedies and the fever still remains high, the child may not be responding. Adding another therapy, such as massage, may help.

Massage

Note: See page 72 for information on massages.
• If the temperature is rising, you feel that a fit is imminent and other remedies have not worked – Spinal stroke.
• Emergency massage to stop a fit – Hollow of heel.
• To restore consciousness – Nose-upper lip. With a blunt pencil or similar object, massage the point midway between the nose and the

Noses upper-lip massage

upper lip (see illustration). This increases the blood supply to the brain.

External remedies

• If your child will not take the herbal tea advised above – rub 1 5mls teaspoon of the tinctures of Catmint and Rue into the abdomen every 2 hours.

91

COLDS

Colds are among the most common ailments, affecting children and adults alike. They can occur at any time of year, but are especially common during winter.

In Chinese medicine, colds are considered "superficial" since they do not pose a great threat to the system. There are two main types: one has a "chilly" nature and is often seen in winter; while the other is the "hot" type and is more often seen in summer.

Causes and factors

Colds are due to a disturbance of the immune system. The external cause which triggers this is usually invasion by a virus – but the virus cannot usually take hold unless there is already an imbalance in the body. Adults are more prone to colds when they feel depressed and harbor negative emotions, but babies and toddlers usually succumb because their immune systems are immature and not yet very strong.

The imbalance may arise from changeable weather, such as a sudden fall in temperature, or exposure to wind, which chills the child. In addition there is usually some accumulation of "latent cold" (page 26) due to a damp climate or the change from summer to winter. The "hot" type of cold, seen in warm weather, is linked to an imbalance of internal heat, often "latent heat" (page 26) in going from winter to summer. A further factor which can aggravate all these effects is when your child is extremely tired, weak or very stressed.

Young children often get their first colds when they start at playgroup or nursery school. Here they come into contact with other children, who catch colds and pass them on.

92

General symptoms

The typical cold starts with tiredness and irritability, a slight runny nose and sneezing. Often the child has a sore throat that worsens over the next three days, so that in some cases the nose runs like a tap, with a clear, watery discharge. In some children the discharge may be thicker and grey, yellow, or even green. During this stage, which usually lasts at least three days, the face is puffy, the appetite and sense of smell are dulled, and sometimes the hearing is affected as the ears become blocked by a mucous discharge. You may notice your child feels "heavy", irritable, or dispirited.

After this the cold gradually subsides over the next three days – hence the old saying: "Three days to come, three days to stay, three days to go".

In some children the nasal discharge persists, or tends to return, or the child keeps catching colds and never seems to shake them off completely. Such cases are known as chronic colds or chronic catarrhal (mucous) conditions. They often occur

OTHER CAUSES OF COLD-LIKE SYMPTOMS

Symptoms resembling a cold may occur at other times, indicating the response of the immune system:
- in the early stage of many infections, for example, mumps, measles, chickenpox and whooping cough,
- during the week following immunization, especially against polio and whooping cough (page 27), or
- when teething (page 158).

after an initial severe cold or sometimes after a cough, and they are one of the commonest of the "echo" patterns of illness (page 25).

Symptom profiles: types of cold

Treatment depends on the type of cold, so take note of your child's symptoms in order to make an accurate diagnosis, as shown in the table below. Sometimes a cold progresses through the various types, for example, from watery to catarrhal.

Complications

In healthy children, a cold stays in the head. If your child has a predisposition to lung problems the cold can "go down" to the chest, where phlegm (catarrh) settles and produces the symptoms of a phlegm-type cough (page 96).

In certain children, a cold in the head can rapidly develop into an asthma attack; and adenoids (page 95) and certain types of earaches (page 118) are often connected with colds.

TYPES OF COLDS	
Watery cold	Clear, thin nasal discharge that runs like a tap White facial color Child is depressed
Catarrhal (mucous) cold	Thick nasal discharge, either white, grey or green Dull facial color, sometimes green around the mouth, with red cheeks Tongue coating is often grey and sticky Child is irritable
"Hot" cold	Nasal discharge is thick, sticky and yellow Nose is often painful Hot forehead, often red cheeks Rapid pulse Tongue coating is often thin yellow Child is restless and "clingy"
Chronic cold	The cold comes and goes, but never seems to clear up Nasal discharge varies from thin and clear to thick Swollen glands, poor appetite In severe cases the child is prone to chronic coughs or even asthma

TREATMENT FOR COLDS

Mild colds are hardly worth treating. The symptoms cause little discomfort and it is best to let your child fight the attack unaided.

Severe colds are certainly worth treating, especially if there is a family history of lung problems. By timely treatment, a severe cold can be prevented from turning into a cough, thereby reducing the chance of establishing an "echo" disease.

For a chronic cold, treatment usually needs to be on a deeper level, and herbs are recommended. Symptoms may worsen for 7-10 days before they improve.

Tissue salts

Note: See page 64 for information on tissue salts.

These are the treatment of first choice for most colds, since they are gentle in action, and many colds do not need a deep-acting remedy.
- For watery colds – Nat. mur.
- For catarrhal colds – Kali mur., Combination J.
- For "hot" colds – Ferr. phos., Kali sulph., Combination Q.
- For chronic colds – Kali sulph., Silica, Combination Q.

Herbs

Note: See page 40 for dosages and cautions for herbs.
- For watery colds – Bayberry (*Myrica cerifera*) and Ginger (*Zingiber officinale*). Ginger may be replaced by Cayenne pepper (*Capsicum frutescens*).
- If the nose runs like a tap, add Cleavers (*Galium aparine*) to the above herbs.
- For catarrhal colds – as for watery cold, administer the above with the addition of Garlic or Lemon. Elecampane (*Inula helenium*) or Golden seal (*Hydrastis canadensis*) may be helpful in stubborn cases.
- For "hot" colds – Sage and Lemon tea, Eyebright (*Euphrasia officinalis*).
- For chronic colds – Golden seal, Elecampane and Hyssop (*Hyssopus officinale*). Golden seal and Elecampane clear mucus from the system, while Elecampane and Hyssop help the lungs and nasal passages.
- If the glands are swollen, add Blue flag (*Iris versicolor*) and Poke root (*Phytolacca decandra*) at twice the standard dosage to the remedies for chronic colds.

Homoeopathy

Note: See page 54 for dosages and cautions for homoeopathic remedies.
- For watery colds, especially if the child catches them frequently or is rather anxious and sensitive – Ars. alb.
- For watery colds, especially if the eyes and nose are smarting – Euphrasia.
- For watery colds, especially if the child is weak and dispirited – Ferr. phos.
- For catarrhal colds, especially in damp weather – Gelsemium.
- For catarrhal colds, especially when triggered by change from hot to cold – Dulcamara.
- For catarrhal colds, especially when the child is very emotional – Kali bich., Pulsatilla.
- For catarrhal colds, especially when there is much phlegm and also signs of heat – Nux vomica.
- For "hot" colds, especially if there is great heat – Kali iod., Rhus tox.
- For "hot" colds, if a fever develops – Aconite, Belladonna (page 57).
- For chronic colds – Sulphur, Calc. carb., Silica.

ADENOIDS

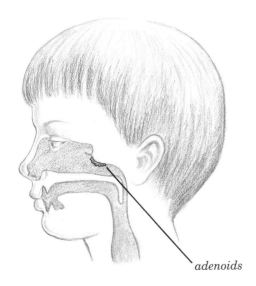

adenoids

The position of the adenoids in the nose.

In some children the adenoids swell and restrict the normal flow of air through the nose. This leads to characteristic nasal speech and a tendency to "mouth-breathing" and snoring.

Causes and recovery

In natural medicine, swollen adenoids are considered to be due to accumulation of phlegm (mucus or catarrh). In many children the phlegm is obvious and they suffer from a continuously runny nose. In others the phlegm becomes so thick that it cannot flow, and its presence is only confirmed by subtle diagnostic features such as enlarged neck glands and a special quality to the pulse. Such thick mucus is nearly always due to the "echo" pattern (page 25).

Natural treatments can help, and should produce effects after two or three weeks. The mucus softens, leading to more nasal discharge, and the spirits and appetite improve. If you see no change after four weeks, consult a practitioner.

Surgery

Should your child still be troubled by swollen adenoids after six months of natural treatment by a practitioner, it may be worth considering surgical removal, the orthodox treatment for certain cases of enlarged adenoids. This is a routine, low-risk operation, provided the child is otherwise reasonably healthy. Do not regard the natural treatments as wasted. If you start with natural medicines, and surgery eventually becomes necessary, you will help your child to become much stronger for the operation and to recover more quickly afterwards.

TREATMENT FOR ADENOIDS

Natural treatments aim to clear the "echo" pattern of illness. A phlegm-reducing diet (page 36) is also essential.

Herbs and homoeopathy

Treat as for chronic cold (see opposite).

Massage

Note: See page 72 for information on massages.
● Daily massage of acupuncture points (which are situated along energy channels, page 14) can considerably improve the circulation of energy in the adenoids and speed up the healing process.
● Massage down either side of the child's nose, using your thumb and forefinger, about 50 times.
● Thumb to elbow, using your thumbs, for about 3 minutes.

COUGHS

Coughs vary in their nature and severity, from little more than a tickle in the throat that lasts for a few days to a severe cough that may develop into bronchitis, pneumonia or asthma.

Causes and factors

On the physical level, many coughs are caused by viruses or bacteria that inflame the respiratory tract and trigger the over-secretion of mucus. Inflammation which leads to the feverish type of cough is nearly always caused by bacteria; antibiotics (which kill bacteria) have made these coughs much less dangerous than in former times.

Weather and season As the weather changes from hot to cold, from dry to damp, and as the seasons change, the body has to adapt. A delay in adaptation can give rise to "latent heat" or "latent cold" (page 26), opening the way for infections.

DANGER SIGNS

Seek help when you are worried. Call the doctor if your child:
- develops a high fever (above 40°C, 104°F),
- becomes progressively disinterested and lethargic,
- wheezes or has other difficulties in breathing, or
- has pain in the chest.

If your family often has coughs, you will know what to look for. If this is your first child, or the first time your child has had a bad cough, do not hesitate to call the doctor or take the child to hospital.

Internal causes and emotions It is easy for infection to occur when the body is tired or run down, as happens when your child has had insufficient sleep, is going through a growth spurt, or is upset by immunization, especially whooping cough or polio.

Emotional factors that can make a child more prone to coughs are mainly "negative" feelings such as irritability and depression. Similarly, an emotional upheaval, such as a new baby arriving or a parent's absence from home, can deeply upset children.

Types and patterns of cough

Various terms describe the type of cough. An acute cough comes on suddenly, within a day or two. A chronic cough persists, perhaps for many weeks, sometimes getting better and sometimes worse.

A productive cough brings up lots of phlegm (catarrh or mucus). This may be thin and watery or thick and gluey. Adults can usually learn to cough up the phlegm and spit it out, but children often swallow it. Your child may make rattling or gurgling sounds in the throat and chest, and in severe cases, it seems as if he or she is "drowning" in phlegm.

In a non-productive cough, very little or no phlegm is brought up. The cough is usually rather harsh and hard, and in some cases "croupy" (noisy or "crowing"). The breathing may be wheezy and your child may complain of tight feelings in the chest.

Five commonly-seen patterns of coughs are described here: feverish, watery, catarrhal (phlegm or mucous type), hard (or croupy) and chronic. If your child's cough does not clearly fit one of these patterns it is wise to seek the advice of a practitioner.

Preventing coughs

In winter, avoid overheating your house. The transition in going from a hot house to freezing temperatures outside can stress the body and produce croupy coughs that are particularly difficult to cure.

Certain foods, especially cow's milk, cheese, roast peanuts, sugar and bananas, generate phlegm and should be avoided during a cough. Children who suffer from chronic coughs should avoid these foods altogether for two or three weeks. After this, they may be reintroduced gradually in small quantities.

Many coughs take hold because of a negative outlook. Try to encourage a positive approach in your child, with plenty of activity, fresh air and sunshine throughout the year. Fresh air and exercise are important, but do not expose your child suddenly to cold winds or rain, especially without suitable clothing. The body may be overstressed and put out of balance as a result, which could open the way for another cold or a similar infection in the future.

TREATMENT GUIDE

When treating your child with natural medicines, you will probably find that any remedy that benefits the lungs helps to reduce the symptoms of a cough. However, the more accurate your diagnosis, the more successful the treatment. This list of features below will guide you in diagnosis. Other points to observe include any variation in the severity of the cough under different conditions, such as warm or cool air, and whether your child has had an immunization (page 27) in the past month.

Note that the herbs recommended for each type of cough may be administered by rubbing the tincture into the abdomen.

The massages given for asthma (page 104) are helpful for all types of coughs, and particularly chronic coughs. Eucalyptus oil may be used in the massage and is beneficial to coughs, as is Comfrey oil on the chest.

FEATURE OF COUGH	REFER TO
Long-term illness	Chronic cough
Accompanied by fever or painful chest	Feverish cough
Accompanied by difficulty in breathing	Asthma or Hard cough
Accompanied by yellow phlegm	Feverish cough
Accompanied by white phlegm	Catarrhal cough
Accompanied by clear phlegm	Watery cough
Hard-sounding and "croupy"	Hard cough, Whooping cough or Feverish cough
Accompanied by a skin rash	A common childhood infection such as measles

Feverish cough (includes bronchitis)

Symptom profile The illness comes suddenly, and is obviously due to infection. Symptoms include:
■ a hard-sounding cough which may keep the child awake at night,
■ there is often a slight fever, the forehead feels hot to the touch, and there may be sweating and a red face,
■ sore, inflamed throat, and
■ a nasal discharge or a cough with thick, yellow phlegm.
    This type of cough is called "attack by heat" in Chinese medicine. It may occur in spring when the weather turns suddenly warm, or in the heat of summer; it may also progress from another cough.

Recovery You should notice some change in your child's mood soon after treatment, and if the remedy is right, perspiration starts within one hour. This is a good sign, since it shows that the body is fighting the infection. At this stage the cough "softens" and becomes more productive. When the fever has largely faded, this type of cough may evolve into the catarrhal pattern: treat accordingly. Keep a close watch on your child, because a feverish cough can develop into bronchitis or pneumonia, which needs specialist help.

TREATMENT FOR FEVERISH COUGH

Herbs

Note: See page 40 for dosages and cautions for herbs.
    The aims of treatments are to bring down inflammation, reduce phlegm (if necessary) and calm the cough.
● To clear fever and reduce inflammation – either Pasque flower (*Anemone pulsatilla*), Lobelia (*Lobelia inflata*), or Pleurisy root (*Asclepias tuberosa*) prepared as a standard diluted tincture. Or use Elderflower (*Sambucus nigra*), Plantain (*Plantago major*) or Marshmallow leaves (*Althea officinalis*) prepared as a tea.
● To reduce phlegm – either Elecampane (*Inula helenium*) or Echinacea (*Echinacea purpurea*).

● To calm the cough – Lobelia.
● Home prescription – Pasque flower 2 drops, Pleurisy root 20 drops, Lobelia 10 drops. Give every 2-4 hours in water, until improvement. If there is constipation, add 10 drops Black root (*Leptandra virginica*) to each dose. If the child is tearful and frightened, add 2-4 drops of tincture of Motherwort (*Leonurus cardiaca*).

Homoeopathy

Note: See page 54 for dosages and cautions for homoeopathic remedies.
● Sense of suffocation, a short dry cough which may develop into a croupy cough, and the sudden onset of fever with shivering – Aconite.

● Tightness and pain in the chest, dry cough with wheezing, profuse perspiration – Bryonia.
● Violent cough which starts as a tickle, headache, face red with fever, skin is hot to the touch – Belladonna.
● Tearful nature and green nasal discharge – Pulsatilla.
● Wracking cough which leads to retching and vomiting – Nux vomica.

Tissue salts

Note: See page 64 for information on tissue salts.
● Ferr. phos. may help in the early stages, acting as a tonic to give the child energy to fight the illness.

Watery cough

Symptom profile This type of cough usually comes on quite suddenly. Typical symptoms include:

■ the child coughs up watery phlegm,
■ clear phlegm (catarrh) comes from the nose; it may be viscous like glue or runny like egg white,
■ the cough is often worse lying down, as the lungs tend to become clogged with secretions,
■ a pale facial color, sometimes alternating with flushing, and
■ the child often feels cold and "shivery", and the cough is usually noticeably better if he or she wears warm clothes.

This type of cough is called "attack by cold" in Chinese medicine. It can appear during cold, wet weather, which acts to lower the reaction time and strength of the body's immune system and produce the weak, shivery feeling.

Recovery After treatment, the first changes should be in your child's mood. He or she starts to throw off the negative feelings that always come with watery phlegm, and shows positive interest. Soon the remedy works through to the symptoms, which should start to diminish after about one or two hours.

The effects of the remedy may wear off in three to six hours. It is advisable to repeat the dosage after this time interval until the cough clears – which is usually within a few days. If the cough progresses to another type, treat as necessary.

TREATMENT FOR WATERY COUGH

Herbs

Note: See page 40 for dosages and cautions for herbs.

The aims of treatment are to warm the system, stimulate the body's immune defences and clear the wet secretions from the lungs.
● To warm the system – Aniseed (*Pimpinella anisum*), Fennel (*Foeniculum vulgaris*), Ginger (*Zingiber officinale*) and Prickly ash (*Xanthoxylum americanum*). Give as a tea. Select 2 or 3 herbs, 1 level teaspoon of each, and sweeten the tea with honey if required.
● To warm the system (older children only) – Cayenne pepper (*Capsicum annum*), add tincture to the tea above or put 3 drops in food.
● To clear clogging secretions from the lungs – Horehound (*Marrubium vulgaris*) and Coltsfoot (*Tussilago farfara*). Standard dosage, added to the tea above.
● For nasal congestion – add standard dosage of Eyebright (*Euphrasia officinalis*) to the tea above.

Homoeopathy

Note: See page 54 for dosages and cautions for homoeopathic remedies.
● Anxiety and restlessness, fear of suffocation, the child likes frequent sips of cold water and he or she feels worse around midnight to early morning – Ars. alb.
● The child keeps on getting watery coughs – Ars. alb.
● The child goes stiff and blue during bouts of coughing, there is persistent nausea with a mouth full of saliva and no thirst – Ipecacuanha.

Tissue salts

Note: See page 64 for information on tissue salts.
● Nat. mur. or Combination J often helps this type of cough.

99

Catarrhal (mucous) cough

Symptom profile A catarrhal cough comes on quite suddenly and may be due to infection. Symptoms include:
■ the child coughs up thick, white phlegm (catarrh or mucus), and thick white, or even grey, phlegm comes from the nose,
■ the cough is often worse lying down,
■ the child's face tends to be grey,
■ he or she is not much affected by being kept warm, but is often worse when exposed to cold air, and
■ sometimes there is diarrhea.

   Like a watery cough, this is also a "cold" type, although there is usually a constitutional factor which predisposes to phlegm production. Avoid mucus-producing foods as much as possible in this pattern of cough (page 36).

Recovery The effect of natural treatments depends largely on how catarrhal your child is. As with a watery cough, his or her mood should soon change, but in catarrhal conditions this occurs more slowly, and it takes longer for the healing effects to work through to the symptoms. In a mild attack, symptoms should lessen while the treatment is being taken, and the cough generally clears in a few days. If it persists, or returns, it may have become a chronic cough (page 102).

Hard (croupy) cough

This cough develops when there is inflammation of the larynx (voicebox) and trachea (windpipe), which leads to the phlegm being very thick and difficult to bring up. This croup is only present in severe cases. The illness usually comes on quickly and has often progressed from another pattern of cough, but it can drag on for weeks. It may develop in the week or two following immunization for whooping cough or diphtheria.

TREATMENT FOR CATARRHAL COUGH

Herbs

Note: See page 40 for dosages and cautions for herbs.
   The aims of treatment are to clear phlegm from the lungs and reduce its production. If herbs are too heating, such as Capsicum, there is a danger of drying the phlegm into hard knots.
● To clear phlegm from the lungs – Elecampane (*Inula helenium*), Hyssop (*Hyssopus officinale*) and Coltsfoot (*Tussilago farfara*).

● To reduce the production of phlegm – Golden seal (*Hydrastis canadensis*). Caution: Do not give Golden seal on its own, but only with other herbs that assist the lungs, as above.
● Home prescription – Elecampane, Hyssop, Golden seal, Coltsfoot, 3 drops of tincture of each taken 3 times daily in water.
● Garlic is especially helpful for coughs, in food or administered as a foot poultice (see opposite).

Homoeopathy

Note: See page 54 for dosages and cautions for homoeopathic remedies.
● The cough is loose in the morning and dry in the evening, the phlegm is thick and yellow or green, and the child is tearful and emotional – Pulsatilla.
● The phlegm is sticky and stringy, and may be yellow – Kali bich.
● Much phlegm and rattling in the chest, difficulty in

Symptom profile The hard cough may come in bouts lasting around five minutes. Typical symptoms of this type of cough include:

■ the child's throat is tickly rather than inflamed, but may become sore due to so much coughing,

■ in severe cases there may be crouping ("crowing", noisy breathing), but in mild cases this does not happen,

■ there is usually no fever, except after a coughing bout, and

■ usually no nasal discharge, but the nose is blocked and the child breathes through the mouth.

General care and recovery If your child has this cough pattern, the characteristic emotion is likely to be irritability. This can feed on itself, with the cough causing irritation, leading to more coughing.

It is important to keep calm and help your child to overcome irritation and anger. If such emotions have a basis in daily life, such as problems at school or family tensions, it is a good idea to talk about these and bring them into the open. Bach flower remedies may then be of help.

One of the first signs of improvement after treatment is that the cough "softens" and becomes more productive. Continue giving the same remedy if there are no others available. However the cough may change its character, and so it may be better to treat as for a catarrhal cough.

This cough can also cause irritation in the rest of the family, since the hard, barking cough is often worse in the evening and at night. The remedies may not speed recovery, but they are helpful in reducing the symptoms, especially during the night. This allows your child to rest, sleep, and build up energy to fight the illness. It also allows parents and other members of the household to rest and get some sleep, which contributes to lessening the tensions and irritations in the family. (For treatment see next page.)

---

breathing, and a pale or bluish face – Antim. tart.
● Loose cough with white or yellow phlegm, the child is selfish and irritable with hot hands and feet – Sulphur.

Tissue salts

Note: See page 64 for information on tissue salts.
● Kali mur. or Combination Q are recommended.

To make a garlic poultice, crush a small piece of garlic into a paste with a little cooking oil. Place this on the sole of the foot (far left). Cover with a bandage (left), and leave on overnight.

101

TREATMENT FOR HARD (CROUPY) COUGH

Herbs

Note: See page 40 for dosages and cautions for herbs.

The aims of treatment are to reduce the spasmodic nature of the cough, soften the phlegm and clear the lungs
• To reduce the spasmodic nature of the cough – Lobelia (*Lobelia inflata*), Black cohosh (*Cimicifuga racemosa*), Wild cherry (*Prunus serotina*) or Thyme (*Thymus vulgaris*).
• To soften the phlegm and clear the lungs – Elecampane (*Inula helenium*) or Bloodroot (*Sanguinaria canadensis*).
• Home prescription – Wild cherry syrup 20mls, Lobelia tincture 5mls, Elecampane tincture 5mls, Coltsfoot (*Tussilago farfara*) tincture 5mls, give one-quarter of a teaspoon (1ml) 3 times daily.
• Thyme baths (page 132) are especially helpful for babies.

Homoeopathy

Note: See page 54 for dosages and cautions for homoeopathic remedies.
• If the onset is sudden, the cough is dry and barking, and the child is restless – start with Aconite, 2 doses at 30 minute intervals. If there is no change in a few hours, try Spongia.
• Loud rasping cough which wakes the child, the phlegm is difficult to bring up and the child is choked and frightened – Spongia.
• When a head cold has gone onto the chest, there is a hard tickly cough and a thirst for cold drinks (which may be vomited back), and the child may be chilly and/or perspiring – Phosphorus.
• A deep, hoarse cough which is worse at night as soon as the child lies down, a tickle in the throat brings on a coughing bout, and the cough itself is spasmodic, with gasping and retching – Drosera.

Chronic cough

Causes One common cause of a chronic cough is treatment of a feverish cough by antibiotics. These drugs relieve the initial attack, but they do not clear the underlying mucous condition and they tend to weaken the immune system.

Polio immunization may give rise to a chronic catarrhal cough, while whooping cough can trigger a chronic barking cough. These coughs can appear any time up to four weeks after immunization, and may recur as the "echo" pattern (page 25). To determine whether your child has the "echo" pattern, examine the neck glands (see illustration opposite).

A chronic croupy cough may appear shortly before your child learns to speak (the "terrible twos"), when it is sometimes an expression of frustration at being unable to communicate and express wishes clearly. Other causes include the "liver congestion" (page 23) pattern of illness.

Symptom profile The typical symptoms of a chronic cough include the following:
■ the cough persists, sometimes seeming a little better but then becoming worse,
■ it may clear up completely, only to return soon after,
■ there may be continued attacks which in some cases may have to be treated by antibiotics,
■ any phlegm is usually thick,
■ your child's face is often grey, although in some cases he or she has red cheeks and is "green" around the mouth, and
■ the appetite is poor.

General care and recovery When suffering a chronic cough, your child may not remember what it is like to be healthy and happy. So it helps to combine remedies with positive measures to improve vitality such as fresh air, activity and laughter. If he or she continues to suffer from a chronic cough, month after month, it is important to consult a practitioner of natural medicine.

In the first instance, natural treatment may expel copious phlegm, so that the cough worsens and there is mild diarrhea for a week or so. In some children this aggravation may be quite severe, in which case the remedy should only be given in the morning, and in small doses for the first week or two. To avoid this problem, give only the herbs to clear phlegm from

In "echo" chronic coughs, the neck glands remain swollen.

the chest for the first two weeks, as described under Treatment below, and add the other herbs later.

TREATMENT FOR CHRONIC COUGH

Herbs

Note: See page 40 for dosages and cautions for herbs.

The aims of treatment are to clear phlegm from the chest and reduce its production.

• To clear chest phlegm – Hyssop (*Hyssopus officinale*), Coltsfoot (*Tussilago farfara*) and Elecampane (*Inula helenium*).

• To reduce production of phlegm – Elecampane and Golden seal (*Hydrastis canadensis*). Caution: give Golden seal only with herbs that assist the lungs.

• Home prescription – Elecampane, Hyssop, Golden seal, Coltsfoot, standard dosage of each, 3 times daily.

• In "echo" pattern – add to the above prescription Poke root (*Phytolacca decandra*) and Blue flag (*Iris versicolor*), at 3 times standard dosage

• In "liver congestion" – add Black root (*Leptandra virginica*) to the prescription.

Homoeopathy

Note: See page 54 for dosages and cautions for homoeopathic remedies.

• The child coughs up yellow phlegm, the cough is worse in warm air, there is a yellow nasal discharge and often a sore throat – Merc. sol.

• The cough worsens with changes in the weather – Kali carb.

Tissue salts

Note: See page 64 for information on tissue salts.

• The cough worsens when the weather changes from dry to wet, it is most severe in the early morning, with thick greenish phlegm – Nat. sulph.

• There is sticky yellow phlegm, which is worse in a warm room – Kali sulph.

Bach remedies

Note: See page 66 for information on Bach remedies.

These remedies can be very useful for a chronic cough, especially if linked to deep emotional uneasiness.

ASTHMA

Asthma is a condition in which breathing becomes difficult. The common pattern is for a child to seem "well" most of the time, but suffer from periodic asthma attacks. The attacks are usually brought on by some "trigger" factor, such as a respiratory infection, allergy or emotional stress. A healthy child can cope with these factors, but the asthmatic child's constitution is usually out of balance in some way.

In an attack of asthma, the child's breathing gradually becomes labored and a wheezing sound is heard with each breath. This may gradually become worse over a few hours, until the child is struggling for breath. This stage is very serious, and unless immediate action is taken, the skin takes on a pale blue colour (especially noticeable around the lips) as the oxygen level in the blood falls.

The child may well now be in a state of panic, struggling and terrified, as he or she fights for air. This stage can last for several hours. In many cases, and especially with treatment, it slowly passes, and breathing gradually eases. However, in a minority of cases, an untreated asthma attack can become so serious that immediate medical help is required.

Causes and factors

Asthma occurs when the airways in the lungs become blocked to the passage of air, and the muscles in the airway walls go into spasm (uncontrolled contraction) and narrow the tubes. The airways may be blocked by over-production of phlegm, as in a respiratory infection. In a baby the airway walls are soft and may collapse. In older children there may be a general bodily tendency of the muscles to go into spasm, especially in the tense, nervous type of child.

Accumulation of phlegm In Chinese medicine, it is said there is always phlegm (mucus or catarrh) in asthma. In many children the phlegm is obvious, since even between asthma attacks they suffer from nasal discharge and other signs of phlegm. In other children the phlegm is thick and knotted, and the only signs are a subtle nature to the pulse (detectable by a practitioner) and swollen glands.

The origin of the phlegm may be an "echo" pattern disease (page 25), when the child has repeated respiratory infections but the phlegm never clears completely. Or phlegm may accumulate from a sluggish digestion, when mucus builds up due to "liver congestion" (page 23).

Weak lungs or energy A child with strong lungs will not get asthma. Weak lungs may be due to hereditary factors (asthma in the family, or tuberculosis in an earlier generation), or to repeated past infections. If the body's overall energy is low, the child is prone to infections (page 14). Moreover, the tissues are softer, and the airways may be more likely to collapse.

Emotional factors Emotional factors in asthma are important in children over about three years old, but less so in babies. The emotional factors are those which are likely to give rise to a general stiffening of the muscles in the chest, and a general tendency to spasm. Especially common are unexpressed anger, tension picked up from other family members, a sense of loss which can occur when parents separate (or even think of separating), or a feeling of being over-protected and "smothered" by parents. Sometimes these feelings have a real basis in life; at other times they are due to incorrect perceptions by the child.

Tendency to allergies Asthma attacks are often triggered by an allergic reaction, for example, to house mites and house dust, molds, artificial colorings and flavorings in foods, and foods such as bitter apples, tomatoes and oranges. Some asthma sufferers are allergic to animals such as cats, dogs, or horses.

Principles of care

Asthma is a profound disease, affecting the whole constitution. Some relief may be obtained by using the remedies described below. But you are strongly advised to consult a practitioner of natural medicine to find the correct treatment.

Other illnesses Coughs and colds often bring on attacks of asthma. If these are treated with natural medicines in the early stages, the lungs are strengthened and an asthma cure is correspondingly quicker. If your child has eczema as well as asthma, try to avoid corticosteroid ("steroid") creams. These may be strikingly effective in stopping eczema (page 174), but in doing so can push the eczema in and aggravate the asthma.

IMPORTANT ACTIONS

Asthma attacks often occur at night. You may already know how to control the attacks, with orthodox drugs (such as an inhaler) from your physician, and other techniques described here. However, if the various remedies do not seem to be working, and you are seriously concerned about your child's breathing, seek medical assistance at once. Call early rather than late.

Exercise Exercise encourages fresh air in the lungs and so strengthens the immune system. Be aware that vigorous exercise may cause wheezing and bring on an asthma attack, but gentle exercise such as walking should be encouraged. At the same time, plenty of sleep helps any illness. At night, the body's tissues are restored and deep-seated diseases cured.

Diet This is especially important. Avoid mucus-producing foods (page 36), particularly milk and cheese. For babies and toddlers, give easily-digested foods, and avoid "rough" foods such as brown bread, which may encourage liver congestion. Some children are affected by refined sugar, while others react to food additives.

Family situation A child grows within its family, and from it derives the energy for growth and development. Asthma imposes a great strain on the family, which may in turn aggravate the asthma. It is always helpful if family members can discuss openly with each other the main sources of stress in their lives.

Over-stimulation Activities such as watching exciting television programs and playing computer games are great stimulants. For the "spasmodic" type of asthma, keep these activities to a minimum.

Posture Body position can be vital. Sitting up straight is generally advisable, and cannot be overemphasized for those with asthma. Pay special attention when the child is learning to write, so that he or she adopts the habit of good posture when working at a desk. If bad habits develop when reading and writing, consult a teacher of the Alexander Technique.

TREATMENT FOR AN ASTHMA ATTACK

In the sudden (acute) attack, the aim is to ensure that your child can breathe. If you can do this by natural means, then he or she will be stronger and better able to shrug off the attack next time. If you need to resort to orthodox medicine, do so – and be prompt in your action. Take any measures required to counter the attack.

Various natural therapies may help. If the child does not respond to one, try another. Certain therapies may be given at the same time. For example, acupuncture may be given at the same time as homoeopathy or healing.

Herbs

Note: See page 40 for dosages and cautions for herbs.
• The following herbs may be of assistance – Lobelia (*Lobelia inflata*), St John's Wort (*Hypericum perfoliatum*), Valerian (*Valeriana officinalis*), Blue Cohosh (*Caulophyllum thalactroides*). Select 2 or 3 herbs, always including Lobelia, and give the standard dosage every 15 minutes. The herbs help to relax muscles and thus relieve the spasms.
• In babies, when the attack is mild, a Thyme (page 132) bath may be helpful.

Homoeopathy

Note: See page 54 for dosages and cautions for homoeopathic remedies.
• Pruss. ac. given every 15 minutes may avoid the need for drugs by inhaler.

Bach remedies

Note: See page 66 for information on Bach remedies.
• Red chestnut is often indicated; alternatively give the Bach Rescue remedy.

Massage

Note: See page 72 for information on massages. The severity of an asthma

Shoulder massage for asthma attack

attack can be greatly relieved by 3 simple massages, given promptly at the onset of the asthma attack.

Keep calm yourself and take control firmly but gently, reassuring the child. Help him or her to relax in any way you know how, so that vital energy is not dissipated in crying. Asthma attacks commonly occur at night, when your concentration may be lacking, so practice the massages during the day.
• Scapular massage, continued for about 5 minutes.
• Chest massage, also given for about 5 minutes.
• Shoulder massage. Find the points midway between the backbone and the outer edge of each shoulder. Press down firmly with your index fingers and rotate vigorously (see illustration). This may be uncomfortable for the child, but if you can continue, it may well stop the asthma attack.

External remedies

• Comfrey ointment (*Symphytum officinale*) rubbed into the chest is helpful, and can be combined with massage.
• The herbal remedies mentioned above may be administered by rubbing into the abdomen.

Encourage your child to sit up straight with shoulders back, so that lungs and chest can work easily and efficiently.

It can take a long time to cure asthma – six months, perhaps even one year. Do not be surprised if your child has some relapses. When these occur, try not to hold off orthodox drugs and inhalers for too long. During the treatment of such a long-term condition, you may feel that you have failed by returning to the use of such drugs. However, this attitude can be dangerous. Often, taking a small dose of an inhaler early in the attack can avoid the necessity of larger doses when the attack has built up.

Natural treatments and orthodox drugs

Several orthodox or conventional medical drugs are used to treat asthma. They are powerful and have saved many lives. But, like all strong medicines (including strong herbs) they have side-effects. Many parents wish to "wean" their children off these drugs, and this is often possible with the help of natural medicines. Generally speaking, natural medicines are quite compatible with orthodox drugs.

However, it must be stressed that any reduction of the dosage of an orthodox drug must be done gradually, over a period of many weeks, and preferably in consultation with the medical practitioner. **Never stop orthodox drugs suddenly**.

The first aim of natural treatment is therefore to stop the symptoms of asthma, while continuing with orthodox medical drugs. The next step is to reduce the orthodox drugs. Finally, the natural medicines can gradually be reduced.

TREATMENT BETWEEN ASTHMA ATTACKS

The aim of long-term treatment is still to make sure the child can breathe during attacks. In addition, natural treatments aim to strengthen the lungs, clear phlegm, increase energy, and ease tension. If possible, seek the help of a practitioner. Asthma is a profound disease and may be difficult to treat in the home. Never stop orthodox drugs suddenly.

Herbs

Note: See page 40 for dosages and cautions for herbs. For all types of asthma, give herbs to strengthen the lungs and clear phlegm. If your child has very clogged lungs, start by giving the lung-strengthening herbs first, then add the phlegm-clearing herbs after 2 or 3 weeks.

Continued on next page

• To strengthen the lungs – select two from Hyssop (*Hyssopus officinale*), Coltsfoot (*Tussilago farfara*), Horehound (*Marrubium vulgaris*), Liquorice (*Glycyrrhiza glabra*).

• To clear phlegm – Golden seal (*Hydrastis canadensis*), Elecampane (*Inula helenium*).

• If the phlegm is thick and knotted (often seen in "echo" diseases), then after giving these herbs for 2 to 3 weeks, use the following to soften the phlegm and clear the glandular system – Blue flag (*Iris versicolor*), Poke root (*Phytolacca decandra*). When you first give these herbs, there may be a temporary increase in the amount of phlegm. Do not give them during an attack.

• If the phlegm originates from a digestive disturbance ("liver congestion" pattern) there may be foul-smelling diarrhea and possibly constipation alternating with diarrhea. In these cases, avoid any "rough" or raw foods (page 36) and give Black root (*Leptandra virginica*).

• To relax the child – Lobelia (*Lobelia inflata*), Hops (*Humulus lupulus*), St John's Wort (*Hypericum perfoliatum*), Thyme (*Thymus vulgaris*). Select two herbs, standard dosage.

• Thyme baths (page 132) may also be given.

• The herbs mentioned above may be administered by rubbing into the abdomen.

Homoeopathy and tissue salts

Note: See pages 54 and 64 for information on homoeopathy and tissue salts.

Homoeopathy is difficult to prescribe in the treatment of asthma, especially if the symptoms between attacks are mild. See also Coughs (page 96).

• For generally strengthening the constitution – Sepia. Other remedies should be chosen on the basis of the symptoms present. Here are some suggestions:

• Phlegm – Nat. sulph. (green sputum), Ars. alb., Sambucus nigra, Kali mur. (white sputum), Calc. phos. (tough gluey sputum).

• Weak lungs – Ipecacuanha, Calc. fluor.

• Spasms, tension – Aconite, Chamomilla, Kali phos. alternating with Mag. phos.

Bach remedies

Note: See page 66 for information on Bach remedies.

Bach remedies are especially helpful in the home treatment of asthma. They, perhaps more than any other remedy, offer a gentle way to cure your child. Consult a practitioner for advice.

Massage

Note: See page 72 for information on massages.

• Thumb to elbow massage.

• Daily friction massage of the chest and back helps to strengthen the lungs.

• Back pinch-pull massage, and the same technique on the abdomen.

Relaxation techniques

Older children often get tense through overwork at school; tension can also arise through allergy to foods. General relaxation techniques can therefore help.

Tension should not occur in babies. If your baby becomes nervous and tense, this probably comes from the environment. You may well be aware of tension within yourself, so look for ways to help you relax.

Other therapies

Acupuncture and hand healing (sometimes called spiritual healing) have been very effective in curing asthma.

Results of treatment

you should notice some changes in your child within about a week of starting treatment. He or she should be more active, and although there may be a cough or cold, this helps to expel the phlegm, and each time recovery from an asthma attack should be easier.

HAY FEVER (AND RHINITIS)

The term "hay fever" was originally used for symptoms arising from exposure to dust in hay-making. Nowadays it covers various sorts of allergies, including pollen, feathers (in pillows), animal hair and house dust. The term "allergic rhinitis" is sometimes used instead, meaning nasal inflammation and discharge caused by an allergic reaction. Seasonal rhinitis (typical hay fever) occurs at a certain time of year, usually spring, early summer or late summer and autumn, when most plants produce their pollen. Perennial rhinitis comes on at any time and is often linked to tiny mites in house dust and animal hair allergies.

Symptoms

Hay fever is an over-reaction of the mucus-producing membranes, mainly in the nose, to irritation by pollens and other substances. In mild cases the inner part of the nose becomes inflamed, and the child has mild sneezing. In severe cases the nose is very itchy and perhaps painful, so that the child sneezes continuously, has a runny nose with a watery discharge, and suffers from itchy, watery eyes which are sensitive to light. He or she may have swollen eyelids and a tickly throat. Often there is great difficulty in concentrating because of the irritation.

In some children, hay fever can become more severe and spread down the respiratory tract, giving rise to an irritating cough. In children who are prone to asthma, this can sometimes trigger an asthma attack.

During periods of high pollen count, when typical hay fever is at its worst, sufferers may have to spend most of their time indoors, even lying down in a darkened room in order to get relief.

Causes and factors

In orthodox medicine, hay fever is considered to involve body chemicals like histamine involved in the inflammatory reaction. A susceptible child is allergic or "extra-sensitive" to normally harmless substances such as pollen. Pollen that comes into contact with the mucous membranes (nose, eyes and throat) releases histamine and other chemicals, which causes irritation and inflammation.

In Chinese medicine, hay fever is viewed as a combination of excessive phlegm (mucus) in the body and an accumulation of heat in the respiratory system, of which the nose is part. The heat can come from many sources, a few of which are outlined here.

Latent heat The body produces more heat in winter than in summer. If the transition during spring is delayed, excess "latent heat" builds up (page 26). This may be released by a fever, or remain in the system as a factor which predisposes to hay fever. Similarly, longer-term latent heat may be caused by immunization, or a severe, feverish illness in early childhood.

Echo heat Sometimes a child has a severe respiratory infection such as a bad cold but never completely throws it off, especially if treated by antibiotics. The infection may leave a mild inflammation of the mucous membranes in the nose, sinuses and throat, which is part of the "echo" pattern of illness (page 25). There may be no significant symptoms – until the extra irritation by pollen brings on hay fever.

Over-excitement If a child becomes over-excited or over-stimulated, energy rushes into the head, where it may accumulate

109

and cause the build-up of heat. Typically, over-stimulation can be caused by too much television, going to bed too late, and generally too much mental activity without balancing physical activity.

Food and allergies Some foods, such as sugar, and many artificial colorings and preservatives may cause an allergic reaction. In addition, "warming" foods (page 34) such as red meat are likely to aggravate hay fever. The allergy that "triggers" the attack of hay fever is an airborne substance such as hay dust, pollen, house dust, tiny particles of house mites (in house dust), mold spores or fragments of animal hairs.

Anger Some practitioners of complementary medicines might not ask what a child is allergic to, but whom. We may say that certain people "get up one's nose". Anger is an important component of hay fever. Children under seven years usually have few inhibitions and express their anger freely; so if they suffer hay fever, they may be acting out the anger of someone else in the family. After this time, the anger is usually their own.

Timing of preventative treatment

If possible, start treatment at least three months before the hay fever season begins. This gives your child a good

TREATMENT FOR HAY FEVER

If there is a lot of thick phlegm, or other pronounced physical symptoms, herbs are the treatment of first choice. If you feel there is a strong emotional component then homoeopathy, tissue salts or Bach remedies are preferred.

Herbs

Note: See page 40 for dosages and cautions for herbs.
• To clear phlegm – Golden seal (*Hydrastis canadensis*), Elecampane (*Inula helenium*) and Black root (*Leptandra virginica*), 3 drops of tincture of each in a cup of water, 3 times daily.
• To clear heat from the nose and eyes – Eyebright (*Euphrasia officinalis*), Pasque flower (*Anemone*

pulsatilla) and St John's Wort (*Hypericum perfoliatum*), dosage as given above.
• To relieve anger and reduce tension – St John's Wort, Valerian (*Valeriana officinalis*) and Hops (*Humulus lupulus*), dosage as given above.
• Home prescription – Golden seal, Elecampane, Eyebright and Valerian, 2-5 drops of tincture of each in a cup of water, 3-5 times daily.

Homoeopathy

Note: See page 54 for dosages and cautions for homoeopathic remedies.
• For itchy, watering eyes; the child is irritable and worse for open air, lying down and bright light – Euphrasia.

• If the child is fearful and the hay fever is worse in cool weather – Ars. alb.
• If the eyes are sore and painful, the nose is stuffed up, and the child is angry, and worse at night and out of doors – Nux vomica.
• When the nose streams like a tap and the child is a "wet blanket" – Nat. mur.
• If the child cannot concentrate and is mentally exhausted, better after eating but worse with mental exertion – Anacardium. This remedy is useful for school-aged children at summer examination time.
    Other remedies which may help include Allium cepa, Sinapis nigra (for a depressed, gloomy child), Sabadilla and Rhus tox.

chance of eliminating the seasonal latent heat, and of reaching the deeper causes of hay fever. If this is not possible, the remedies given here may well be effective, but must be given several times daily during the hay fever season.

General care

- Avoid mucus-producing foods as far as possible, and especially cheese, milk and peanuts (page 36).
- Avoid foods that tend to be irritating and stimulating, especially red meats, highly spiced foods, and sugar.
- Avoid foods with artificial colorings, flavorings and preservatives.
- When considering immunizations, remember that they may aggravate any tendency to hay fever (page 27).
- Try to keep your child calm, and avoid over-stimulation (such as too much television and video games) without balancing physical activity.
- During spring, before the usual hay fever season, make sure your child gets plenty of fresh air and exercise, preferably exercise that stimulates perspiration. This helps to overcome the seasonal "block" and release latent heat.
- Try to talk through any emotional problems with your child, including family tensions and possible difficulties at school or among friends.

Tissue salts

Note: See page 64 for information on tissue salts.
- For general treatment – Combination H. Of its ingredients, Mag. phos. is antispasmodic and helps to relax the child, Nat. mur. controls water balance and reduces sneezing, and Silica relieves the itchy nose and oversensitivity.
- If there are other signs of heat – add Ferr. phos.

Bach remedies

Note: See page 66 for information on Bach remedies.
  Bach remedies are often particularly effective in treating hay fever. Consider your child's temperament and one of the following remedies may be indicated: Impatiens, Holly, Beech or Agrimony.

Counselling

Sometimes you may be only too aware of anger in your family, but feel powerless. Yet something can always be done. Professional counsellors can help you and your child to direct the energy of anger and other strong emotions into constructive channels.

Visualization

After the age of seven, hay fever may be due to suppressed anger (page 18). The dawning awareness which causes the anger and the hay fever, can also cure.
  In visualization, sit with your child in a peaceful and quiet place, with eyes shut. Ask him or her to imagine a scene of cool mountains. When the scene is clear in the child's mind, he or she imagines breathing in cool, pure mountain air through the nose, which soothes the irritated nasal membranes. Spend about 5-10 minutes like this, several times daily. You might make a tape recording for your child to follow.

111

SORE THROATS AND TONSILLITIS

Tonsillitis is inflammation and swelling of the tonsils at the back of the throat. The condition can be acute or chronic.

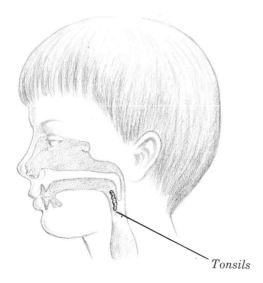

Tonsils

The tonsils are ridges of glandular tissue at the back of the throat. They are involved in fighting illness in the development of antibodies, and in other aspects of the immune system.

Symptoms

Acute tonsillitis flares up suddenly. The tonsils are red, swollen, inflamed – and above all, painful. Your child may complain that swallowing hurts. There is usually a fever and also phlegm, either coughed up or as a nasal discharge.

In chronic tonsillitis, there are recurrent attacks of acute tonsillitis. Between attacks the tonsils are enlarged but not usually painful. The salivary glands at the sides of the jaw are swollen, and your child probably has a poor appetite and is easily tired. Complications are rare in tonsillitis. If the tonsils swell so much that the child can no longer swallow, seek immediate medical help.

Causes and factors

Acute tonsillitis is the result of bacterial or viral infection as a consequence of a weakened immune system. In springtime epidemics, streptococcal bacteria are usually to blame and they attack the tonsils directly. This may be due to changes in the body while adapting to warmer weather, and is often a way to expel "latent heat" (page 26). At other times of the year tonsillitis may be linked to an infection of the ears, eyes or nose.

Body condition The tonsils are near the meeting point of the windpipe (trachea), which takes air to the lungs, and the gullet (oesophagus), which conveys food to the stomach. In Chinese medicine the tonsils are thought to relate to both lungs and stomach. The lung connection is the most common, since tonsillitis may result from inflammation of any mucous membrane relating to the lungs – in the chest, nose and ears. The stomach connection is less common and often due to accumulation of "heating" foods (page 32).

Environment The tonsils filter poisons that affect the head. If your child is continuously exposed to external poisons, such as tobacco smoke or chemical fumes, tonsillitis is more likely.

Emotions The throat is the organ related to the voice, and therefore to the expression of ideas and feelings. Thus any problem of the throat, and especially tonsillitis, is likely to be linked to some obstruction in the normal expression of feelings. At all ages the commonest emotion behind the condition is anger, which has to be suppressed or "swallowed". Tonsillitis is rarely seen before the age of about two

TREATMENT FOR ACUTE TONSILLITIS

Herbs

Note: See page 40 for dosages and cautions for herbs.

Many herbs beneficial in "hot" fevers and "hot" coughs also help acute tonsillitis, because they act to cool the mucous membranes.

- Marshmallow (*Althea officinalis*), Plantain (*Plantago major*), Catmint (*Nepeta cataria*), Elderflower (*Sambucus nigra*), Ragwort (*Senecio jacobaea*), Indigo (*Baptisia tinctoria*). Use on their own, or in combination.
- Home prescription – Plantain, Catmint and Poke root (*Phytolacca decandra*), 20 drops of tincture of each in water, every 3-4 hours if fever or 3 times daily if no fever.
- Poke root is specific for the throat, but use in small quantities and with other herbs; on its own it can generate more phlegm.
- If the tonsils are very swollen – add Cranesbill (*Geranium maculatum*) to the above remedies.
- If the tonsils have yellow spots on them, or the child has spots, boils or styes – add Echinacea (*Echinacea purpurea*), 30mgs in each dosage, to the above remedies.
- If fever is an important symptom – add either Elderflower or Catmint to the prescription.

Homoeopathy

Note: See page 54 for dosages and cautions for homoeopathic remedies.

- If there is thick yellow phlegm, a sensation of a firm lump ("apple core") in the throat, and the child is chilly and smells bad – Merc. sol.
- If there is a sensation of a hot ball in the throat, the right tonsil is worse, and the child is hoarse but not particularly chilly or bad-smelling – Phytolacca.
- If the child complains of a pricking sensation in the tonsils, a bitter taste in mouth, coughs up lumps of mucus, and is sensitive and prone to tears – Silica.
- If there is burning in the throat, and the child experiences a burning heat and is covered in sticky sweat – Phosphorus.
- If there is fever and red face – Apis. mel.

Tissue salts

Note: See page 64 for information on tissue salts.
- In the first stage, before there is swelling, but there is pain – Ferr. phos.
- When there is swelling – add Kali mur.
- If the child is thin and very cold – Silica.
- If the tonsils have a discharge – add Calc. sulph.

Bach remedies

Note: See page 66 for information on Bach remedies.

Bach remedies may be of great help in treating acute tonsillitis, especially if there is a strong emotional factor. The following remedies often help: Holly, Beech, Agrimony, Chicory.

Massage

Note: See page 72 for information on massages.
- Massage the point between the bases of the thumb and index finger with a blunt instrument such as a retracted ballpoint pen. This may be uncomfortable, but massaged with enough vigour it can have a striking effect on the pain of tonsillitis.

Gargles

- If the child is old enough to gargle – Poke root (*Phytolacca decandra*), American cranesbill (*Geranium maculatum*) and Sage (*Salvia officinalis*), a 5mls teaspoon of tincture of each in a glass of water. Each herb helps even on its own.

years, because before this time, the idea of communicating by speech has not been formed. The illness is very common at about two to three years, and again at six to seven years (page 18).

Prevention

To obtain a lasting cure, try to establish why your child has developed tonsillitis. If you feel that it occurs primarily because your child's body is unable to fight off infection, adopt measures to strengthen general health (page 12).

If the tonsillitis is due to "latent heat", then plan ahead for next spring. Give a cleansing diet at this time (page 22).

If you think the illness is primarily emotional in origin, there is a great opportunity for you to help your child to handle and express emotions.

General care

Acute tonsillitis may be painful but it is rarely serious, especially when treated by natural medicines, unless there are signs of scarlet fever also. If your child is otherwise healthy and seems to be coping with the attack, let it run its course. Avoid mucus-producing and heating foods (page 36). And resist the indiscriminate use of antibiotics. Consult a doctor or other practitioner if tonsillitis persists for more than about four days without abating, or if the child is in great distress.

Chronic tonsillitis follows the "echo" pattern (page 25), so take measures to help your child conquer this.

If your child has chronic tonsillitis and also shows signs of weakness, recurrent diarrhea or bed wetting, these problems should be treated by a practitioner.

TREATMENT FOR CHRONIC TONSILLITIS

See Treatment for acute tonsillitis (page 113), for massages and gargles.

Herbs

Note: See page 40 for dosages and cautions for herbs.
• For chronic tonsillitis (and all echo illnesses) – Poke root (*Phytolacca decandra*), 50-100mgs of dried powdered herb, 3 times daily for 3 months. Other herbs to clear the echo pattern may also be given (page 44). These soften hardened phlegm in the system, which appears during the first weeks in the nose, on the chest and occasionally in the bowels (causing loose stools). Some children react with a violent phlegm-producing cough or diarrhea, in which case stop giving the herbs for a week and restart at a smaller dose. Also, discontinue these herbs during an acute attack of tonsillitis.
• If there is a lot of thin watery phlegm – add Hyssop (*Hyssopus officinale*) or Coltsfoot (*Tussilago farfara*).
• If there is a lot of thick phlegm – add Golden seal (*Hydrastis canadensis*) to reduce it, with Elecampane (*Inula helenium*) plus Hyssop to clear phlegm from the lungs. Administer 3 times daily for 3 months.

Homoeopathy

Note: See page 54 for dosages and cautions for homoeopathic remedies.
• Banyta carb may help.

Tissue salts

Note: See page 64 for information on tissue salts.
• If there is soreness in the throat which comes and goes – Calc. phos.

RED AND SORE EYES (AND CONJUNCTIVITIS)

Most eye problems involve the thin membrane covering the white of the eye (the conjunctiva) becoming pink or red, perhaps with swelling and watering. There are three basic patterns, and each requires a different approach.

Sore eyes without infection

The whites of the eyes may become red and sore, but without being infected.

External causes include a foreign body in the eye, such as an insect or piece of grit, injury, exposure to wind (especially dry wind), over-exposure to chlorinated water (as in some swimming pools) and eye strain, perhaps from reading or watching a bright television in poor light.

The chief internal cause of inflammation of the eyes is heat. This may be "latent heat" (page 26), particularly in springtime, or heat that has accumulated in the body during hot weather, heat from food (page 32) or simply over-tiredness.

For sore eyes without infection, provided that the eyes are not too red and there is no pain, treatment is aimed at soothing the eyes.

Acute infectious conjunctivitis

Under certain conditions, sore eyes can quickly develop into acute infectious conjunctivitis. The delicate covering over the eye, the conjunctiva, becomes painful and bright red, as though smeared with blood. There is usually a thick discharge of pus from the eye. The infecting agents are usually bacteria, sometimes viruses.

Acute infectious conjunctivitis is not serious provided it lasts only a day or two. If it continues for much longer, it can have more serious effects. So if the treatments described here are not successful within a

few days, consult a practitioner (orthodox or natural). Orthodox medical treatment uses an antibiotic drug, which may repel the attack and prevent eye damage.

Chronic sore eyes

In some children, the eyes tend to be red and a little sore; sometimes the condition improves, while at other times there may be sudden flare-ups. There are two main causes: insufficient energy in the eyes, and excess internal heat.

Insufficient energy in the eyes may arise from your child's habits. Some children are natural "listeners" rather than "lookers" and do not use their eyes much. Others "look" with great attention and bring energy to the eyes. Another possible cause is a bad attack of measles.

Internal heat usually arises from three main causes: latent heat as already mentioned (page 26), the "echo" pattern of illness (page 25) or the "liver congestion" pattern (page 23).

The symptom of chronic sore eyes, in itself, is not serious. However, since it usually indicates that the energy in the eyes is weak, the eyes may be prone to other disease and may well give later trouble. The aim of treatment is to cure the underlying condition and bring energy back to the eyes. If the treatments given here do not help, you are strongly advised to consult a practitioner.

General care and aims of treatment

Do not let your child rub the eyes. This only makes them more sore. Massaging around the eyes may help to cool them (see Treatment). If the eyes become very crusty, clean them with cotton buds (balls or swabs) and sterilized water.

115

Ensure that the child is not constipated. Avoid heating foods (page 34), especially red meats and particularly garlic, since one of its side-effects is sore, red eyes. Eggs are beneficial for external application, but they may well make the eyes worse when eaten because of their congesting effects on the liver.

Acute infectious conjunctivitis is usually very contagious, so keep your child away from school. Ensure that his or her towel, sheets, clothes and bathroom things are kept separate, away from those of the family. Make sure that he or she washes hands frequently. Careful hygiene should prevent the infection spreading. If it continues for more than three days, consult a practitioner.

Sore eyes, acute or chronic, are not usually serious. But, because our sense of sight is so valuable, it is always wise to obtain expert help if problems occur.

TREATMENT FOR RED AND SORE EYES

External treatments

These general measures help to soothe all types of sore and/or red eyes.
- Lay the child down and place a cool moist tea-bag on each closed eye for about 10 minutes.
- Cut a hardboiled egg in two and remove the yolk. Lay the child down and place the white egg-halves one over each closed eye for 10 minutes.
- Wash the eye with Eyebright (*Euphrasia officinalis*) tea. Infuse a 5mls teaspoon of herb in a cup of hot water, allow to cool, strain the liquid into an eye cup and use in the recommended way.
- Eyedrops containing herbs such as those mentioned here are now available at many pharmacies.
- Wash the eye using a cup of boiled, cooled water with 5 drops of tincture of Eyebright.
- Make an eye lotion by soaking Eyebright herb in

Witch hazel (*Hamamelis virginiana*) distillation. Add to boiled, cooled water as for Eyebright, above.
- Herbs which can replace Eyebright in the above prescriptions are Purple loosestrife (*Lythrum salicaria*), American cranesbill (*Geranium maculatum*) and Marigold (*Calendula officinalis*).

Herbs

Note: See page 40 for dosages and cautions for herbs.

Herbs and other internal treatments help to cool the heat in the system, especially in and around the eyes.

Continued on next page.

Bathe your child's eyes gently with clean water and cotton wool. Never put undiluted herbal tinctures on the eyes.

- Eyebright (*Euphrasia officinalis*) is treatment of choice, taken internally as well as applied externally.
- Chrysanthemum tea is especially beneficial. Available from Chinese stores, either loose or as sachets of "chrysanthemum crystals". For school-aged children, 1 sachet 3 times daily in water. For babies, 1 level 5mls teaspoon of crystals in water, 3 times daily.
- Marshmallow (*Althea officinalis*) as a tea.
- If there is a discharge from the eyes – add Golden seal (*Hydrastis canadensis*) to any of the above prescriptions.
- Treat diarrhea, constipation or other problems as appropriate.
- If the latent heat is due to an "echo" illness, see page 25.

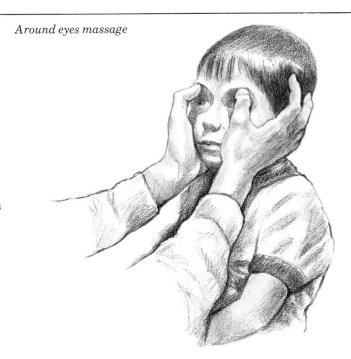

Around eyes massage

Homoeopathy

Note: See page 54 for dosages and cautions for homoeopathic remedies.
- If there are sudden attacks, a sensation of sand in the eyes, the eyes are red and inflamed, and the problem may be due to wind or bright light – Aconite.
- If the eyes are swollen, red and watery with sudden piercing pains – Apis mel.
- If there is a burning sensation in the eyes, they are red and watery, but better in warm air – Ars. alb.
- If the eyes are burning, watery and red, but feel better in warm air, and the child sneezes repeatedly – Allium cepa.
- If the eyes water copiously but occasionally become gummed with sticky mucus – Euphrasia.
- If there is thick, yellowish discharge from the eyes, an itching and burning which makes the child want to rub them, and this becomes worse in warm air – Pulsatilla.

Tissue salts

Note: See page 64 for information on tissue salts.
- To reduce inflammation – Ferr. phos.
- If there is a whitish discharge – add Kali. mur.
- If there is a yellowish discharge – add Nat. phos.

Massage

Note: See page 72 for information on massages.
- Around eyes, to help cool them and ease inflammation. Hold the child's head in your hands, and with your thumbs, stroke around the bone above each eye, which is on the bottom edge of or just below the eyebrow (see illustration). Older children can self-massage the same spot using the thumbs knuckles. Continue for about 5 minutes.
- Jingming massage. Pinch the top of the nose at the corner of the eye with thumb and forefinger, and vibrate gently for 2 minutes (page 7).

117

EARACHES AND OTITIS

Ear infections and earaches of various types are very common in childhood, and they can cause great distress. The commonest form of the problem is otitis media, inflammation of the middle ear. It is usually caused by bacterial or viral infection. Otitis media can be a complication of a nose or throat infection because the germs easily travel from the back of the throat along the eustachian tube.

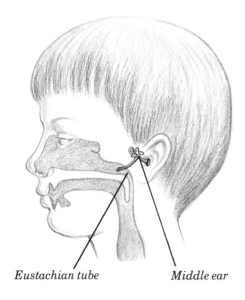

Eustachian tube   *Middle ear*

Symptoms

Acute otitis media This is the term for a sudden attack of otitis media. Often you notice early signs in your child the day before, such as irritability and restlessness, but it sometimes strikes without warning. He or she complains of earache and perhaps pain just below the ear as well. Babies cannot explain where the pain is, and they often put the hand up beside the ear as they cry in distress. Commonly, attacks occur at night and are sometimes accompanied by fever. The diagnosis is established when a practi-

tioner inspects the ear with an otoscope, a light-and-lens device. Without treatment, the inflammation and pain last from a day to a week or longer.

Chronic otitis media This is a long-term condition where the inflammation returns again and again, with repeated episodes of pain. In the secretory type of chronic otitis media, mucus (phlegm or catarrh) builds up in the middle ear, so that the child becomes hard of hearing even between episodes. The glands under the ears swell and there may be a runny nose and cough. In the purulent type, there is an intermittent discharge of brown wax or sometimes pus from the ear.

Glue ear Another long-term form of otitis media, when a thick, yellow, purulent discharge (resembling glue) comes out of the ear. The "glue" gums up the middle ear and affects hearing, so at school age it can inhibit learning.

Causes and factors

Otitis media is often brought on by an infection of the ear itself, or it progresses from an inflammatory disease which affects the head. It may be triggered by over-exposure to cold wind, swimming, or getting water in the ear while taking a bath. Several internal factors cause a predisposition to ear infections:

Internal heat This comes from inflammation of any sort, such as teething, a "hot nature" in babies, "latent heat" (page 26), the "echo" pattern of illness (page 25), or over-excitement and tiredness in older children. Spicy food may give rise to heat in children, as can too much sugar or too many sweets. In babies, heat may be generated by indigestion, particularly when linked to the "liver congestion" pattern of illness (page 23).

Enlarged glands If the child's lymph glands in the region of the ear are permanently enlarged and congested, then the flow of lymph slows, and the tissues in the ear are not properly nourished – so infection can easily take root. A typical pattern of events is for acute otitis media to be treated in the orthodox way with antibiotic drugs; this reduces the inflammation, but the drugs tend to create congestion in the glands, which can take several months to ease. Often, before this occurs, another infection starts.

Phlegm Phlegm that collects in the ears is an ideal breeding ground for bacteria. It can arise from a number of sources: chronic nasal congestion, chronic chest problems such as bronchitis, or any of the mucus-producing foods (page 36) that encourage phlegm or pus.

SOME CAUSES OF INTERNAL HEAT

Excess internal heat tends to produce ear problems in which there is a tendency to inflammation, usually with red cheeks, irritability, restlessness and often insomnia. Although seemingly straightforward, the causes are many and varied. Each requires a different treatment, often involving lifestyle changes. Here are some suggestions:

Cause	Remedy
Over-excitement and over-stimulation both generate inflammation which may flare up in the ears	Keep your child calm, avoid stimulation (especially television); Lobelia (*Lobelia inflata*) and St John's Wort (*Hypericum perfoliatum*) may help
Over-tiredness, when inflammation can occur anywhere in the body	Fresh air, exercise, early to bed
"Latent heat" from seasonal or sudden weather change (page 26)	Try Lobelia and Hypericum, or homoeopathic Nux vomica
"Echo" pattern heat from a past infection or immunization (page 25)	Consult a practitioner of natural medicine; for immunization, see page 27
"Liver congestion" pattern (page 23)	As for diarrhea or constipation
Diet too rich – excessive spicy and greasy foods, too much meat	Give blander foods
Emotional origins	Try to find out what is upsetting your child; Bach remedies may then help

Immunizations An immunization (page 27) may produce inflammation, fever, and phlegm in some children, especially for polio, whooping cough or measles.

Emotions Earache is so disturbing that it may generate panic, which itself causes tension and aggravates the condition. Other emotional factors, especially suppressed anger, begin to feature as causes for otitis media after the age of around seven, when an awareness of individuality arises (page 18).

General care

Earache, particularly at night, can be extremely distressing for both child and parents. Above all, keep calm. Visualize your child as being well and happy, and try to communicate your thoughts. Stay with your child and give reassurance.

There is something particularly distressing about pain in the ear. As a parent, your natural reaction is to try and help – in any way. Most children respond to being given something to take or do, so do

TREATMENT FOR EARACHES AND OTITIS

Whether you choose homoeopathy, Bach remedies or tissue salts, give the remedy every 15 minutes. You should start to see some improvement after 1 hour – if not, change the prescription.

Chronic otitis media is difficult to treat in the home; consult a practitioner.

Herbs

Note: See page 40 for dosages and cautions for herbs.
• For acute attacks – St John's Wort (*Hypericum perfoliatum*), Black root (*Leptandra virginica*) and Hops (*Humulus lupulus*), in combination to lower fever and reduce inflammation. These may not take effect for 4-6 hours, so combine them with external treatments described opposite.
• If there is a purulent discharge – add Echinacea

(*Echinacea purpurea*) to the above prescription.
• If there is panic – add Passion flower (*Passiflora incarnata*) or a few drops of Bach Rescue remedy to the above prescription.
• For the secretory type of chronic otitis media – 2 drops Golden seal (*Hydrastis canadensis*), 6 drops Poke root (*Phytolacca decandra*) and 6 drops Blue flag (*Iris versicolor*), in water 3 times daily. Continue this prescription for 2-4 months, since it can take this long to clear the glands.
• For the purulent type of chronic otitis media – Echinacea to clear the pus. There is usually inflammation as well, so combine with herbs for this (see table on page 119). After about a month of treatment the pus may have subsided, so treat as for the secretory type of otitis media.

Homoeopathy

Note: See page 54 for dosages and cautions for homoeopathic remedies.
• For acute attacks, when the child has a red face, much heat and pain – Belladonna.
• For acute attacks with severe pain, when the child is frantic and wants to be carried, one cheek is red and there may be teething – Chamomilla.
• For acute attacks, with an earache accompanying a sore throat, tenderness behind the ears, and the child is chilly and always feels cold, and he or she wants to be wrapped up and warm – Hepar. sulph.

Tissue salts

Note: See page 64 for information on tissue salts.
• For acute attacks of earache – Ferr. phos.

not hesitate to try a natural remedy. If earache persists for several days, and your child is really distressed, he or she may also have constipation (page 148).

In chronic otitis media, avoid giving mucus-producing foods (page 36).

Orthodox treatment

Orthodox medical treatment of otitis usually involves the use of antibiotic drugs. If the pressure builds up in the middle ear, the surgeon may pierce a small hole in the eardrum. This allows the fluid and pus to drain out of the ear. It is preferable to letting pressure rupture the eardrum, because the drum can naturally repair a small, neat, surgically-made hole, but has more difficulty in mending a large tear from a rupture. If there are frequent discharges or a continuous discharge from the ear, it is common to insert a small tube or washer called a "grommet" or "shunt" into the eardrum, to maintain a permanent hole through which fluid can drain out of the ear.

- If there is thick phlegm – add Kali mur.
- If there is watery phlegm – add Nat. mur.
- If there is a thin discharge from the ear – add Calc. phos.
- If there is a thick discharge – add Kali sulph.

Bach remedies

Note: See page 66 for information on Bach remedies.
- For acute attacks – Rescue remedy, either as the stock or in cream, applied to the painful parts just below the ears. This often stops panic and reduces inflammation.

Massage

Note: See page 72 for information on massages.
- For an acute attack – Sanjiao channel. Hold the child's hand in your left hand

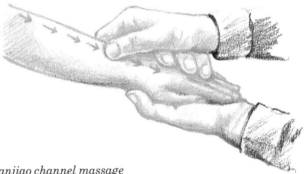

Sanjiao channel massage

(if you are right-handed) and gently massage down the outside of the forearm, from the elbow to the back of the hand, along a line midway between the two long bones (see illustration). 30-50 times, repeat on other side.
- Also Spinal stroke.

External herbal remedies

- For acute attacks –
Plantain (*Plantago major*), 5 drops of tincture dropped into the affected ear every 2-4 hours until relief is obtained. If oil of St John's Wort (*Hypericum perfoliatum*) is available, add the tincture to one-quarter of a teaspoon (1ml) of this oil. Plantago is specific for ear problems, taking away the inflammation and pain.
- Witch hazel (*Hamamelis virginiana*) is almost as effective; use as for Plantain.

121

The Childhood Diseases

The disorders described in the following section are common in childhood, and rare thereafter. Once a child has suffered them, it is almost unknown for them to recur in later life. For example, if your child catches measles, it is extremely unlikely that he or she will ever catch it again in the future.

In orthodox medicine, each of the diseases is considered to be due to invasion of the body by bacteria or viruses ("germs"). The body reacts by producing antibodies that destroy or neutralize the invaders, and the child becomes immune to the disease in the future.

In natural medicine, each of the "childhood diseases" is viewed as marking a transition in a child's life. It is a step in the process of growing up. As a child takes this step on the spiritual, emotional and

Spend time with your ill child doing undemanding tasks, such as quiet reading, and avoid too much stimulation.

mental levels, there is a corresponding reaction in the physical body which usually involves the "throwing out" of accumulated poisons and the appearance of a skin rash. The process is described in detail for measles (page 126), where the transition is most marked and has a deep effect on the child's spirit. The other childhood diseases involve the same sort of process, but it is usually milder and less far-reaching. Modern immunizations interfere with this situation (page 27).

Natural medicines are effective in treating these ailments because they work on levels other than the physical. They reach out to the emotional, mental and spiritual spheres, and can be of great assistance in helping your child through these life transitions. On the practical level, this means natural remedies can effectively reduce the severity of illness and speed healing.

Infection and incubation time

The childhood diseases are infectious, in the sense that they are transmitted from child to child. There is a period between contact with an infected person, when the illness is "caught", and the appearence of the actual symptoms. This time is termed the incubation time. It is characteristic for each disease, usually being between one and four weeks.

This can be a worrying time for parents and children, especially if they are afraid of the suspected disease. It is hoped that the following pages will give confidence. With correct treatment by natural medicines, there should be little to fear.

If your child has not been immunized against a certain disease, and he or she comes into contact with a child who has it, then it is usually too late for conventional immunization to give protection. In fact, immunization during this time can increase the disease's severity. The opposite applies to natural medicines. The incubation period, between catching the disease and the appearance of symptoms, is the best time to give remedies, and thereby reduce the severity of the attack.

Complications

Any infectious disease brings with it the risk of complications. For otherwise strong and healthy children, the danger of serious complication is extremely small. However, it is always wise to be very cautious. Contact a medical practitioner if you feel that the illness does not seem to be running its expected course, or if your child takes a turn for the worse. Be alert for warning signs such as delirium, a high fever and perhaps a febrile fit (page 90), or chest pains and breathing difficulties.

Some of the more common complications of the childhood diseases, and ways to avoid them, are described for Measles (pages 124-125). The preventative measures also apply to the other infections.

Meningitis is a much-feared complication, although it is far less common today than in previous decades. It involves inflammation and swelling of the meninges, the thin layers of tissue around the brain, which puts pressure on the brain itself. Warning features are nausea and vomiting, drowsiness, confusion, aches in the head or neck, a stiff neck, fear or pain when in bright light, and possibly a deep red rash on the body. Contact a medical practitioner urgently if you suspect meningitis.

General care

Children who are about to come down with an infectious illness are often vague, off-color and listless, and perhaps more sensitive and irritable. Be on guard for such early-warning signs. If you are aware that an infection is prevalent in the local community, often at a nursery group or school, then you can give natural remedies to lessen the severity of the symptoms, should they develop.

In this respect, homoeopathy is especially useful in the home. Each infection has its specific remedy, such as Morbillinium for measles, Phytolacca for mumps, and Pertussin for whooping cough. These remedies are usually at 30X potency.

MEASLES

Measles is a childhood illness caused by a virus infection (page 122). It can occur at any age, but is most common between one and three years. One attack of measles usually gives immunity for life, but a few children get measles twice, and in rare cases three times.

The virus can be passed by physical contact, or spread through the air by coughing or sneezing. There follows an incubation period (page 123) of one to two weeks before your child begins to show signs of illness.

In developed countries, measles has lost most of its severity. In less developed regions, it can be a serious illness, sometimes with dangerous complications. In Chinese medicine, measles is viewed as being different from most other childhood diseases, in that it is beneficial to the child. This philosophy is discussed further on page 126 and page 27.

Symptoms

First stage The first signs of measles are usually those of a cold, with watery eyes, runny nose, sneezing and coughing. The child is usually irritable and miserable. Typically, the temperature rises over a day or two, before the skin rash appears. The presence at this stage of small white, raised spots inside the mouth (Koplik's spots), if noticed in time, confirms the diagnosis of measles.

Second (rash) stage The rash usually develops on the fourth day after symptoms begin. It often appears first behind the ears and then spreads in one or two days to cover the whole body. In mild cases it takes the form of a few red dots here and there; in severe cases the red dots multiply and join, so that there are whole areas

DANGER SIGNS

Obtain medical help at once if your child has measles and then develops more serious symptoms, such as:
- chest pain, with shallow breathing or wheezing as in asthma,
- delirium, loss of consciousness or coma, or
- an extremely high temperature, perhaps with febrile fits (page 90).

of livid red with a few "islands" of yellow-green skin between. The child is usually very irritable and distressed. The eyes are often swollen and red, and he or she may be sensitive to bright light.

A day or two after the full rash develops the child may become listless, with dulled consciousness, as though drugged. There may be a cough with yellow phlegm, and a red tongue with yellow coating. As the rash spreads, the fever rises – to 40°C, 104°F or more. This stage of the illness usually lasts from three days up to about one week.

Third (recovery) stage Gradually the child's temperature comes down and the rash changes colour from livid red to duller purple-red. Over the next week the rash fades. During this time, the child often seems confused and distant.

Complications – and avoiding them

Poisons in the system A 16th-century Chinese text says of measles: "The poison must come out." The more heat-poison that has accumulated in a child's body, the more severe measles is likely to be, and the higher the risk of complications. Sour of heat-poison include oranges, red meat, and artificial colorings and flavorings, these should be avoided as far as possible for young children.

Phlegm reduction The phlegm that accumulates in the lungs during measles is an ideal breeding ground for bacteria. As a result, the most common complication is bronchopneumonia, where a secondary infection invades the bronchi (main airways in the lungs). The bronchi become inflamed and the child has severe pain in the chest, often accompanied by shallow breathing or even asthma. This is a serious condition and you should seek immediate medical help. Measures to strengthen your child's energy (page 14) and avoid the build-up of phlegm, or mucus, help to prevent this complication.

Brain activity Another possible complication is encephalitis (inflammation of brain tissue). The child may become delirious or even lapse into a coma. This serious and possibly fatal condition is much less common than it was many years ago, but if it occurs, obtain help at once. A child who is already "hot-headed" is more likely to develop this complication (although the risk is still very small). This is one reason why it is important to try and raise your child in a calm and peaceful atmosphere, encouraging his or her imagination by reading, painting, outside play, and even simple daydreaming.

Diarrhea It may happen that the poison which appears on the skin, as a measles rash, afterwards affects the intestines and causes diarrhea (page 151). This can be serious in babies, and requires treatment. Take your baby to a practitioner of natural medicine or to an orthodox physician.

"Echo" symptoms

If the attack has been very severe, your child may be left with an "echo" of measles (page 25). There are three common symptoms. One is night terrors: instead of being calmer and more peaceful after the illness, he or she is tearful and timid, sleeps badly and wakes in fear. A second echo symptom involves the skin: a mild form of eczema (page 174) may persist, which worsens when the child is tired. Thirdly, there may be impaired vision: the poison which affects the brain also influences the optic nerve from the eye. In severe cases the whole eye and its function become impaired. If your child shows these echo symptoms, consult a practitioner of natural medicine or go to an orthodox physician for an eye check.

General care and recovery

As soon as measles is confirmed, put your child to bed in a darkened room. There may be no sign of the eyes being affected, as yet, but this measure helps to prevent eye damage. Spend time with your child, giving comfort and encouraging him or her to remain calm. Read stories to your child rather than allowing television, since the latter can put a strain on both eyes and brain.

As your child's temperature starts to fall, his or her appetite should gradually return. Provide simple foods at first, in small quantities. Cereal, porridge or baby food is recommended initially. As he or she eats more and the digestion strengthens, a more varied diet can be given.

Measles is an important transition in your child's life and should be allowed to run its course. Do not send your child back to school too soon – keep him or her

125

resting at home for two to three weeks. Above all, fresh air and an optimistic attitude during the recuperation stage will make a huge impact on your child's life and considerably reduce the chances of complications.

The perspective of Chinese medicine

In Eastern medical philosophy, poisons are believed to accumulate in the baby's body during life in the womb. After birth, the body at some time attempts to rid itself of the poisons. This leads to the many childhood diseases with eruptive rashes, and in particular, measles.

Since the 16th century, it has been realized in Eastern medicine that measles is connected with infection. However the basic function of the disease is the same: the infection is regarded as the necessary agent for poisons to "come out". So, although the dangers of measles are clear, the illness is seen as a step towards overall health.

Measles as a transition The impact of measles can be best understood by observing changes in your child's behavior, attention and attitude before and after the illness. Often, he or she is restless and irritable for some weeks or months before developing measles – as though a storm is brewing. The family and other people around the child often greet the appearance of measles with relief, because at last the cause of the problem is evident.

As the rash develops, and the disease goes into its second stage, the child becomes more confused and irrational. This is the most dangerous phase, and it represents the transition point.

At this time, the body turns the corner as the poison leaves and the immune

IMMUNIZATION AGAINST MEASLES

Those who support immunization against measles point to the infection's discomforts and the risk of dangerous complications such as encephalitis, and even death. Those who argue against immunization point to the loss of this infection's severity in recent years. Today, for the otherwise healthy child, measles is no longer the dangerous disease it was in previous times. Also, there are dangers from immunization itself – including the faint but possible risk of brain damage or death. Each side can produce statistics to support their argument.

As discussed above, it is believed in Chinese medicine that measles represents the expulsion from the body of poisons accumulated during pregnancy. If these poisons cannot be released, because of immunization against measles, they may affect the child's behaviour – tending to make him or her more selfish, irritable, greedy, restless and impatient. Moreover, the poison stays as "latent heat" and may predispose the child to other disorders later in life (page 26). Having measles provides the body with the natural and necessary opportunity to rid itself of these poisons.

system gains the upper hand against the invaders. Then, as the crisis passes and the fever subsides, the child's awareness returns – but with a different outlook. The negative and irritable behavior has gone, and he or she is emotionally delicate and open to new influences. The child sees ordinary and familiar things in life for the first time, but through new eyes, as though he or she has had a form of spiritual experience. On the physical level, the poisons accumulated during life in the womb have been expelled. At the higher emotional and mental levels, negative forces such as greed and selfishness have also been expelled. So a child who has measles is afterwards less self-centered and more open-hearted, and often more able to express his or her individuality. The personality becomes rounder and fuller, and more joyful and contented, as a step towards maturity and adulthood.

TREATMENT FOR MEASLES

In the first stage, the aims are to stimulate the immune system so that it can deal with the measles virus quickly, and to bring the rash to the surface. In the second stage, remedies assist in bringing down the fever and clearing the rash. The aim in the third stage is to build up the body's resistance and strength.

Herbs

Note: See page 40 for dosages and cautions for herbs.
• First stage – Yarrow (*Achillea millefolium*) as a tea, 1 teaspoon of dried herb infused (not boiled) in a cup of water, sweetened with honey. Add 1 drop of tincture of Pasque flower (*Anemone pulsatilla*) to the tea to help bring out the rash. Poke root (*Phytolacca decandra*) is an alternative to Pasque flower, as 5 drops of tincture in each cup of Yarrow tea.
• Second stage – Echinacea (*Echinacea purpurea*), 1 100mgs tablet (or 1ml of tincture) 3 times daily, to help clear the rash. Also Catmint (*Nepeta cataria*), infuse 1 teaspoon of dried herb in a cup

and give 3 cups daily, to help bring down the fever. Keep giving both these herbs, even though they may not have a dramatic effect, until the rash disappears completely.
• If there is a cough – add Lobelia (*Lobelia inflata*), 5 drops of tincture, to the Catmint tea.
• When the rash starts to fade and the temperature begins to fall – return to giving the child Yarrow tea in addition to Echinacea and Catmint.
• After the rash has disappeared – Barberry (*Berberis vulgaris*), 5 drops of tincture, together with Gentian (*Gentiana lutea*), 5 drops of tincture, in water, to restore appetite and strengthen the body.

Homoeopathy

Note: See page 54 for dosages and cautions for homoeopathic remedies.
• After exposure to another measles sufferer but before symptoms appear – Morbillinum 30X daily for 3 days, to reduce the severity of the possible attack.

• First stage – the remedies for fevers (page 84) are appropriate, such as Aconite, Belladonna and Gelsemium.
• First stage, if there are eye symptoms – Euphrasia.
• Second stage, when there is a hard dry painful cough, great thirst and a high temperature – Bryonia.
• Second stage, for a child who is too weak to throw out the poisons – Zincum metallicum.
• Second stage, if the child has high fever, red face and possibly delirium or fits – Stramonium.
• Second stage, if the face is puffy and the child is in a stupor and makes piercing screams, because the rash has "gone in" rather than coming out – Apis mel.
• Second stage, when the child is weepy, with sensitive eyes, diarrhea and a cough with yellowish phlegm – Pulsatilla.
• Third stage, if there are helps, as for fevers.
• Third stage – Sulfur often residual chest symptoms and signs of heat – Phosphorus.

127

MUMPS

Mumps (parotitis) is a virus infection of the parotid glands. These are two of the six salivary glands, and are just below and in front of the ears. The infection is commonest between the ages of three and ten years, and the virus is spread by others who have mumps. The course of the infection may be aggravated by accumulation of "latent heat" (page 26) and phlegm (mucus), by diet, particularly red meats and dairy products; and by emotional factors such as a rigid outlook, stubbornness and suppressed anger.

Symptoms and general care

Mumps has an incubation period (page 123) of 12-24 days. Typically, your child will have mild discomfort in one parotid gland and be somewhat irritable. The gland swells over the next day or two, the jaw becomes stiff, and it is difficult to open the mouth, but the associated pain is usually relatively mild. In severe cases the gland can become very inflamed and painful, causing a general fever. After about a week the swelling subsides. It may then develop in the gland on the other side, and the pattern is repeated.

Your child is infectious to others from just before the swelling first appears until the last swelling subsides. Keep him or her at home during this time. A child usually builds up immunity after the infection (page 122).

During the illness, keep your child warm and quiet. He or she need not be confined to bed, but activities should be undemanding. Provide a light diet, avoiding dairy products, eggs, sugar and red meat. Fruit juice drinks, such as apple juice with cloves, or lemon with honey, help to relieve any throat pain.

In mild cases it is hardly worth giving remedies, since the swelling and discomfort are small. In severe cases, however, remedies are certainly worthwhile. If there is fever, treat this as appropriate (pages 84-89).

Complications The main complication of mumps is orchitis, painful inflammation of the testicles in boys. It is rare, and tends to occur after puberty. Children should be exposed to mumps after the age of three, in order to catch the infection and acquire immunity, thereby avoiding a more serious attack after puberty.

TREATMENT FOR MUMPS

Herbs

Note: See page 40 for dosages and cautions for herbs.
• During the infection – Poke root (*Phytolacca decandra*), either one-quarter of a teaspoon (1ml) of tincture 3 times daily in warm water, or a 100mgs tablet 3 times daily.
• During an epidemic, and if the child has not had mumps –

Poke root to reduce the severity of a possible attack. Give for 2 weeks dosage as above. An alternative is Red clover (*Trifolium pratense*).
• For constipation – add Black root (*Leptandra virginica*) to Poke root.
• For fever and constipation – add Senna (*Cassia acutifolia*) to Poke root.
• For orchitis – Poke root.

Homoeopathy

Note: See page 54 for dosages and cautions for homoeopathic remedies.
• During an epidemic, and if the child has not had mumps – 1 dose of Phytolacca 30X or Parotidium 200 to reduce the severity of an attack.
• If there is heavy sweating without relief, offensive

RUBELLA (GERMAN MEASLES)

Rubella is a mild infection caused by a virus. It is so mild that in some children it comes and passes unnoticed. It is highly infectious and has an incubation period (page 123) of two to three weeks.

It is very important to keep any child with suspected rubella away from expectant mothers, especially those in the first four months of pregnancy. If a pregnant mother catches rubella during this time, there is a high risk that her child will be born with a handicap such as brain or eye damage. For this reason, immunization against rubella is routine in many countries during childhood, and this is fully recommended for girls (page 28).

Symptoms

The infection usually starts with a mild rash on the chest, which may look like a few spots of chickenpox or simply a skin irritation. Soon after, the glands in the neck swell, especially those at the back of the neck. There is phlegm (mucus or catarrh) in the nose and chest, sometimes with a loose cough, and a slightly raised temperature (above 37°C, 99°F). Aches and pains in the joints may occur.

In severe cases, which are rare, the temperature may reach 38.5°C, 101°F, and there is perspiration and the child feels uncomfortable.

The rash and fever persist for a few days, during which time the child is infectious to others. The symptoms then gradually subside.

General care

Keep your child at home while there is a rash, and for three days afterwards. If the fever is high, he or she should rest, preferably in bed, and remain quiet for the next week or two.

Avoid mucus-producing foods (page 36), spicy dishes and red meat at this time.

Treatment for rubella

Rubella is usually such a mild illness that only rarely does it warrant treatment. If the body temperature is high and there is much phlegm, treat your child as necessary (pages 84-89). However, be alert for complications (page 123) and seek urgent help should these occur.

breath and a thickly coated tongue – Merc. sol.
• If the swellings feel stony-hard, the child cannot swallow anything hot, and pain shoots into the ears on swallowing – Phytolacca.
• If the swellings are soft but painless, yet there is stinging throat pain – Apis mel.
• If the left gland is highly inflamed – Rhus tox.

• For a high fever with red face, when the right gland is more swollen, the throat is bright red, and the child is sensitive to cold and has shooting pains – Belladonna.
• If there is continuous phlegm, and the other salivary glands below the lower jaw swell – Baryta carb.
• If the fever lingers, and to prevent orchitis – Pulsatilla.

External remedies

If the salivary gland is very swollen but not red and inflamed, apply finely-chopped fresh Ginger root (*Zingiber officinale*) for 20 minutes at a time, as a poultice on the skin. Stop the applications if the skin becomes red.

129

CHICKENPOX

Chickenpox is a viral infection spread by contact with infected people, with an incubation period (page 123) of 10-14 days. (The same virus may cause shingles in later life.) It is a mild disease, but in children the rash and spots can cause irritation out of all proportion to their severity. Chickenpox is similar to measles (page 124), although it is a less severe illness, in that it is a way for the body to expel accumulated poisons.

Symptoms and general care

For a day or two your child is irritable and "clingy", and may have the cold-like symptoms of sneezing and a runny nose. The first spots can appear anywhere, on the arms or face, but the chest is especially common. The spots are soft red mounds about three millimeters across with watery blisters in the center, and usually they itch. Often there are just a few spots for the first day or two, then more appear. In severe cases the whole body is covered with raised red mounds, which are hot and itchy. At this stage the child is feverish and distressed, and wants to scratch. If the spots are scratched, they ooze watery fluid – but they go on itching. This stage may last over a week, possibly accompanied by a cough.

Gradually the symptoms subside. Normally there are no side-effects or complications, unless the spots are badly scratched and become infected, when the "pock mark" scars may persist for many years. After the attack, your child should have lifelong immunity.

The severity of chickenpox can be reduced by ensuring that poisons do not build up in the body. Follow the general principles given for measles (pages 124-126). During the feverish stage, keep your child quiet, preferably in bed. Cotton gloves tied on the hands will help to prevent a baby or young child scratching the skin, since this may leave permanent scars. Cotton garments worn next to the skin are most comfortable.

TREATMENT FOR CHICKENPOX

Homoeopathy

Note: See page 54 for dosages and cautions for homoeopathic remedies. This is the treatment of choice.
- During an epidemic, before the illness develops, 1 dose of Variolinum 30X to relieve symptoms should they occur.
- Alternatively, give Rhus tox. 3-5 times daily for 1-2 days after contact with an infected child.
- During the early stages, when the child is anxious and feverish but the rash has not appeared – Aconite.
- If the child has a high fever, red face and very hot skin – Belladonna.
- Give Rhus tox. as soon as the first spots appear and continue until all spots go.
- If there is phlegm, alternate Rhus tox. with Sulfur.

External remedies

Note: See page 40 for dosages and cautions for herbs.
- A bath containing tea made from Burdock (*Arctium lappa*) and Peppermint (*Mentha piperita*) soothes irritation.

Bach remedies

Note: See page 66 for information on Bach remedies.
    Bach remedies may help to relieve the rash irritation. Chicory, Hornbeam or Cherry Plum is often indicated.

130

WHOOPING COUGH (PERTUSSIS)

Whooping cough is due to infection by bacteria, and the illness has an incubation period (page 123) of 7-10 days. It tends to occur in epidemics during childhood, and is a serious illness, particularly for babies under one year. Infection is passed from one child to another by droplets from coughing or sneezing.

Internal factors

Weak lung energy If a child's lung energy is weak, then any infectious cough is likely to become more severe; this is true of whooping cough. There are two main causes of weak lung energy. One is an inherited tendency. For example, there may be asthma or tuberculosis in the family. The second is a history of repeated coughs, which may have lowered the energy of the lungs, or left the child with lung problems of the "echo" pattern of illness (page 25)

Liver congestion Whooping cough rarely progresses to the second whooping stage (see below) unless "liver congestion" (page 23) is present. This leads to the build-up of the characteristic slimy mucus or phlegm and gives rise to vomiting. Liver congestion is a particular problem for babies under a year old.

Symptoms

First stage: onset At its onset, whooping cough is indistinguishable from an ordinary cough. There is nasal mucus (phlegm or catarrh) and the cough is worse at night. There may be a slight fever and the child has watery eyes.

These symptoms last for up to two weeks. After this time, a child who is otherwise healthy and strong may get better; however, if there are underlying problems such as liver congestion, the disease may progress to the second stage.

Second stage: whooping After about two weeks, the cough increases in intensity and becomes more spasmodic. Eventually there are bouts of uncontrollable coughing, which alarm both child and parent. Your child may try to sit up and hold onto something for support when coughing severely.

Typically, in each coughing bout there is a first breath which sounds like a long whistle, followed by a series of short, suffocating, spasmodic coughs, finishing with the "whoop" as the child draws breath again. The face turns a deep red or purple color during this time, the veins stand out in the neck and the eyes bulge. One bout may follow another, with no time to recover breath in between. Sometimes there is a small amount of bleeding from the nose or mouth.

After several coughing bouts the child may bring up thick, slimy mucus, followed by an attack of vomiting. He or she is exhausted after each bout, but usually recovers quickly and is relatively happy and cheerful between attacks.

The sight of a child going through whooping cough is truly alarming, and places a great strain on parents and those around. It seems as though he or she will suffocate or burst a blood vessel when coughing. In spite of appearances, this very rarely happens. The second stage may last as long as two to three months, slowly fading with time.

Third stage: recovery As the child recovers, the cough gradually becomes less severe; the whooping, spasmodic nature subsides; and it is usually looser and productive

131

(page 96). Nevertheless the child often remains weak due to the prolonged strain of coughing and vomiting.

This stage may last another one to three months, but in some children the cough never completely clears, and returns periodically over many years as an "echo" form of the disease.

If your child is slow to recover, take him or her to a practitioner of natural medicine. A recurrent hard cough that has been left behind and recurs as an "echo" disease can usually be treated effectively, even after several years.

Severity and complications

Babies under one year are affected particularly badly by whooping cough, because the respiratory system is still maturing, and they are at greatest risk from complications. As the child gets older, he or she becomes stronger, and attacks are generally less serious and less severe.

Complications are not common, but are serious when they occur. They include bronchopneumonia, lung collapse and fits (page 90). Babies risk a hernia, from the strain of coughing. If complications occur, urgent professional action is required. Natural medicine is very effective in many cases, but if a practitioner is not available, then take your baby or child immediately to an orthodox medical practitioner or to hospital.

General care and diet

Reassure your child by remaining calm and confident, and explaining what is happening. Even very small children can be helped in this way. Although they may not understand what you say, they will be comforted by your confidence.

Consider letting the child sleep in your bedroom. An unwell child usually feels reassured if he or she is in the same room as the parents, and will not be so frightened upon waking in the night, with coughing and nausea or vomiting. If this is not possible, leave the doors open between your rooms, and consider using a nightlight (even if your child does not normally have one). Also, place towels and a basin near the bed, in case they are needed urgently at night.

Babies should be laid to sleep in the semi-prone position, chest down and with head to one side, to avoid the danger of choking on vomit in the night.

Thyme baths (page 134) are very helpful for babies and children with whooping cough. The vapours and fragrance help to ease the throat and lungs, so producing a calming effect.

Avoid over-exciting your child, and try to make sure that any sleep lost at night is made up during the day.

A baby or child with whooping cough should be kept away from other children for six weeks after its onset, to reduce the risk of spreading infection to others.

Try to follow these dietary guidelines:
- Avoid mucus-producing foods (page 36).
- Give warm vegetable soup daily, to provide extra vitamins and to help the body's natural protection. Raw and cold foods should be avoided.
- Attacks of coughing commonly occur at night. The main meals should be breakfast and lunch, with little to eat in the afternoon and evening. This allows the stomach to empty by evening and therefore reduces the chances of vomiting after coughing at night.
- If your child becomes hungry in the afternoon, limit food to dry crackers and water. Avoid citrus juices such as orange and grapefruit juice, since the "sharp" taste and acidic nature of these fruits may well aggravate vomiting. Give diluted apple juice or honey instead.

Prevention

There are three approaches to prevention. One is immunization (discussed on page 28). A second is to avoid contact with children who have the disease. The bacteria are transmitted in saliva, either by direct contact between children or when sneezing or coughing. By avoiding contact with infected children, your child can be protected – at least, in principle. In particular, babies under one year who have not been immunized should be kept away from infected children.

The third approach is to strengthen the child, so that any attack of whooping cough is mild. The infection progresses to the second (whooping) stage only in babies and children who are weak, or who already have some build-up of phlegm in the system due to liver congestion. So, to prevent a bad attack, the body should be strengthened, the digestion regulated, and phlegm cleared. This can be done in a number of ways, as described in the first part of the book. In particular, ensure your child gets fresh air and exercise.

TREATMENT FOR WHOOPING COUGH

Herbs

Note: See page 40 for dosages and cautions for herbs.
- To prevent the infection by strengthening the body and clearing phlegm – a combination of Coltsfoot (*Tussilago farfara*), Elecampane (*Inula helenium*) and Golden seal (*Hydrastis canadensis*). Some phlegm may be expelled at first, with a productive cough and loose stools, but this should fade after a few days. If there are signs of liver congestion, add Black root (*Leptandra virginica*). For further advice, consult a herbal practitioner.
- First stage – treat as for a cough (page 98), with the addition of Sundew (*Drosera rotundifolia*), which is specific for whooping cough, to the prescription.
- Second stage – a combination of Hyssop (*Hyssopus officinale*), Coltsfoot, Lobelia (*Lobelia inflata*), Black cohosh (*Cimicifuga racemosa*) and Wild cherry (*Prunus serotina*). This helps to allay the spasmodic cough. Give 15-30 drops of the mixture in warm water, 3-5 times daily. Of the

Continued on next page

133

five herbs, Wild cherry has the most pleasant flavour, and if your child is averse to herbs, a syrup of Wild cherry on its own will suffice.

- If there is vomiting – add 5 drops of Black root to each dosage of the above combination.
- If your child appears anxious – give a tea made from Lemon balm (*Melissa officinalis*).

Homoeopathy

Note: See page 54 for dosages and cautions for homoeopathic remedies.

- To strengthen the body and clear phlegm, in order to prevent a bad attack – Pertussin 30X, one dose in spring and one in autumn. Consult a practitioner before giving this remedy, as reactions can be severe.
- First stage – Aconite or Belladonna, as for a cough.
- Second stage, when the cough is provoked by a tickle in the throat or lying down, and the child has contracting pains below the ribs when coughing – Drosera.
- Second stage, when the child tries to eat but then coughs and vomits after the first mouthfuls, and the cough is dry and painful – Bryonia.
- Second stage, when the child cries before the cough in anticipation of pain, there is coughed-up blood, nosebleed and bloodshot eyes – Arnica.
- Second stage, if the child gasps with repeated crowing

whoops, there is spasmodic vomiting, the face and lips turn blue, there are cramps in the fingers and toes, the fingers are clenched during coughs, and the child feels better after drinking water but worse in the middle of the night – Cuprum metallicum.

- Third stage, when the child has a "rattling" cough but is too weak to expel the phlegm, and coughs and gasps as though choking and suffocating – Ant. tart.
- Third stage, when the cough is dry, harsh and persistent – Sanguinaria.
- Third stage, when the chest seems full of phlegm but this is not brought up despite the coughing, and there is also persistent nausea – Ipecacuanha.
- Third stage – one dose of Pertussin 30X may be given to eliminate the "echo" effect.

Bach remedies

Note: See page 66 for information on Bach remedies.

- At night, leave a glass of water with a few drops of Rescue remedy next to the child's bed. A few sips will help overcome the panic so often experienced by a child with whooping cough.
- Other remedies may be added according to the disposition of the child. Consider the following: Cherry plum (especially useful when there is a lot of

spasmodic coughing), Hornbeam or Mimulus. In the later stages, Gorse and Olive are often needed.

Massage, baths and external remedies

Note: See page 72 for information on massages.

- Second stage – Thyme baths are a considerable help in reducing the severity of the cough. Make an infusion of 2-3 5mls teaspoons of Thyme in boiling water. Leave standing for 5 minutes, then strain into the bath water. The child has a bath in the normal way. Children usually enjoy this and find the bath very soothing.
- After the bath, massage Comfrey ointment or oil into the chest and back. This helps to relax and expand the lungs.
- Apply a Garlic poultice to the feet (page 101). Garlic oil, when absorbed into the blood, aids the expulsion of thick phlegm. Do not leave the garlic on too long, as it may cause blistering.

Other therapies

Acupuncture is especially helpful in treating whooping cough. The spasmodic cough usually subsides a day or two after treatment and begins to loosen, then clears over a week. Treatment should be given 2-3 times weekly to ensure a speedy recovery.

Digestion and Energy

The body's digestive system is intimately involved with the the production and distribution of energy (page 14). Its function is to convert food into energy which can be used by the body. In babies and children this is particularly important, because large amounts of energy are needed for growth and development. In infancy, especially, the digestive system is working close to maximum capacity.

The relationship between food and energy production is the main reason why natural medicines are so effective in the treatment of digestive and associated disorders. For, although food provides energy, it also requires some energy to be digested. If the energy is not flowing well in the digestive system, problems may occur. Natural medicines can reverse this process and restore the natural flow of energy, thus returning the child to good health. This can be seen in the range of treatments advised in this section, from gentle massage that helps to wind or burp a baby after feeding, to the stronger remedies for sudden digestive upsets in older children.

Energy imbalances and blocks also often underly behavioural problems such as sleeplessness or tantrums. Information on these problems is also included in the following pages.

Food as a "lever"

Most parents instinctively understand the importance of a good diet, and they go to great lengths to ensure their children eat healthily. However, some children use food and mealtimes as a "lever" to get their own way. The following pages, and the first part of the book, discuss some of these aspects. They should help you, as a parent, to keep alert for adverse reactions

Mealtimes should be funtimes. However, some children turn them into a battle of willpower against parents.

or allergies in your child, and to know when to remain firm and when to yield over the often vexed question of diet.

As a general principle, we have found that many children know what kinds of food are good for them – but they do not know what is bad for them. So if your child repeatedly refuses a certain food, it may mean that the food simply does not agree with his or her digestion. On the other hand, children usually need to be restrained in their exuberant demands for sweet and sugary foods, "junk foods", carbonated drinks, and brightly-coloured items loaded with artificial preservatives, colourings, and flavourings.

BREASTFEEDING PROBLEMS

Most babies benefit from taking only breast milk for at least the first four to six months after birth. If possible, breastfeeding should continue until the child is a year old, gradually supplementing the milk with solid foods after about four to six months. However, many mothers experience difficulty in carrying out such a plan, even though they wish to. The following simple remedies should help to overcome common problems.

Milk production In Chinese medicine, it is said that a mother's milk is produced from her blood; it takes one drop of blood to provide one drop of milk. This is not meant literally, but to give some idea of the amount of energy needed to feed a hungry baby. It also provides an insight into the factors which can reduce the milk supply. Anything which leads to anaemia – weak digestion, inadequate food, lack of sleep, exhaustion, worry and strain – is likely to reduce the supply of milk. Similarly, anything which affects the mother's flow of energy, involving foods, moods or activities, is passed directly to the baby. If she drinks coffee or alcohol, some of this is passed to her baby. Similarly, indigestion or worry is also transferred.

Insufficient milk First, make sure your own diet is healthy and adequate. Foods that significantly affect milk production are shown on the right. Second, ensure that you get enough rest. It takes energy to make milk, and you must conserve this whenever possible.

Insufficient milk at two months The supply of milk commonly decreases temporarily at about two months after birth. It is important at this stage to keep putting your baby to the breast, because the activity of

---

FOODS TO INCREASE MILK PRODUCTION

Brewer's yeast, up to three 10mls spoonfuls (dessertspoons) daily, may be added to breakfast cereal

Dill seeds, as a tea sweetened with honey

Fennel seeds, as a tea or in stews

Lettuce (but do not eat lettuce if your baby's digestion is "cold", page 32)

Fenugreek, in salads or stews

Turnip (although eating turnips can give your baby "wind" or "gas")

Peanuts, Watercress, Raspberries

Goat's rue (*Galega officinalis*)

Alfalfa, Nettles

Mistletoe (*Viscum album*)

Milk thistle (*Silybum marianum*)

FOODS TO DECREASE MILK PRODUCTION

Dried figs, Lentils

Basil (*Ocimum basilicum*)

Mint (*Mentha piperita*)

Cranesbill (*Geranium maculatum*)

Sage (*Salvia officinalis*), which has an especially strong effect in reducing milk

---

sucking stimulates the flow of milk. Do not worry that your baby is getting insufficient food. A healthy baby has considerable reserves and will not be harmed by a few days on a reduced diet. You have to work through the problem together – and it will really be worth it. Make sure you get enough rest during this time. For example, rest while your baby is sleeping, in order to build up your energy.

It may help, at this stage, to talk to mothers with slightly older babies. They will usually offer advice and encourage you to continue breastfeeding.

Massage can increase the circulation of energy to the breasts and aid milk production. The main massage point is at the corner of the nail of the little finger on either hand. Stimulate this yourself by gentle biting, or allow your baby to do this by nibbling at your little finger.

Homoeopathy can also help during this difficult phase. Remedies include Calc. carb., especially for a mother who feels tired and has a tendency to put on weight and become flabby; and Aguus castus, for a mother who feels apprehensive and timid, and lacks confidence.

Milk gives the baby indigestion Many foods that you eat are passed on almost directly to your baby. So a food which is difficult to digest or causes "wind", or "gas", in adults, is likely to do the same for a baby. In particular, watch out for turnips, lettuce, and beans. If you eat baked or undercooked beans, they may give your baby flatulence. So try soaking beans overnight and throwing away the water they have soaked in before cooking; also, cook the beans thoroughly and include some cloves in the food, which helps to reduce flatulence.

If you suffer from indigestion yourself, consult a practitioner, since the complaint is likely to be passed to your baby. Give yourself plenty of time for feeding, and try to remain as calm as possible.

Homoeopathy can help this problem, but the prescriptions are complicated, so consult a practitioner.

Sore nipples and milk congestion

Make a herbal remedy from 50 grams of Squaw vine (*Mitchella repens*) simmered in half a litre of water. Strain off the fluid and add it to an equal volume of cream. Boil the mixture to reduce it to a pasty consistency, and apply it to the nipples after each nursing. Hypercal ointment, available from some natural medicine suppliers, is another soothing application for sore or tender nipples.

Some mothers find that homoeopathy is useful for easing soreness. Remedies include Chamomilla, especially when the nipples are inflamed as well as tender, and the mother feels irritable from the pain; Lycopodium, when the nipples crack and bleed; Phytolacca, when the nipples are cracked and painful and the pain seems to shoot down the spine; and Silica, when the sore nipples give a constant burning pain.

"Milk fever" is the name given to inflammation of the breasts, which may become so strong that it affects the whole body and makes the mother feverish. It is due to milk becoming congested and infected in the breasts. Orthodox medical treatment is to give antibiotics and to apply hot compresses. Often, mothers are advised to stop breastfeeding for a time. However with natural medicines it is not usually necessary to stop breastfeeding.

Homoeopathy is the treatment of choice. The following remedies are often found to help: Belladonna, especially when there is excessive milk production and the mother's fever is high; Bryony, when the breasts are hot, hard and painful, the energy seems to be stagnating there, and the mother is angry; and Phosphorus, when the mother is extremely tired, pale and apprehensive.

137

COLIC

Colic is a form of "indigestion" or "abdominal cramp" that occurs mainly in babies and young children. It not usually serious, and most children eventually grow out of it. However, some simple remedies can relieve the problem.

Symptoms

Typical symptoms of colic include:
- the baby or child cries for up to two hours after feeding,
- he or she writhes in agony, sometimes sweating from the scalp,
- the face is often pale, and blue-grey just between the lips and nose,
- there may be flatulence, and "wind" or "gas" is passed at both ends, and
- gurgling noises from the abdomen.

Causes and factors

Colic is caused by a spasm (uncoordinated contraction) of the muscles in the intestines, due to difficulty in digesting food. There are two common patterns of the problem – "liver congestion" and "cold digestion". Usually the child suffers from a combination of both.

The liver congestion pattern of illness is described on page 23. Some commoner causes are overfeeding, immunization, teething, not burping (winding) the baby after feeding, and in weaned babies, too many different foods, too much coarse food (such as brown bread or raw vegetables), or too much rich food.

"Cold digestion" is an imbalance in the body, similar in nature to that caused by exposure to cold. In Chinese medicine, colic is said to occur because the cold causes muscular contraction, which leads to pain, in the same way that cold weather can bring on muscular cramps. This type of colic is made worse by eating "cold" foods – both physically cold ones, such as milk from the refrigerator, and energetically cold foods (page 34).

The most common causes for this pattern are an anaesthetic given during childbirth, exposure to cold, eating too much cold food, catching a "cold" disease, and immunization. In older children the problem may be brought on by extreme emotions or mental stress.

General care and diet

Several precautions can lessen the chance of colic, or reduce its severity.

Ensure that your baby or child eats fairly slowly and takes enough time over meals. Avoid giving bananas, yogurt, lettuce and other very cold foods. (If you are breastfeeding, do not eat these foods yourself.) Also avoid "windy" or "gassy" foods such as cucumbers, turnips, green peppers, onions, and beans. (Likewise do not eat these types of foods yourself if you are breastfeeding.)

Some children find cow's milk hard to digest, so try giving goat's milk or soya milk for a while to see if there is any improvement. Cow's milk can be made more digestible by simmering it for 15 minutes with half an onion. Persist for several days to allow the cow's milk to work out of the system.

If you are breastfeeding, try not to rush around too much. Give yourself time during the day to relax, especially around feeding times. For a mother with other children, it may help to feed the baby at a different time. If you are weaning your baby, and colic begins with the first solid foods, it may help to include some root Ginger and a pinch of ground Cloves in the food (see Treatment).

TREATMENT FOR COLIC

Herbs

Note: See page 40 for dosages and cautions for herbs.
- For mild, intermittent colic – give a home-prepared "gripe-water" consisting of a tea or syrup made from Dill seeds (*Anethum graveolens*) or Fennel seeds (*Foeniculum vulgaris*) with a little Ginger (*Zingiber officinale*) and Cloves (*Eugenia aromatica*), sweetened with honey. Cloves is especially helpful for reducing flatulence.
- When the colic is more severe – select three herbs from the list below: one to clear liver congestion, one to soothe the stomach and one to act as an antispasmodic. Prepare a mixture of equal parts of the mother tinctures, and give 2-3 drops of tincture, diluted in a cup of water, after each feed.
- Black root (*Leptandra virginica*) – specifically for liver congestion.
- Sweet sedge (*Acorus calamus*) – stimulates the stomach and intestine, helping the baby to pass stools and wind.
- Oregon grape (*Berberis aquifolium*) – a general digestive tonic which helps to relieve liver congestion.
- Barberry (*Berberis vulgaris*) – assists the stomach in the early stages of digestion.

- Gentian (*Gentiana lutea*) – as for Barberry.
- Prickly ash (*Xanthoxylum americanum*) – warming and a tonic to the digestion.
- Blue cohosh (*Caulophyllum thalactroides*) – an antispasmodic, which helps to relieve intestinal cramps.
- Wild yam (*Dioscorea villosa*) – as for Blue cohosh.
- Balm (*Melissa officinalis*) – as for Blue cohosh.
- German chamomile (*Matricaria chamomilla*) – as for Blue cohosh.

At first the colic often worsens slightly. If it becomes much worse, reduce the tonic by half and double the quantity of antispasmodic in the prescription.

Homoeopathy

Note: See page 54 for dosages and cautions for homoeopathic remedies.

- For liver congestion pattern, when the colic is associated with teething and the child is tense and irritable – Chamomilla.
- For liver congestion pattern, after rich food and when the child is irritable – Nux vomica.
- For cold pattern, when the upper part of the abdomen is bloated – Carbo veg.
- For cold pattern, when the lower part of the abdomen is bloated – Lycopodium.

Massage

Note: See page 72 for information on massages.
The following should help, daily before or after feeding.
- Stomach channel.
- Rotating abdomen (see illustration and page 74).
- General back massage.

Rotating abdomen massage

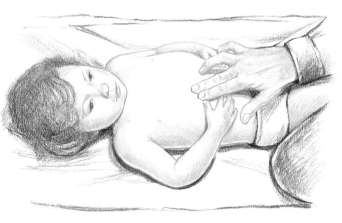

139

VOMITING AND NAUSEA

Vomiting means being sick, or "bringing up" stomach contents. It occurs when food in the stomach cannot continue along the digestive tract to the intestines. The stomach contracts, and since the food cannot go down, it comes back up. Although unpleasant, it is not usually serious – provided it does not become prolonged, or forceful ("projectile") when it may be due to a problem such as pyloric stenosis.

Nausea means feeling sick in the stomach, but not actually being sick. The patterns and treatment for nausea and vomiting are similar.

Vomiting and nausea are symptoms, and because they are closely related to the activity of the rest of the digestive system, they should never be considered in isolation. Look at the whole pattern of your child's digestion, and if relevant, consult the sections on constipation (page 148) or diarrhea (pages 151 and 156).

DANGER SIGNS

Call the doctor promptly if any of the following signs occur:
- your child's temperature goes above 40°C, 104°F,
- he or she vomits continuously for more than 24 hours,
- he or she becomes dehydrated, with sunken eyes and loose skin,
- he or she stops putting on weight due to long-term vomiting, or
- there is pain in the lower right abdomen, which may be appendicitis.

Patterns of vomiting Successful treatment depends on accurate diagnosis. Consult the checklist of questions and become familiar with your child's case, and turn to the relevant pages for that pattern.

PATTERNS OF VOMITING AND NAUSEA

Pattern	Key symptoms
Infection	Sudden onset of vomiting, often accompanied by fever
Undigested food or excitement	Child has eaten too much rich food or has been overexcited
Constipation	The vomiting keeps coming and going, sometimes better and sometimes worse; accompanied by constipation
Internal heat	Red face, "projectile" vomiting (vomit ejected with great force)
Phlegm	Vomit is runny and clear like water, or a frothy fluid
Weak stomach	Child vomits a little after feeding
Emotion	Child is very irritable and emotional

CHECKLIST OF RELEVANT QUESTIONS

■ What is being vomited? Undigested food, partly digested food, bile (yellowish or dark, bitter fluid), water?
■ When does the nausea or vomiting occur? After meals, after certain foods, at a specific time of day or night?
■ What are the stools like? Constipated, normal, diarrhea green, yellow, with a normal or bad smell?
■ What is the child's facial color? Red, yellow, green, white, grey?
■ Are there other symptoms? Abdominal pain, fever, chills?
■ What is the child's emotional state? Excited, angry, distressed, afraid?

In breastfed babies, the symptom of vomiting may be due to a condition of the mother, in which case she should also receive treatment. Consult a practitioner of natural medicine.

Infection pattern

Infections usually strike suddenly. With little or no warning, the child empties the contents of the stomach (which often includes most of the last meal). In mild cases he or she is almost unaffected by the vomiting and seems quite cheerful afterwards. In severe cases the vomiting continues for 24 hours or more, by which time the child is bringing up little more than a clear fluid. The problem rarely continues for longer than a day or so in babies and young children.

TREATMENT FOR INFECTION PATTERN OF VOMITING

In mild cases it may be better to give no treatment. If the vomiting continues for more than several hours, these remedies should help.

Herbs

Note: See page 40 for dosages and cautions for herbs.
● Gentian (*Gentiana lutea*) or Black root (*Leptandra virginica*). Use with caution if there is diarrhea. Both these herbs help to settle nausea and vomiting but are rather bitter to the taste.
● To calm an agitated child – mild herbal teas such as Balm (*Melissa officinalis*) or Chamomile (*Anthemis*

nobilis). Peppermint (*Mentha piperata*) is an alternative.

Homoeopathy

Note: See page 54 for dosages and cautions for homoeopathic remedies.
● For epidemic "gastric flu" – Baptisia.
● If the child is chilly, or there are intermittent sweats with chills afterwards – Ars. alb.
● If the child is angry and restless – Chamomilla.

Tissue salts

Note: See page 64 for information on tissue salts.

● If there is fever – Ferr. phos. If the child vomits bile add Nat. sulph. If the vomit is watery, add Nat. mur.

Bach remedies

Note: See page 66 for information on Bach remedies.
If vomiting continues unabated for a day or more, your child may become very agitated and distressed. Besides seeking help, give the Rescue remedy. If he or she is listless, consider Clematis.

141

In mild attacks the infection passes. During a serious attack the vomiting usually stops, but is replaced by diarrhea. If the vomiting continues for more than about 24 hours, seek assistance as promptly as possible.

The following symptoms usually occur:
■ sudden onset, often with no warning,
■ usually the vomiting does not last long, but may progress to diarrhea, and
■ there is often an epidemic which is "going round" the local community.

Undigested food or excitement pattern

Undigested food is often a cause of vomiting. The food may be too rich, or your child may be allergic to it. Typically, a baby vomits soon after feeding whereas older children bring back the food several hours later (usually in the night!). If a child is too excited or stimulated, either when eating or shortly after, energy leaves the stomach and there is not enough left to digest the food. The food sits in the stomach for some time, and is then brought back.

The following symptoms usually occur:
■ abdominal discomfort or pain,
■ nausea that gradually builds up and leads to vomiting,
■ the child is emotional and weepy, and
■ there is a thick grey or yellow coat on the tongue.

If your child continues to suffer from this kind of vomiting, it may be linked to "liver congestion" (page 23). Follow the general advice for this problem.

TREATMENT FOR UNDIGESTED FOOD PATTERN OF VOMITING

Mild cases usually need no treatment, especially if undigested food is vomited. In older children, the food may have been partly digested and passed through the stomach to the intestines; although there is a need to vomit, only yellowish fluid comes up.

Herbs

Note: See page 40 for dosages and cautions for herbs.
● Gentian (*Gentiana lutea*), Black root (*Leptandra virginica*), and Barberry (*Berberis vulgaris*). Give 10 drops of tincture of each in a glass of water, sipped frequently so that the whole glass is taken over 6 hours.

● Chamomile or Melissa tea helps to settle and calm a very excited child.

Homoeopathy

Note: See page 54 for dosages and cautions for homoeopathic remedies.
Give 3 doses at 30-minute intervals, then 3 hourly doses, then 3 doses 2-hourly.
● If the childs vomits after eating too much, or too quickly, or eats when upset, and there is a sensation of weight in the stomach which does not seem to move up or down – Nux vomica.
● If "cold" energy foods like melon and grapefruit are brought up – Ars. alb.

● If the child weeps and wants comfort, and vomiting occurs after eating "party" foods such as ice cream and cakes – Pulsatilla.

Tissue salts

Note: See page 54 for information on tissue salts.
● Kali sulph. or Nat. phos.

Results of treatment

With the first sips of herbs, or the first pills, the retching should subside, to be replaced by nausea. This should then fade over the next few hours.

Constipation pattern

Constipation is the main cause of recurrent vomiting in babies. There is no room for all the food consumed, so some of it comes back. The main treatment should be directed towards relieving this problem (page 148).

Internal heat pattern

A build-up of internal or "latent" heat (page 26) can cause recurrent vomiting in babies and young children; it is more common in hot climates. It may be due to the "echo" pattern of an infectious disease (page 25), but more commonly results from heat transmitted from mother to child during pregnancy (page 17).

The following symptoms usually occur:
■ the child is well for weeks, then suffers several bouts of vomiting,
■ sudden, violent ("projectile") vomiting soon after a meal,
■ the child often has a large appetite, which may return straight after vomiting,
■ he or she does not seem to feel the cold, and is often red-faced and hot,
■ there may be slight constipation, and
■ thirst and insomnia.

This pattern can be difficult to cure, and it may require the help of a practitioner.

TREATMENT FOR INTERNAL HEAT PATTERN OF VOMITING

Herbs

Note: See page 40 for dosages and cautions for herbs.
● For reducing the heat – Meadowsweet (*Filipendula ulmaria*), 5 drops of tincture; or Marshmallow syrup (*Althea officinalis*), a 5mls teaspoon; or Pasque flower (*Anemone pulsatilla*), 1 drop of tincture.
● Combine one of the above with a herb to soothe the stomach – Gentian (*Gentiana lutea*) or Barberry (*Berberis vulgaris*), 2-3 drops of tincture.
● If there is also blockage or "liver congestion" pattern – add Black root (*Leptandra virginica*), 2-3 drops of tincture, to the above prescription.

Give the herbs for 1-3 months on a regular basis, even if the vomiting attacks end before this, since it takes time to clear such a deep-rooted problem.

Homoeopathy

Note: See page 54 for dosages and cautions for homoeopathic remedies.
● When the orifices are red, burps are smelly, and the child desires sweets – Sulphur.
● If the child is always hungry, with a smell of bad food in the mouth, much saliva and a yellow coating on the tongue – Merc. sol.

Massage

Note: See page 72 for information on massages.
● Stomach channel.
● Rotating abdomen.

Massage twice daily for 1 month, then once daily or every other day for 2 months.

Results of treatment

The first sign of effective treatment is a more even mood. Wild children calm down, while subdued ones become more assertive. Gradually, over a period of weeks, the remedies work through to the physical level, and symptoms subside.

If vomiting attacks occur about once a month, they may be due to an "echo" of whooping cough or to whooping cough immunization (page 28). In this case, give the treatment described here for about 2 months, then 1 dose of homoeopathic Pertussin 30X.

143

Phlegm pattern

Phlegm (mucus or catarrh) accumulating in the stomach can give rise to intermittent attacks of vomiting, because it interferes with the normal digestion of food. This pattern is often seen after an attack of whooping cough or as a reaction to immunization against this disease.

The following symptoms usually occur:
- the child may be well for weeks but then suddenly suffers an attack,
- vomiting a watery fluid or phlegm,
- in prolonged attacks the vomit may be yellow or green, but is still watery,
- discomfort for some hours or even days before the vomiting attack,
- other signs of phlegm, such as a nasal discharge, cough or asthma (below), and
- the face is pale or grey.

Avoid all mucus-producing foods (page 36) in this type of vomiting. And if your child also suffers from a chronic cough or asthma, consult a practitioner of natural medicine. Herbs that treat vomiting can aggravate asthma during the first few weeks. If there is no local practitioner, start by treating the cough or asthma as described on page 96 or 104. When this condition improves significantly (which usually takes at least ten days), add the herbal remedies for vomiting gradually, in small dosages – once daily to begin with, working up to the full dosage over a week.

TREATMENT FOR PHLEGM PATTERN OF VOMITING

Herbs

Note: See page 40 for dosages and cautions for herbs.
- Golden seal (*Hydrastis canadensis*), Black root (*Leptandra virginica*) and Gentian (*Gentiana lutea*).

A discharge of phlegm is common at first, with some nasal discharge, cough or loose stools. Provided your child is otherwise healthy, these soon pass. In severe cases the child may vomit phlegm immediately after being given the herbs, but usually feels better afterwards. Provided the vomiting is not too violent, treatment should be continued until all symptoms have gone, which may take 2-3 months.

- If the glands are swollen – this indicates an "echo" disease. After two weeks of treatment with the remedies above, add Poke root (*Phytolacca decandra*) and Iris (*Iris versicolor*), 3 times the standard dosage of each. Continue the treatment for 2 months or more as necessary.

Homoeopathy

Note: See page 54 for dosages and cautions for homoeopathic remedies.
- If there is constant nausea, the chest is full of phlegm, and the tongue is clean but wet – Ipecacuanha.
- If there is nausea and retching, the face is pale or blue with a cold sweat, the tongue has a thick white coat, and the child wants to lie down – Ant. tart.
- If the child vomits watery mucus, and afterwards is weak and cold – Ars. alb.

Tissue salts

Note: See page 64 for information on tissue salts.
- Kali mur., Nat. mur. or Calc. fluor. is suitable.

Results of treatment

As phlegm starts to move in the body, the child may vomit more, or have diarrhea or a productive cough. If he or she then feels better, continue treatment. If not, stop for a few days and begin again cautiously.

Weak stomach pattern

This type of vomiting is caused by weak digestion. There may have been a difficult birth, or the child may lack vitality – after a long illness, for example. Vomiting occurs because the stomach acids are not strong enough to digest the food. If the child is generally strong but has a weak stomach, the main symptom is spitting up or regurgitating small amounts of food after a meal ("posseting"). If the child lacks vitality, symptoms include:

- a pale face, blue above the mouth,
- sleeping a lot during the day,
- vomiting undigested food or milk,
- loose stools that may contain undigested food, or occasional constipation and lack of appetite and weight gain.

Diet is an important part of treatment. Give easily digested foods, and small amounts each time. If your child has a weak stomach, this can be strengthened. It is particularly important to provide regular meals with no snacks in between, and to ensure food is fresh and healthy, with very little sugar. In addition, try to build up your child's general health by encouraging plenty of fresh air, activity and exercise.

Energy is also important. If your own energy is low, your baby may be affected. In this case, consult a practitioner of natural medicine yourself.

TREATMENT FOR WEAK STOMACH PATTERN OF VOMITING

Herbs and massage are the treatments of choice. Homoeopathic prescribing may require a practitioner.

Herbs

Note: See page 40 for dosages and cautions for herbs.
- To strengthen the digestion – fresh Ginger root (*Zingiber officinale*). For a young baby, add it to milk; if you are breastfeeding, take Ginger tea yourself. For older children, add it to food.
- Fennel seeds (*Foeniculum vulgaris*) also strengthen the digestion. For babies and children alike, make a tea from 1 level 5mls teaspoon of seeds in one-quarter of a litre of water, and sweeten this with honey.

You should see some improvement within a week of starting treatment. These herbs can be given over a long period and will continue to strengthen your child.
- Other herbs – Gentian (*Gentiana lutea*), Barberry (*Berberis vulgaris*) and Fringe tree (*Chionanthus virginica*), 5-10 drops of the combined tinctures, given 3 times daily.
- Prickly ash (*Xanthoxylum americanum*) or Yarrow (*Achillea millefolium*) may also be helpful.

Homoeopathy

Note: See page 54 for dosages and cautions for homoeopathic remedies.
- If there is vomiting or diarrhea after eating, and digestive upset after eggs – Ferr. metallicum.
- If the child tends to eat too quickly, and is hungry when nervous – Anacardium.
- If the appetite is good but the child remains thin and is very sensitive – Nat. mur.

Tissue salts

Note: See page 64 for information on tissue salts.
- Nat. mur., Calc. fluor. or Ferr. phos. is suitable.

Massage

Note: See page 72 for information on massages.
- Abdominal massage.
- Stomach channel massage.
- Back pinch-pull massage.

145

Emotion pattern

The two most common emotions which cause vomiting are anger ("it makes me sick to think of it"), and anxiety and stress ("sick with worry"). Anger is not a common cause of vomiting in babies and children, but it sometimes underlies problems just before a young child learns to speak (page 18). Stress vomiting may occur before an important event, such as an examination.

Vomiting due to anger in babies and toddlers is indicated by:
■ white face,
■ swollen abdomen,
■ the baby or child bursts into a rage and is wilfully destructive,
■ there is often diarrhea alternating with constipation, and

■ he or she vomits undigested food hours after the meal, otherwise, the baby is usually of a strong disposition.

In older children, symptoms of vomiting due to stress are:
■ an attack before an important event,
■ the tongue has a red tip, and
■ he or she is likely to be sensitive and highly strung.

Stress vomiting in older children is not really a medical problem, though it is often treated as such. It is more concerned with adapting and learning to focus energy, without over-concentration. In such situations the Bach remedies are especially helpful. Above all, do not "pressure" this sort of child. Try to spend time with your child, helping him or her to direct energy in a more relaxed and even way.

TREATMENT FOR EMOTION PATTERN OF VOMITING

Herbs

Note: See page 40 for dosages and cautions for herbs.
Try a relaxing herb tea:
● If the child is often angry – Chamomile (*Anthemis nobilis*).
● For the tense, single-minded child – Vervain (*Verbena officinalis*).
● If the child is nervous and has headaches – Lemon balm (*Melissa officinalis*) or Lime flowers (*Tilia europaea*).

Homoeopathy

Note: See page 54 for dosages and cautions for homoeopathic remedies.

● When the child feels anxiety in the "pit of the stomach" – Ars. alb.
● If the vomiting is from sudden fright or bad news – Aconite.
● If the child vomits from anticipation or excitement – Arg. nitricum.
● If the child is very angry – Chamomilla.

Bach remedies

Note: See page 66 for information on Bach remedies.
● Holly or Beech may help.
● For older children, Vervain may be indicated according to the emotional bias.

Results of treatment

Herbs work more on the physical level, to relax your baby or child and ease tension, especially if you can help by talking about the anger that he or she feels. Homoeopathic and Bach remedies act to bring the anger to a more conscious level. Then the child can express his or feelings and overcome them, instead of bottling them up inside, with consequent ill effects.

146

TRAVEL SICKNESS

"Travel sickness" (or "motion sickness") includes nausea or actual vomiting due to travelling in a car, boat or plane. It affects adults and children alike, although children are more susceptible. There are two causes, one physical and one functional.

The physical cause involves weak muscular activity in the stomach, so that digestion slows or ceases. It usually arises from the "weak stomach" pattern of vomiting (page 145), or it may arise from constipation, or anxiety and "nerves". The functional cause is due to the sense of balance not working properly. We have two balance organs, one inside each ear, which act like spirit levels. The eyes also contribute to the sense of balance, so that we can actually see if we are standing up straight. Travel sickness occurs when messages to the brain from these two systems are different. If the inner ears can sense the rocking of the boat, but the eyes are looking at the inside of the boat – which apparently stays level – the brain becomes confused. This affects the nervous system, and may cause vomiting.

TREATMENT FOR TRAVEL SICKNESS

Actions

● Good posture is essential. If your child curls up or slumps, then energy cannot flow to the stomach.
● Discourage reading or games that involve looking down, as this takes the eyes away from the horizon.
● Encourage your child to look out of the window (in a car or plane) or at the horizon (at sea).
● Keep a car window open at all times; at sea, take frequent walks on deck.
● Special bracelets are now available that massage the Neiguan point on the arm (see Massage).

Herbs

Note: See page 40 for dosages and cautions for herbs.
● Prepare a compound tincture of Sweet sedge (*Acorus calamus*), Woodruff

Neiguan wrist massage

(*Asperula odorata*) and Wormwood (*Artemisia absinthium*). Give 2-3 drops in half a cup of water every 15 minutes.

Massage

Note: See page 72 for information on massages.
● Neiguan wrist massage. Find the point one-sixth of the way up the forearm from the crease of the wrist to the inside of the elbow, on the inside of the forearm, midway between the two long bones (see illustration). Massage with your index finger for 1-2 minutes. Repeat on the other forearm.
● Stomach channel massage.

Homoeopathy

Note: See page 54 for dosages and cautions for homoeopathic remedies.
● The remedy of choice is Nux vomica, given every 15 minutes if necessary.
● Other remedies are Bryonia if the child is generally motion-sick; and Cocculus if there is nausea, faintness, dizziness and aversion to food.
NOTE: Avoid peppermint sweets while giving a homoeopathic remedy, since these neutralize its effect.

147

CONSTIPATION

Most babies and children have a bowel movement and pass stools every day or so. If the interval is much longer than this, it can be regarded as constipation. Sometimes a baby or toddler does not pass anything for several days; when the stools are finally passed, they are loose, soft and runny. This is termed constipation alternating with diarrhea. Commonly, constipation is combined with other digestive disturbances, because one of the main problems that babies face is consuming enough food to grow.

In general, two conditions give rise to constipation: "weak digestion" and "liver congestion".

"Weak digestion" pattern

In weak digestion, the vitality is low and the intestinal muscles do not have quite enough strength to produce regular bowel movements. This can be caused by any of the factors that give rise to the "weak" pattern of illness (page 21). For example, some children are born with low energy; a traumatic birth or the use of drugs during childbirth can affect the baby. After birth, causes include a food allergy or the aftereffects of infection or immunization.

The "weak" child usually has a pale face and tends to sleep a lot during the day. He

DANGER SIGNS

Take your child to the doctor as soon as possible if:
- he or she has not passed stools for four days,
- the abdomen becomes swollen,
- the constipation causes pain, or
- he or she becomes distressed, or listless and apathetic.

or she may sleep for a long time at night too, but often wakes for a brief sip of milk or water before falling asleep again. The cries of a "weak"-type baby are not very strong.

"Liver congestion" pattern

The "liver congestion" pattern of illness is described on page 23. The child has enough vitality and energy, but the liver congestion prevents the normal flow of digested matter through the system, and accumulated food in the intestines interferes with normal digestive function. In rare cases there is a physical blockage, as by worms (page 162). Should you suspect any type of physical blockage, take your baby or child to a medical doctor immediately.

This pattern occurs in "strong"-type children (page 21) who often have red cheeks with green around the mouth, and sturdy, powerful muscles. A baby of this type is boisterous and active, with a strong and piercing cry.

Causes and factors In general, the physical causes are those described for the liver congestion pattern of chronic diarrhea (page 156).

Emotional causes also play their part, especially in toddlers and children. Toddlers have many problems adapting to the many life changes that occur all the time. This can produce deep emotional upset, even though your toddler may not show it. He or she might then feel the need to "hold on" and not relax the bowels. Additional factors might be the arrival of a younger brother or sister, emotional stress between parents, a parent starting work or changing jobs, starting school, and severe fright or upset.

Diapers and toilet training

Toilet training marks an important stage in the complex relationship between parent and child, when the parent expects the child to behave in a particular way. The child then conforms or rebels, according to his or her nature.

A common problem for two-year-olds is being able to pass stools only when wearing a diaper. This is sometimes called the "Peter Pan complex", since it suggests that the toddler wishes to stay as a "baby" and not progress through to the next stage of childhood.

Diet and routine

Regular bowel habits are aided by regular eating habits. Provide the same-sized meals at about the same time each day. Avoid between-meal snacks. Even the smallest baby should have at least two hours between meals (page 31).

Babies and toddlers up to about three years old should eat easily-digested foods. Avoid too much brown bread, bran, muesli and raw vegetables. Foods such as these are difficult to digest at this age and tend to accumulate in the intestines, slowing down muscular activity. The digestive system is not yet able to cope with too much roughage. Also, the roughage provides bulk to the diet, but it has less value in terms of vitamins and other nutrients.

After the age of three, some bran and other "rough" foods can be introduced. By the age of about seven years, most children can eat the same foods as adults. Indeed, by this stage, roughage (fiber) in foods often helps to cure constipation.

Aluminium is becoming recognized as harmful to the body, even in small amounts. In the weak pattern of constipation, especially, avoid aluminium cooking utensils. Minute traces of aluminium may get into the food and possibly aggravate the weakness.

FOODS THAT HELP RELIEVE CONSTIPATION

For babies and toddlers: Maple syrup, syrup of figs, stewed prune juice, fresh pears.

For older children: Figs, prunes, slippery elm, bananas, pears, licorice root.

TREATMENT FOR CONSTIPATION

The treatment of constipation is notoriously difficult. Some of the remedies described here may provide relief, but it might be necessary to consult a practitioner of either natural or orthodox medicine. Do not hesitate to seek advice if your child is having problems.

Herbs

Note: See page 40 for dosages and general cautions for herbs.

Special cautions: Use herbal laxatives with great care for your baby, because of the danger of prolonged diarrhea. This is especially relevant if your baby is weak and pale-faced. It is wise to seek the advice of a herbalist or other qualified practitioner. Also, herbal laxatives should never be given regularly to babies and children. If you appear to

Continued on next page

149

find that any laxative is needed regularly, it means you have not found the cause. Seek help from a practitioner of natural or orthodox medicine. In addition, avoid repeated use of Senna, as this may irritate the bowels.

• Many commercially-produced herbal laxatives are available. Subject to the cautions on the package, and those outlined here, they can be safely given to babies and children. If you are not satisfied with the results of one brand, try another with a different combination of herbs. Some herbs promote muscular activity and the passage of food in the bowel, while others help to soften and moisten the stools.

• General herbs for all types of constipation – Butternut (*Juglans cinerea*) or Cascara (*Rhamnus purshiana*) stimulate bowel activity. Start with 1 standard dosage 3 times daily, and double or triple this after 4-5 days as necessary.

• For the weak pattern – add a simple tonic to the herbal prescription. For example: Gentian (*Gentiana lutea*), Barberry (*Berberis vulgaris*) and Licorice (*Glycyrrhiza glabra*), 3 times daily.

• If there is great weakness – Stone root (*Collinsonia canadensis*) may help over 1-2 months.

• For the liver congestion pattern – add Black root (*Leptandra virginica*) which works slowly and gently on the digestive system. Give standard dosage 3 times daily for 1 week or more.

Homoeopathy

Note: See page 54 for dosages and cautions for homoeopathic remedies.

• For the weak pattern, if there is no urge to pass stools for several days, and finally when the stools come they are dry and hard, and often the child feels that not all of the stools have been expelled – Alumen.

• For the weak pattern, if there is much desire to pass stools but these cannot be fully expelled, and the child is rather sensitive and shy in nature – Silica.

• For the liver congestion pattern, if the child feels at ease and does not seem troubled by constipation, the stools are pale and smell like bad eggs – Calc. carb.

• For the liver congestion pattern, if there is alternating constipation and diarrhea, or the child keeps wanting to go but little is passed, and he or she is irritable and angry – Nux vomica.

• For the liver congestion pattern, when the stools are irregular, hard and dry, and the child is irritable and sensitive and tends to hide or withdraw when pride is injured – Nat. mur.

• For a child who is normally well but who suffers constipation after a fever – Sulphur or Bryonia.

Bach remedies

Note: See page 66 for information on Bach remedies.

Bach remedies are one of the most effective treatments for habitual constipation in older children. They are also helpful for babies, although it is more difficult to determine the correct remedy.

• For a child who has problems in making the transition to a more grown-up way of life – consider Walnut.

• If the child is jealous of a younger brother or sister – Holly may be indicated.

• If the child is worrying about going to a new school – Walnut can ease the transition, or use Larch to give confidence.

• If the child is frightened, the remedies for fear will help.

Massage

Note: See page 72 for information on massages.

This can give very effective relief for all ages, and especially for babies.

• Down sacrum.

• Rotating abdomen (clockwise).

• Up the Stomach channel.

ACUTE DIARRHEA

The term "diarrhea" describes a wide range of conditions where the stools are loose. It ranges from diarrhea alternating with constipation (page 148), where the stools are runny but only passed every three or four days, to serious infections such as dysentery, where watery stools may be passed many times each day.

Diarrhea may be acute or chronic. In the acute form, a child who does not normally get diarrhea suffers a sudden attack. In chronic diarrhea the problem comes and goes (page 156).

Causes and factors

Infection Epidemic infection (a "stomach bug") is the commonest cause of diarrhea during childhood. In babies and young children, almost any infection may affect the digestive system, so that any epidemic passing through the community can bring on diarrhea. Such epidemics are common after a prolonged period of damp weather.

Cold food Both physically cold foods, such as ice cream and iced drinks, and also "cold energy" foods (page 32), can be difficult for the stomach to "heat up" and so lead to a sudden attack of diarrhea. Fruit and fruit juices have a similar effect, as do some antibiotic drugs.

Rich or indigestible food Foods that are too rich (such as greasy fried potatoes and lots of red meat), or spicy (such as strong curries), or highly flavored, or "rough" and difficult to digest, may cause a sudden attack of diarrhea as the body expels the undigested food.

Food poisoning This has become an increasing problem, with the increase in pre-cooked meals and "cook-chill" catering,

the spread of salmonella bacteria through foods such as undercooked chicken and eggs, and listeria infection involving foods such as certain soft cheeses made from unpasteurized milk.

Dysentery is also spread by infected food, but is rare nowadays in developed countries, due to improved standards of public and personal hygiene.

Sunstroke When the body gets very hot, blood is diverted from its interior to the skin, to assist cooling. This may leave the digestive system without enough blood to function well, and if there is already a weakness in that area, the child may get diarrhea. This is particularly likely when he or she drinks too much cold water when very hot.

Over-stimulation In older children, physical diseases are often a reflection of their physical state. Physically, diarrhea is a symptom of being unable to digest and absorb food; emotionally, it is related to problems in coping.

For example, it is extremely common for people to get diarrhea when travelling abroad. On the physical level this is caused by unfamiliar foods and foreign infections to which the body has little resistance. On the mental and emotional level, there is a wealth of new impressions which may lead to a mild form of "culture shock". The difficulty in "digesting" and absorbing new ideas and impressions causes a disturbance on the mental level, which can give rise to diarrhea on the physical level. This type of transition becomes a problem particularly when children first go to school. They face the unfamiliar surroundings of the classroom without the emotional security of parents close at hand.

151

Fright When a child has a severe fright, it can drain energy from the digestive system, or stimulate the nerves and hormones controlling bowel evacuation (as in adults), bringing on diarrhea.

Patterns of acute diarrhea

When treating acute attacks of diarrhea by orthodox medicines, it is sometimes necessary to determine the nature of the infecting agent, in order to select the correct drug. However, when treating diarrhea by natural medicines, it is not usually necessary to know the exact nature of the infecting agent, or whether it is viral or bacterial – or even if there is an infecting agent at all. But it is very important to determine the pattern and severity of the problem, and the way that it is affecting your child, so that the correct assistance can be given.

There are two main patterns of acute diarrhea: "cold" and "hot".

DANGER SIGNS

Diarrhea is relatively dangerous for babies and young children, since it may lead to loss of body fluids and salts, and dehydration. Contact your doctor immediately if:
■ your child becomes dehydrated (with sunken eyes and flaccid limbs),
■ he or she seems listless and begins to lose weight,
■ he or she is failing to thrive and put on weight, or
■ you have any other worries about your child's digestive system, or his or her general health.

"Cold" pattern

The "cold" pattern of acute diarrhea can be caused by physically cold foods and drinks, cold energy foods (page 34), exposure to cold, some epidemic infections, or possibly dysentery.

Typical symptoms include:
■ abdominal pain of a cramping nature, nearly all the time,
■ the child is sensitive to cold and likes to be kept warm with covers and a hot-water bottle,
■ sudden onset of diarrhea, usually in less than a day,
■ the stools are loose, often containing undigested food, but they do not smell particularly bad,
■ a pale face,
■ there may be a mild fever with a hot head, but the temperature is unlikely to be higher than 38.5 °C, 101°F, and
■ the child is generally lethargic, listless and difficult to rouse.

"Hot" pattern

The feverish or "hot" pattern includes diarrhea from sunstroke (page 182). It can also arise from rich or spicy foods, and some epidemic infections, including dysentery and typhoid.

Symptoms of this pattern include the following:
■ a red face,
■ abdominal pain, mainly when the stools are passed,
■ high fever (above 39°C, 102°F) accompanied by sweating,
■ the child is very irritable and may become distressed,
■ the stools smell terrible, and
■ the anus is sore and inflamed and may cause discomfort on passing stools.

Onset and recovery

Infection Diarrhea due to an epidemic infection starts suddenly. Sometimes the child is pale and irritable for a day beforehand, but at other times the first attack comes without warning. There is no typical progression for this type, which may be gone in 24 hours or continue for a week. Since the infection is likely to have affected other babies and toddlers in the area, it can help to ask local doctors, schools and playgroups in order to estimate likely progress.

If you know in advance what form the epidemic is taking, you can administer treatment before your child becomes ill. This often averts an attack, or reduces its severity when it does develop.

Cold food Diarrhea due to cold or cold energy foods, or an abdominal chill, can persist for several days, and in some cases lead to chronic diarrhea. Treatment should produce an immediate change of mood, but the child may slip back if remedies are not continued. It is especially important to ensure that the child does not continue to eat cold energy foods.

Rich or indigestible food If your child eats food that is poorly cooked, or prepared from low-quality ingredients, the stomach may revolt and expel the contaminated food. Normally he or she should feel better after about 12 hours, and no treatment is necessary. If the diarrhea continues, then treatment should make a marked difference within 24 hours.

Dysentery and typhoid Dysentery is an infection by shigella bacteria, which lodge in the intestines and cause acute and violent diarrhea, usually of the "cold" pattern.

This is particularly dangerous for babies and toddlers, because watery stools may be passed up to a dozen times a day, with the risk of dehydration (opposite). Without treatment, the problem can go on for more than a week, and some babies experience great fear or even panic.

Natural remedies can have a striking effect on this condition. Herbal or homoeopathic remedies should be given every 15 minutes, and a significant change in the child's spirit is generally noticed after three or four hours; if not, reconsider the remedies you are giving. The main symptoms should subside after about 12-24 hours.

Typhoid is caused by salmonella-type bacteria. It used to have a relatively slow onset, but nowadays there are strains of bacteria that can bring on symptoms within a few hours. These start with violent abdominal pains, which continue for up to three weeks. The diarrhea pattern is usually of the "hot" type.

Both dysentery and typhoid are serious diseases. If you suspect them, contact your medical doctor urgently as well as giving natural remedies.

General care and recovery

Diet For all types of diarrhea follow these guidelines:
• Avoid giving your child physically cold foods, such as milk straight from the refrigerator, and also "cold energy" foods like cucumber and yogurt (page 34).
• Do not provide fruit more than once a week, and even then, in small quantities. Avoid fruit juices.
• Make sure that mealtimes are regular, with no snacks between.
• Try to serve wholesome, good-quality ingredients and not "junk" food.

153

• Give easily digestible foods and avoid raw and "rough" ones (page 24).

If your child has a generally weak digestion, take measures to strengthen the system (page 23). Fresh air, exercise and early nights help to recover energy.

If your child has had a bad attack of diarrhea, his or her digestive system may have been weakened. It may be advisable to consult a practitioner of natural medicine, to assist convalescence and avoid future traces of the "echo" type of disease pattern (page 25). A herb often recommended for children in this situation and to avoid "echo" illness is Fringe-tree (*Chionanthus virginica*).

TREATMENT FOR ACUTE DIARRHEA

At home, homoeopathy is the treatment of choice.

In mild cases of cold pattern diarrhea, simply wait. If the baby or child passes stools more than 4 times in 8 hours, or remains ill for more than 24 hours, then start treatment. In severe cases, when he or she passes stools every half an hour and is in distress, begin at once.

Herbs

Note: See page 40 for dosages and cautions for herbs.

When treating with herbs, give the child's digestive system about 12 hours to expel any stagnant matter.
• For both cold and hot patterns – Cranesbill (*Geranium maculatum*), Witch hazel (*Hamamelis virginica*) and Oak bark (*Quercus robur*). Give 10-15 drops of tincture of each herb every 2 hours, or a 5mls teaspoon of tincture of each herb rubbed into the abdomen every 2 hours. Half dose for 1-3 years, quarter dose for under 1 year.

• When the child is also exhausted – Beth root (*Trillium pendulum*).
• For the cold pattern in older children – add Cayenne (*Capsicum annum*) as a pill.
• For the hot pattern – add Indigo (*Baptisia tinctoria*).

Homoeopathy

Note: See page 54 for dosages and cautions for homoeopathic remedies.
For the cold pattern:
• When there are green watery stools, the child is fearful and has been exposed to cold winds – Aconite.
• When the child is fearful and feels cold, the stools are offensive-smelling and blackish, and the diarrhea may be linked to excess fruit or food poisoning – Ars. alb.
• When there is diarrhea and vomiting, both coloured grass-green – Ipecacuanha.
• For diarrhea with great exhaustion – Carbo veg.
For the hot pattern:
• When there is "gastric flu" with mild fever and foul-smelling stools – Baptisia.

• When there is a red face and high fever – Belladonna.
• When there is colicky pain, thirst and dry lips – Bryonia.
For emotionally related bouts of diarrhea:
• For "exam nerves" and other important events – Gelsemium.
• For an emotional upset – Arg. nitricum.
• For a very nervous and "high-strung" child – Borax.

Tissue salts

Note: See page 64 for information on tissue salts.
For the cold pattern:
• Watery stools – Nat. mur.
• Slimy stools, often after rich food – Kali mur.
• When the stools are sour, smelly and greenish, and there is diarrhea after eating unripe fruit – Nat. phos.

Bach remedies

Note: See page 66 for information on Bach remedies.
These can help to prevent acute diarrhea from

154

Natural and orthodox medicines

Natural medicines have a striking effect on the course of all types of diarrhea. Two therapies are particularly effective: acupuncture and homoeopathy. Indeed, acupuncture for bacterial dysentery is recommended as the treatment of first choice by the World Health Organisation. The orthodox medical treatment of diarrhea (given below) is simple, and aims to conserve the child's strength so that he or she has enough energy to fight the disease. If your child is very ill, a combination of natural and orthodox remedies is strongly recommended.

developing into a more serious problem or turning into the chronic form.
- If the child is fearful – Mimulus or Aspen.
- If the child is panic-stricken – Rock Rose.
- For listlessness – Clematis.
- For a child who clings to mother or father all the time – Chicory.
- If the child seems very sensitive to outside stimuli (such as noises) – Walnut.

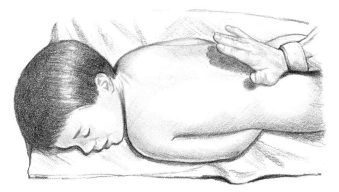

Up sacrum massage

Massage

Note: See page 72 for information on massages.
- For all forms of diarrhea – Up sacrum. Using the heel of your hand, massage firmly up the middle of the sacrum from the tip of the "tail" just above the buttocks to the centre of the back (see illustration). 50-100 times.
- For the cold pattern – Rotating abdomen, Hollow of back, Forefinger, Thenar eminence, and Stomach channel. If there is headache, add Across forehead.
- For the hot pattern – add Elbow to little finger, Across forehead and Up forehead to the above. If the temperature is very high, add Spinal stroke.

Carry out massages every 2 hours in acute attacks, taking 10-15 minutes in total. In milder attacks, massage 3 times daily.

Orthodox treatment

The orthodox treatment ("rehydration") aims to replace body fluids and salts lost in the diarrhea. Commercially available brands of "electrolytes" or "salts", as powders or ready-made fluids, are available at pharmacies. In case of difficulty, make your own solution of sugar, salt and water as follows:
- Boil 200mls (one-third of a pint) of filtered water. As it cools add 1 heaped 5mls teaspoon of sugar, one-eighth of a teaspoon (0.2gms) of bicarbonate of soda, and one-sixteenth of a teaspoon (0.1gms) of common salt. Stir until dissolved and give to your baby or child when cool.

155

CHRONIC DIARRHEA

The general features of diarrhea are described for the acute form (page 151). Chronic diarrhea keeps coming back, sometimes worse and sometimes better, or it continues in a mild way for weeks without much change. The child may be weakened by the attacks, and is usually distressed, but there is not the same feeling of urgency as with severe acute diarrhea. There are two common patterns of chronic diarrhea "liver" congestion" and "weak digestion".

"Liver congestion" pattern

A description of this general pattern of illness is given on page 23, together with basic causes such as overeating and immunization.

In breastfed babies, causes include teething and mother's indigestion; in bottlefed babies they are irregular feeding, milk that is too rich or unsuitable (page 137), or not burping after a feed; and in weaned babies, too many different or rich foods, or too much "rough" food (such as brown bread and raw vegetables).

Typical symptoms of this pattern of diarrhea include:
- the stools are loose and often greenish in color,
- in mild cases the stools smell of sour apples, but in more severe attacks they have a foul and putrid odor,
- the stools may be passed two or three times daily, although sometimes the diarrhea is interspersed with days when no stools are passed (constipation with diarrhea), and
- the child is typically strong and self-willed, with red cheeks and a greenish tinge around the mouth.

In addition, there will be the typical symptoms of liver congestion.

"Weak digestion" pattern

This pattern occurs because the digestive system has difficulty in coping with even simple foods. The weakness may be due to a previous bad attack of acute diarrhea, any prolonged disease, antibiotics, rapid growth, a food allergy, too many late nights, or general weakness in babies (page 21).

In older children, causes include concentrating too hard on schoolwork, so that the energy is diverted from the digestive system to the head, to sustain the long periods of attention. Symptoms are:
- the stools are loose and may come several times a day,
- they may contain particles of undigested food or milk,
- they have a "normal" or pale colour,
- the smell is usually not too offensive,
- a baby is likely to be rather docile and "good", sleeping a lot during the day and causing little trouble, although perhaps waking at night,
- an older child usually desires to get things right and be "top of the class",
- the face is usually rather pale,
- a poor appetite, and
- this pattern is more common among high-strung children.

DANGER SIGNS

Diarrhea is relatively dangerous for babies and young children, since it may lead to loss of body fluids and salts, and dehydration. Contact your doctor immediately if your child shows any danger signs as described for acute diarrhea, page 152.

General care and diet

The measures which help acute diarrhea also benefit the chronic type (page 154).

In the liver congestion pattern, first and foremost, your child's diet must be controlled. Give regular meals, with smallish portions, and no snacks between meals. If your child has a hearty appetite and a strong will, this can present problems; direct the remedies towards reducing the appetite, as for "hot" vomiting (page 143).

In the weak digestion pattern, changes in lifestyle may be advised. It is particularly important to determine the cause of the weakness and treat it. This may involve considerable changes in upbringing, such as insisting on early nights, avoiding certain highly-stimulating friends, cutting down on extra-curricular activities and television, or even considering a change of school. In either pattern of chronic diarrhea, it may be necessary to consult a practitioner.

TREATMENT FOR CHRONIC DIARRHEA

Herbs

Note: See page 40 for dosages and cautions for herbs.
• For both patterns – Tormentil (*Potentilla tormentilla*) and Oak bark (*Quercus robur*), 5 drops of tincture of each, 3 times daily. Half dosage under 3 years.
• For the liver congestion pattern – add Black root (*Leptandra virginica*). Note: give only small dosages 3-6 drops of tincture 3 times daily.
• For the weak digestion pattern – fresh Ginger root (*Zingiber officinale*) mixed into the food or drink is the main herbal tonic for babies. It can be combined with Fennel seeds (*Foeniculum vulgaris*) and honey to make a delicious drink.
• When there is also exhaustion – add Beth root (*Trillium pendulum*).
• Sage (*Salvia officinalis*) tea strengthens the digestion.

Give 1 cup 3 times daily for 2-3 months to babies or children of any age.

Homoeopathy

Note: See page 54 for dosages and cautions for homoeopathic remedies.
• For the liver congestion pattern, if the appetite is poor – Antimonium.
• For the liver congestion pattern, if the appetite is voracious – Sulphur.
• For diarrhea during teething – Chamomilla or Podophyllum.
• For the weak digestion pattern – either Sepia, Silica, Ars. alb., Cinchona, Ferr. phos. or Ipecacuanha. Consult pages 56-63 for details, to select the correct remedy. These remedies have somewhat slower effects, for they rely on the child using his or her own energy to build up strength.

Tissue salts

Note: See page 64 for information on tissue salts.
• For the liver congestion pattern – Nat. phos., or Calc. phos.
• For the weak digestion pattern – Ferr. phos.

Massage

Note: See page 72 for information on massages.
• For chronic diarrhea – Up sacrum, as in acute diarrhea, also Rotating abdomen (anti-clockwise), Zhongwan, Guanyuan, Stomach channel, Thenar eminence.
• For the weak pattern – Back pinch-pull for babies, and general back massage for older children.
Carry out the massages 1-2 times daily for babies and toddlers, daily for children.

157

TEETHING

Problems associated with teething are so common that the expression "teething troubles" has passed into everyday language. Most babies and toddlers have some irritation and soreness as the teeth erupt (grow through the gum). The age at which the different teeth appear varies from one child to another. On average, the front teeth (incisors) erupt at about six months, while the back or cheek teeth (molars) do so at two to three years.

The remedies given here are also helpful for toothache, to give pain relief until the attention of a dentist is available.

They are effective for adults as well as children, particularly in the form of herbal mouthwashes.

Symptoms

Common symptoms include irritability, sore gums, a red cheek on the same side as the erupting tooth, nasal discharge, dribbling from the mouth, digestive upsets, diarrhea and insomnia (page 164) – even with screaming throughout the night. The child is often hot and restless, and a baby will not settle to sleep.

TREATMENT FOR TEETHING

Herbs

Note: See page 40 for dosages and cautions for herbs.
- Chamomile tea (*Anthemis nobilis*). Pour boiling water onto 1 level 5mls teaspoon of dry herb in a mug. When cooled, strain off the herb and sweeten the tea with honey. For babies, 1-2 5mls teaspoons is enough, every 2 hours. Or soak a clean handkerchief in the tea, cool it in the refrigerator and give it to the baby to suck. Older children may like to drink a cup every few hours.
- Syrup of Marshmallow root (*Althea officinalis*) can be added to a baby's food or drink. Give up to 3 level 5mls teaspoons daily.
- For gum inflammation – Meadowsweet (*Filipendula ulmaria*), 5 drops of tincture in a 20mls tablespoon of water, every 2-4 hours.

Homoeopathy

Note: See page 54 for dosages and cautions for homoeopathic remedies.
- Chamomilla 3X or 6X may be used freely during difficult teething bouts. It is available commercially in some areas as "teething granules" (page 185). As with herbal tea, the remedy may be given to suck on a cooled handkerchief.
- If there is also greenish, watery, bad-smelling diarrhea – Podophyllum.
- If the child has stomach pains, wants to be carried, is bad-tempered, and asks for things but refuses when they are offered – Cina.
- If there is a high fever, and a danger of fits (seizures) – Belladonna at standard dosage until the fever subsides. Then change the remedy to fit the new symptoms or gradually reduce as necessary.

Tissue salts

Note: See page 64 for information on tissue salts.
- Calc. phos.
- If the child is feverish or alternately overexcited and very quiet – Ferr. phos.
- Combination R. For the initial stage, give 1 tablet every 30 minutes. Reduce the dosage after either a slight improvement or 6-8 dosages.

Massage

Note: See page 72 for information on massages.
Carry out the following massages 2-3 times during the day, and as necessary at night, for up to 20 minutes.
- Hegu ("end of crease") massage. The Hegu point is on the hand, between the bones in the bases of the thumb and index finger (metacarpal bones). The point itself is

Causes and factors

In Chinese medicine, the gums and digestive system are considered to be related, so that anything that affects the gums can also affect the digestion. When teeth come through, the gums often become inflamed. If the digestive system is strong and functioning well, the inflammation does not spread. However, if the child has a tendency to the "liver congestion" pattern of illness (page 23), irritation from the gums can spread down and cause severe digestive disturbances.

Prevention

The main way to avoid or minimize teething problems is to prevent a build-up of the liver congestion pattern. Make preparations about one month before teething is expected. Details are given on pages 24-25, but in particular avoid overfeeding, and if bottlefeeding, add more water than usual. For older children, avoid rich foods, especially red meats and fatty meals, and also avoid "rough" foods that are difficult to digest, like wholegrain bread, raw vegetables and muesli.

located on the back of the hand, at the lower end of the crease formed when the thumb lies alongside the index finger (see illustration). Massage it with the tip of your finger, gently vibrating for 1-2 minutes. Repeat on the other hand. (The Hegu point is the main anaesthetic acupunture point for the teeth and gums.)
• Forefinger massage, 100 times on each hand.
• Thumb massage. Massage up the palm surface of the thumb, from the "fingerprint" to the end of the thumb, 100 times on each hand.
• Thenar eminence massage, 200 times on each hand.
• Abdominal stretching. The thumbs start in the middle of the abdomen and move outwards, for 5 minutes.
• Rotating abdomen (clockwise), for 5 minutes.
• Below-the-knee massage. Knead the point about 3-4cms

Hegu massage

below the knee, just outside the main shin bone, 30 times on each leg.

External treatments

• For a baby, if there is green nasal discharge and diarrhea – make a combined tincture of equal parts of Black cohosh (*Cimicifuga racemosa*), Hops

(*Humulus lupulus*) and St John's Wort (*Hypericum perfoliatum*). Rub a 5mls teaspoonful into the baby's abdomen 3 times daily. (A baby's skin is permeable so the herbs can be absorbed.)
• Make a mouthwash from equal parts of the tinctures of Meadowsweet (*Filipendula ulmaria*), Poke root (*Phytolacca decandra*) and Golden seal (*Hydrastis canadensis*). Dilute 1:10 tinctures:water and gently rub it on the gums every 2 hours.
• Place a 5mls teaspoon of ground Cloves (*Eugenia aromatica*) on the Hegu point (see illustration). Moisten with a few drops of vinegar and cover with an adhesive bandage or gauze pad overnight.

DIAPER RASH

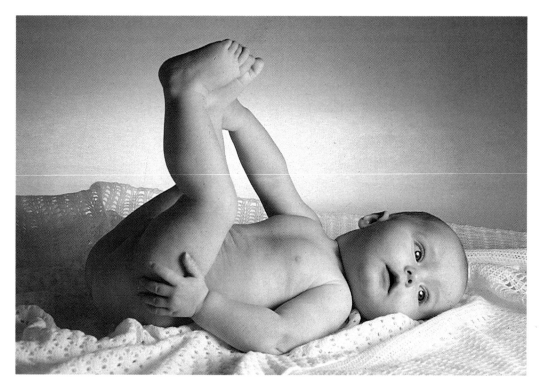

Diaper (diaper) rash is redness and soreness of the skin in the area covered by the
diaper. It is usually concentrated around
the genital area and anus, and spreads
down the legs and up the abdomen. The
skin becomes irritated through prolonged
contact with urine and stools. A baby's
skin is delicate and soft, and is easily
irritated – especially by being kept moist.

Internal causes and factors

The extent and severity of the rash is
affected by the nature of the urine and
stools. If the body is functioning well, the
urine should be "mild" and nearly color-
less. If there is an imbalance, the urine
can become very strong, and also more
acidic – and therefore more irritating.
Similarly, a baby's stools should be "mild"

Allow air to get to your baby's diaper area.

in composition, without a particularly bad
smell. When the digestion is out of
balance, the stools can take on a foul
smell, and are often acidic and corrosive,
and so more likely to produce a rash.

Acidic urine Three main factors cause acidic
urine. One is hot weather, when a lot of
fluid is lost through perspiration, and so
the urine becomes more concentrated and
corrosive. A second factor is spicy food. If a
baby habitually eats such foods, or if the
breastfeeding mother eats rich and spicy
food, the baby's digestion may not be
strong enough to neutralize the spices. As
a result, irritating substances are passed
into the urine. The third factor is the
"liver congestion" pattern (page 23).

Acidic stools Again, three factors cause acidic, corrosive stools. One is enteritis – an infection in the digestive system. When a baby catches a digestive infection and develops diarrhea (page 151), this upsets the balance in the bowels, and the stools are often extremely irritating. Second, when the baby's digestion is over-loaded – by overeating, or eating food which is difficult to digest – the meal is not properly broken down and may become acidic. Third, teething (page 158) may violently upset the digestive system.

Diet and hygiene

Diet Adopt the measures to reduce the "liver congestion" pattern. In particular, give easily-digested food (avoid wholegrain bread and other "rough" foods), do not overfeed, avoid spicy foods, and allow at least two hours between meals. Also, keep your baby awake for about half an hour after eating, and ensure that he or she has enough to drink (preferably plain water rather than fruit juices) in hot weather.

If you are breastfeeding, avoid rich and spicy foods, red meats and wines, which are likely to cause irritation to your baby's digestive system.

Hygiene Good hygiene is the most important single aspect of prevention, as well as treatment. Change your baby's diaper as soon as it becomes dirty. Allow time for the air to get to the affected parts. Try to give your baby several hours a day without wearing a diaper. In severe cases, avoid diapers completely, especially if your baby can spend time outside in warm weather. Use soft, absorbent cloth diapers. Rough diapers are more irritating to the skin.

TREATMENT FOR DIAPER RASH

Herbs	Homoeopathy	External treatments
Note: See page 40 for dosages and cautions for herbs. • To reduce the acidity of the urine – Buchu (*Barosma betulina*) and Cleavers (*Galium aparine*), 2 drops of tincture of each, 3 times daily. Half dose under 2 years. • To help regulate the digestion – Black root (*Leptandra virginica*), Barberry (*Berberis vulgaris*) or Fringe tree (*Chionanthus virginica*). These will only be effective if combined with preventative dietary measures.	Note: See page 54 for dosages and cautions for homoeopathic remedies. • To reduce the acidity of the urine – Merc. sol. • In a baby girl, when the rash is accompanied by a green vaginal discharge – Merc. sol. (consult a practitioner also). • To help improve liver congestion – Lycopodium. • When the urine is scalding and the skin raw – Cantharis. • When the affected skin comes up in raised mounds or pimples – Rhus tox.	• Zinc-and-castor-oil ointment is favoured by many orthodox medical practitioners. • To soothe and cool the skin – Marigold (*Calendula officinalis*) ointment. • Chickweed (*Stellaria media*) ointment is specifically for inflammation in the urogenital area. • It may help to cover the diaper area with a protective cream, to reduce the skin's contact with urine.

WORMS

Various kinds of worms infest children (and adults) across the world. In temperate regions the most common kinds are the digestive parasites, threadworms and roundworms (a type of nematode). It is especially common to catch worms between the ages of two and five years, when children have freedom to roam but are not yet properly trained in hygiene. (The "ringworm" that affects the skin is not a worm but a fungal infection.)

Causes of infestation

Worms reach the intestines after the child inadvertently places eggs in the mouth, most commonly after playing in soil and dirt that is infected, or after contact with an infected animal such as a pet cat or dog. The eggs hatch in the child's intestines and multiply rapidly in a child with a poor or weak digestion. If the digestion is strong, the worms do not multiply and are soon expelled in the stools. Children who have some digestive imbalance, usually "liver congestion" (page 23), are more susceptible.

The diagnosis of worms is confirmed by laboratory analysis of the stools.

Threadworms (pinworms)

The eggs of threadworms (*Oxyuris vermicularis*) come from dirt – on unwashed food, by putting unwashed fingers in the mouth, or from dirty fingernails. They hatch in the intestines into little white worms some 2-13 millimetres long.

The first and main symptom is intense itching around the anus. It occurs chiefly at night, and may prevent sleep. The itching is caused by the female worms, which pass out through the anus at night to lay their eggs.

In some children it is difficult to know whether such itching is due to worms or another cause. The diagnosis can often be confirmed by applying clear adhesive tape (cellophane tape) over the anus in the morning and peeling it off to see if any eggs have stuck to it. When they have multiplied considerably, one or two worms may be seen in the stools.

If the condition is left untreated for months, it can affect the whole constitution. The child becomes listless, with a poor appetite, nausea, vomiting, abdominal pain, diarrhea and slimy, mucus-containing stools.

Roundworms

Roundworms (*Ascariasis lumbricoides*) are pale yellow worms with flat heads, which grow to about 10 centimetres long. Being much bigger than threadworms, they are more of a threat to the child's constitution.

At first, when there are only one or two worms present, there may be no symptoms. The worms lay their eggs in the

---

ADDITIONAL SYMPTOMS

These additional symptoms may be seen when a child suffers from worms of any kind:
- grinding the teeth at night,
- dreams of battles,
- restless, interrupted sleep,
- a dark spot that shows up on the white of the eye, and
- a powdery patch, like eczema, on the cheek. It may appear as a discoloration of normal skin pigment, some 2-3 centimetres across.

duodenum (the first part of the small intestine) and if they multiply rapidly, a knot of worms may build up. At this stage the child suffers severe abdominal pain, with irregular slimy stools, diarrhea vomiting and poor appetite.

Another common symptom is a hard, non-productive cough, because as the embryo roundworms hatch, they migrate to the lungs.

Prevention

Encourage your child in hygiene. Teach him or her never to put hands in the mouth without washing them first, and always to wash hands after playing in soil, dirt and earth, and after petting animals. If there are any signs of the "liver congestion" pattern of illness, this should be treated.

TREATMENT FOR WORMS

There are two approaches to treatment. One is to administer a substance which is poisonous to the worms, but not to the child. The worms are then stunned or killed, and eliminated by passing out in the stools.

The second approach is to strengthen the child's digestion so that the worms are expelled naturally. In practice, this is less effective for getting rid of worms, but it should be considered if a child suffers repeated infestations, along with advice from a practitioner.

Orthodox medical treatment

● Piperazide, an extract from Cayenne pepper (*Capsicum annum*), together with an extract from Senna (*Cassia angustifolia*). The former stuns the worms, while the latter causes them to be passed. This combined extract is available in many areas on the advice of a pharmacist.

Herbs

Note: See page 40 for dosages and cautions for herbs.
● For older children – Cayenne pepper (*Capsicum annum*) may be given with yogurt, but it is very hot! Give one-half of 1 level 5mls teaspoon daily for 1 week.
● A tea made from Wormwood (*Artemisia vulgaris*) or Tansy (*Tanacetum vulgare*) will stun the worms. These herbs have the disadvantage of being intensely bitter.
● Give 5 lemon pips, ground and mixed with honey, daily for 5 days.

Whatever treatment you give, repeat after 2 weeks, to expel the worms which were just eggs or embryos at the first treatment.

Homoeopathy

Note: See page 54 for dosages and cautions for homoeopathic remedies.

● Cina may alter the balance of the body so that the child expels threadworms naturally.
● Other homoeopathic remedies for liver congestion include Aes. hippo., Chelone glabra or Sabadilla. The remedy may be combined with orthodox treatment, to strengthen the digestion.

Side-effects of treatment

A small amount of blood is sometimes seen in the urine after treatment for worms – whether orthodox, herbal or homoeopathic. This is no cause for concern, provided it is definitely linked to the anti-worm treatment and not to urinary problems, and the child does not need treatment for worms more than twice a year.

163

SLEEPING PROBLEMS (INCLUDES CRYING)

If your baby or child wakes at night and cries, there may be other signs which point to a serious health problem. In such cases, take the necessary steps as indicated by the symptoms and the disorder which you suspect is causing them.

What about the child whose health seems good but who repeatedly wakes and cries? It may be of little consolation to know that the problem may not be serious for the child – since it is certainly serious for the parents. Being woken repeatedly in the night and deprived of sleep can drive people to distraction and even violence. Natural medicines can help.

There are four main patterns of insomnia, as described here. Consider the signs and symptoms that your child exhibits, and then refer to the appropriate section for further details and treatment.

"Colic" pattern of insomnia

The child is woken by a cramping pain in the intestines, which comes from the indigestion-type pain of colic (page 138). This pattern is also called "cold digestion" because the colicky pain is similar to that caused by taking too many "cold energy" foods or drinks (page 32), or an inherent tendency to a "cold" type of digestion, or the cold effect of anaesthetics given during childbirth.

Symptoms The characteristic features of this "colic" pattern of insomnia are:
■ the child whimpers, cries or yells before waking, then wakes screaming, or with a dreadful shout,
■ he or she may even cry or scream before being fully awake,

TREATMENT FOR COLIC PATTERN OF INSOMNIA

Diet

Avoid cold energy foods (page 32), especially bananas, which may give rise to colic in babies and toddlers. In a few cases the intestinal pain is caused by inability to digest cow's milk, so try goat's milk or soya (soy) milk.

Herbs

Note: See page 40 for dosages and cautions for herbs.
● In mild cases – 1 cup of simple infusion of Melissa (*Melissa officinalis*) before going to sleep is usually enough.
● In other cases – Sweet

sedge (*Acorus calamus*), Black root (*Leptandra virginica*) and Gentian (*Gentiana lutea*) should be used together, mixing equal quantities of the mother tinctures. Give 3-6 drops of the mixture for babies, rising to 12 drops for children, in water or dilute fruit juice.

The symptoms may be aggravated for a few days, especially if the child is flatulent. After the blockage clears, sleep should gradually become calmer.

Homoeopathy

Note: See page 54 for dosages and cautions for

homoeopathic remedies.
● If the child suffers a lot of flatulence, and the upper part of the abdomen is swollen and bloated – Carbo. veg.
● If the whole abdomen is swollen, and the child passes loose stools which may contain particles of undigested food – China.
● If the lower part of the abdomen is bloated and swollen, the child craves sweets and drinks, and he or she feels full after the first mouthful of a meal – Lycopodium.
● If the child is vigorous, wilful and violent, and there are signs of phlegm – Calc. carb.

writhing in agony, sometimes sweating with pain, and restless sleep, often in a face-down position, with teeth-grinding,
■ the face is usually pale, often with a blue-grey colour above the mouth, and
■ sometimes the child is also colicky and flatulent during the day.

"Heat" pattern of insomnia

The child cannot sleep because there is too much heat inside the body. Just as sleep is difficult in hot weather, so an internal imbalance causes the child to become "overheated" in the night, and he or she wakes. The heat can come from many causes, such as great excitement, too much rich or spicy food, constipation, or the "liver congestion" or "echo" patterns of disease (pages 23 and 25). It may also

have come from the mother during pregnancy (page 17). For a lasting cure, the cause should be identified and removed.

Symptoms The characteristic features are:
■ the child has difficulty in going to sleep,
■ he or she wakes up in good spirits and is reasonably content but may be frightened of the dark,
■ usually there is no crying at first (particularly if there is a nightlight), but he or she soon calls for attention, and often lies wide awake for hours, wanting to get up and play,
■ the face is usually red, especially on and round the cheeks,
■ he or she is hot at night, sleeps face-up and may throw off bedclothes, and
■ there may be excessive activity during the daytime.

Massage for all patterns

Note: See page 72 for information on massages.

Massage can be very helpful for all patterns of insomnia. Almost any simple massage helps a child to relax and fall asleep. In babies and toddlers, the massage may be done twice or even three times daily. In older children, carry out the massage in the evening, taking about 10 minutes in total.
● Fingerprints.
● Heel on lower abdomen.
● Zusanli.
● Lifeline. Using your index finger, massage the point at the beginning of the "lifeline"

Lifeline massage

on the palm, near the wrist (see illustration). Stroke gently for 2-3 minutes, and repeat on other hand.
● If there is fever or heat – follow the massages given for

fevers (page 84) or try the Dewpond massage on the palm of the hand.
● If there is fright – Ten kings massage with a ballpoint pen or matchstick.

Other therapies

Acupuncture, cranio-sacral osteopathy and hand-healing have all helped to cure sleeplessness in children.
● An infusion of Chamomile (*Anthemis nobilis*) added to the water in the bedtime bath may help the child to relax.

TREATMENT FOR HEAT PATTERN OF INSOMNIA

Diet

Avoid red meats and rich and fatty foods. Also make sure the child has enough to drink, and is not constipated. Check all foods for artificial colorings or flavorings since your child may be allergic to these.

Herbs

Note: See page 40 for dosages and cautions for herbs.
- Chamomile (*Anthemis nobilis*), Lime flowers (*Tilia europaea*) and Vervain (*Verbena officinalis*) are mild, gentle in action and can be taken regularly by young and old alike. They are available either loose or as "tea bags".
- When the child is irritable, with a red face, and possibly teething – Chamomile.
- If the child is nervous and sensitive – Lime flowers.
- When the child shows intense mental effort, and has difficulty in stopping an activity and settling down – Vervain.

- Stronger herbs are Valerian (*Valeriana officinalis*), Scullcap (*Scutellaria laterifolia*), Motherwort (*Leonurus cardiaca*), Passion flower (*Passiflora incarnata*) or Hops (*Humulus lupulus*). Give separately or together, 1-5 drops of mother tincture of each herb in water or another drink. These herbs are also available in pill form from many manufacturers.
- If the heat arises from constipation – see page 148.
- If you suspect the heat is an "echo" of a fever or immunization, or a form of hyperactivity, specialist help is advised.

Homoeopathy

Note: See page 54 for dosages and cautions for homoeopathic remedies.
- If there is thirst, and the child alternates between being destructive and affectionate – Phosphorus, at any time of the day or night.
- If there are digestive

disturbances (particularly flatulence), or when the child is brooding and prone to tears – Sulphur, given in the morning.
- If the child is emotional and weepy – Pulsatilla.
- If the child is very excited, and during teething troubles – Chamomilla, in the evening or at night (page 158).
- If there is irritability and great mental exertion (such as homework), and particularly in spring – Nux vomica.
- If the child is afraid to go to sleep, and "jerks" when sinking into sleep – Lachesis.

Bach remedies

Note: See page 66 for information on Bach remedies.
- Especially if there is fear of the dark – Aspen.

Massage and other therapies

See Colic pattern, page 164.
- Hops are a great soporific, and a traditional remedy is to put some hops into the pillow.

"Fright" pattern of insomnia

The child cannot sleep because he or she has had a fright or shock – but is unable to express it. The insomnia is often caused by frightening dreams linked to the fear. In some cases the shock may have been experienced by the mother, in pregnancy or just after birth, and transmitted to the child. The shock may have been due to an accident or seeing a frightening movie or TV program.

Symptoms The characteristic features are:
- the child may be afraid to go to sleep, but not afraid at other times,
- restless and agitated sleep, often moaning or talking while asleep, and telling

next day of vivid, frightening dreams,
- he or she may lie awake for hours, and
- pale blue color on the bridge of the nose between the eyes.

"Weak" pattern of insomnia

In this pattern, the circulation of energy around the child's body is generally weak or slow in some way. There is usually no problem in going to sleep, but once asleep, the energy circulation slows down more and more, so that the brain is deprived of its blood supply and the child wakes up. This is linked to the "weak" pattern of disease (page 21).

This type of insomnia may also be related to the blockage of energy circulation in the body, as discussed on page 15.

Symptoms The characteristic features of this "weak" pattern are:
- the child wakes frequently, maybe every two hours or even less,
- he or she is not usually in distress at first, and a small drink of milk or juice is often enough to settle the child at this stage, after which he or she may well go back to sleep very soundly,
- if no one attends, he or she may begin to whimper or cry,
- often the face is very pale, and
- other signs of weak energy or poor circulation include lack of appetite, choosiness over food, a generally weak and tired condition, and a history of illness which may have weakened the child's constitution. In addition, the child may be sleepy during the day.

TREATMENT FOR FRIGHT PATTERN OF INSOMNIA

The Bach Rescue remedy is the treatment of choice.

Television

Limit your child's television viewing. It is not only the violent nature of some programs, but the set's flickering lights which are stimulating.

Herbs

Note: See page 40 for dosages and cautions for herbs.
- Motherwort (*Leonurus cardiaca*) can be effective in calming a frightened child, especially if the fear is obvious rather than being suppressed.

Homoeopathy

Note: See page 54 for dosages and cautions for homoeopathic remedies.
- The main remedy is Arnica, although the symptom picture may indicate a heat-type remedy. In cases of recent shock, the standard 6X potency should be adequate. If the trauma has lasted for many months, higher potencies will be needed.
- If the insomnia is due to a frightening television program or a similar worrying or unsettling event – Stramonium.
- Other remedies include Ars. alb. or Aconite.

Bach remedies

Note: See page 66 for information on Bach remedies.
- For fright pattern – Rescue remedy is the treatment of choice. The insomnia may get worse at first, with digestive upsets. It is common for symptoms of heat to appear (spots on the skin, diarrhea with anal soreness) when the fear is released, but these symptoms soon subside.

Massage and other therapies

See Colic pattern, page 164.

167

TREATMENT FOR WEAK PATTERN OF INSOMNIA

The weak pattern is difficult to cure at home by homoeopathy. If this is your preferred therapy, seek the advice of a practitioner of natural medicine.

Diet

Serve food for your child that is easy to digest. Avoid raw foods and bran, and give white bread rather than brown bread. Keep beans out of the diet if possible, and do not force the child to eat more vegetables than he or she wants. This may contradict healthy dietary advice for adults, but rough, unrefined foods are often too coarse for a young child's digestive system. Such "high-fiber" foods can be introduced gradually at a later stage when they will be of more benefit.

Herbs

Note: See page 40 for dosages and cautions for herbs.
● In babies – give a tea made from Fennel seeds (*Foeniculum vulgaris*) sweetened with honey or even Licorice (*Glycyrrhiza glabra*), just before bedtime, and during the night if needed.
● In babies – stronger herbs are Gentian (*Gentiana lutea*), Hawthorn (*Crataegus oxycantha*) and Golden seal (*Hydrastis canadensis*). Use 3 together at half the standard dosage, as a tonic to aid the circulation.
● For older children – a tea made from Yarrow (*Achillea millefolium*) is a helpful tonic, but tastes bitter. Give 1 cup of infusion made from a 5mls teaspoon of Yarrow, sweetened with honey as required, to taste.

Massage and other therapies

See Colic pattern, page 165.
● For the weak pattern in babies – try the Back pinch-pull massage as described on page 76.

Back pinch-pull massage

General advice for insomnia

Newborn babies Go to your wakeful baby in the early stages, to hold and reassure him or her. By giving the baby a sense of security early on, you can avoid encouraging a fear of abandonment and other imaginary worries. The confidence your baby receives should prove to be of great benefit throughout childhood.

For excitable young babies who are difficult to soothe, it may be helpful to use swaddling, with the hands secured at the sides, so that movement is restrained. This may sound rather cruel and it certainly would be for older babies and children, but newborn babies often derive comfort from being wrapped in this way. Perhaps this is because it was not long since they were constrained during life in the womb.

Routine and sleep habits Older children who have difficulty in falling asleep should be discouraged from reading and mental work for about two hours before bedtime. A short walk or some other break just before retiring may help.

Some children simply get into bad habits over going to sleep. They may keep themselves awake or wake themselves in the night by an effort of will, in order to seek attention and comfort. Often such a child creates a terrific emotional scene if you interfere with these cherished habits. Such a "routine" can be difficult for parents to break, requiring great ingenuity and fortitude. It may help to spend a night or two with friends, or to ask a trusted friend to "babysit", to share the strain and bring a new perspective.

Once you have resolved to break the habit, the Bach remedies can be helpful. Your child may complain vigorously for up to a week – but if he or she goes on for much longer, it usually means that the problem is more than just one of habit. Be assured that parents do get through this difficult time, and nearly all children stop disturbing their parents repeatedly in the night after about the age of five years.

REMEDIES FOR PARENTS

Insomnia and night crying can cause great worry and tiredness in the family. As a parent, you may wish to treat yourself by natural medicines, to break the cycle of tension and exhaustion. A Bach remedy often indicated in such circumstances is Cherry plum. Homoeopathic remedies include Cocculus if you are very irritable, dizzy and with "frayed nerves" from broken sleep; Kali phos. if you feel irritable, have "nervous exhaustion" and simply want to hide away; and Arnica if you cannot get back to a routine of sound sleep due to the habit of staying awake so often.

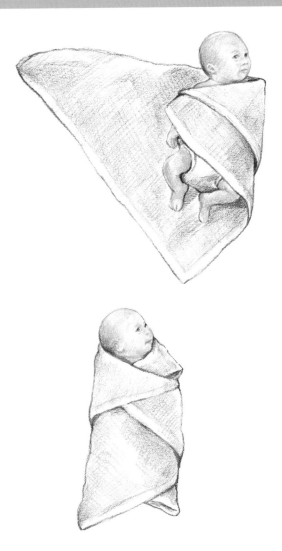

Young babies often derive comfort from being wrapped well, or swaddled, in a suitable sheet or soft blanket. The restraining effect of the swaddling may mimic the restricting sensations in the womb. Ensure the baby's arms are comfortably by his or her sides (top) before wrapping neatly in the blanket (above).

169

BEHAVIORAL PROBLEMS

Some children are the despair of their parents because of their "bad behavior". They seem bent on making lives difficult for those around them. Natural medicines can help many of these children to be more at peace with themselves, and bring out the cheerfulness and warmth that is always there, but that sometimes gets overwhelmed and "buried".

Aggression A degree of controlled aggression is a natural part of the human personality. But some children show needlessly violent behavior. They seem to want to destroy the world about them and inflict pain on people. At play, such a child may repeatedly hit other children, and throw toys and other objects with amazing force. Almost anything can provoke such outbursts of violent behavior.

Tantrums These overwhelming fits of rage may be provoked by a small event, or no event at all. A child in a tantrum usually screams in a loud, piercing voice that goes straight to the heart, and which may cause people to approach and try to help – which is usually viewed by the parents as unwelcome "interference". Often the child throws itself down, arms and legs flailing, and head banging on the floor. A strong child can keep this up for perhaps two hours, before he or she becomes exhausted and (usually) falls asleep.

Breath-holding Like a tantrum, this is a manifestation of great rage, and it may occur as part of a tantrum. Typically it develops as tension builds over some (usually trivial) matter. Suddenly the child draws in a huge breath of air, with the intention of shouting at the top of the voice, but is unable to breathe out. The face turns bright red, and then purple,

and the eyes stare. This state may persist until the child passes out and falls to the floor. A few moments later he or she regains consciousness and continues as normal, though often more subdued. Breath-holding looks dramatic, but it is rarely a threat to health.

Causes and factors

Physical causes Before the age of about three years, a child's digestion is working close to maximum capacity and is easily disturbed. A common problem is the "liver congestion" pattern (page 23). If this is the basis of the trouble, the child usually has an enlarged or swollen abdomen, loose and often foul-smelling stools, and a pale face, perhaps with rosy cheeks or a greenish color round the mouth.

Irrational and wild behavior may be caused by toxins which have accumulated in the body and cannot be expelled. The toxins may have built up in the baby during life in the womb (page 17). This is more likely if the mother has taken certain medicines or been ill at this time. Anaesthetics during a difficult birth or cutting the umbilical cord too soon may also be causes.

After birth, sources of toxins include allergy to a natural component of foods, such as gluten (in wheat); too much sugar in the diet; reactions to immunization (page 27); or artificial colorings and flavorings in food.

Emotional causes Some behavioral problems are primarily emotional in origin. Most mothers have experienced their children reflecting their own moods (page 16). When family tensions run very high, the child may reflect what someone else in the family is actually feeling inside, and act it out. Children who are closest and dearest to their parents are strongly affected by these types of adult emotions.

Spiritual causes Some children fly into a terrific rage when they are crossed, simply because their will is so strong. These children are born with determination and understanding beyond their years. From an early age they have a keen moral sense, and are outraged by events which go against what they believe to be right.

The importance of diet

There are proven links between diet and behavior. So it is always vital to ensure that your child's diet is suitable. Do not overfeed, give regular meals, and avoid "rough" foods such as wholemeal bread, muesli and raw vegetables. Cut down on milk: research shows that too much cow's milk is linked to violent behavior. Eliminate toxins from your child's diet, such as artificial flavorings, colorings and preservatives. Some children benefit from organically grown foods, since they are affected by even minute traces of artificial fertilizers and pesticides.

All sources of toxin or allergy must be eliminated for successful results. It can be very difficult to identify the source of an allergy, but it well repays the effort. A child who shows signs of malicious behavioral may well be allergic to milk, peanuts or oranges.

TREATMENT FOR BEHAVIORAL PROBLEMS

Parents with badly behaved children are strongly advised to contact a practitioner of natural medicine, who will be able to assist in accurate diagnosis. This is the key to successful treatment.

Herbs

Note: See page 40 for doses and cautions for herbs.
• If poor digestion seems to be the cause – Black root (*Leptandra virginica*) and Fringe tree (*Chionanthus virginica*). For a few days after starting treatment, the baby or child may pass some foul-smelling stools, and behavior and sleep patterns may worsen. Do not be discouraged, but continue

giving the remedy. Stop only if the aggravated behavior persists for more than a week.

Homoeopathy

Note: See page 54 for dosages and cautions for homoeopathic remedies.
• If poor digestion seems to be the cause – consider China, Nux vomica, Chamomilla or Calc. carb.

Bach remedies

Note: See page 66 for information on Bach remedies.
Bach remedies can be very successful for behavioral problems. Indeed, their very origins are based on an

individual's emotional and spiritual nature. Consult the relevant pages for details.

"Owning the emotions"

When a child's tantrums and rages are a reflection of those around, the first step is to locate the problem. Next time it happens, stop for a moment and ask yourself: "Who really feels like this?" Is lying on the ground, kicking and screaming, what you would really like to do? Your inner voice may well answer: "Yes, that's just how I feel!" Once the voice answers, often the child suddenly feels better. You have taken back your emotion and "own" it once again.

171

Skin problems and injuries

The body's self-renewing outer covering has many functions. It protects internal organs, insulates from too much heat or cold, and keeps body fluids in and other fluids out. Good personal hygiene is essential to keep the skin healthy and functioning well. And so is a balanced diet that provides the correct nutrients (page 32).

The state of the skin is an indication of the general health. If a skin problem arises, it is usually due to an internal disorder. For example, many of the typical childhood diseases such as measles (page 124) are accompanied by a skin rash or spots, and eczema (page 174) is related to poor digestion. In natural medicine, this is considered to be the result of accumulated poisons being "thrown out" of the body by the disease process.

In traditional Chinese medicine, the skin is said to be the "third lung". The practical consquence of this is that treatments for the skin can affect the lungs. For example, the orthodox steroid drugs used against eczema may sometimes "push the eczema inwards" and contribute to asthma (page 104).

Difficulties of diagnosis

Skin rashes of various kinds are a common childhood problem (see opposite). Besides the rashes that accompany childhood diseases such as chickenpox and rubella, there are many others which come and go in a vague manner. They are notoriously difficult to diagnose, even for experienced practitioners. The rash in such a straightforward disease as measles can occasionally be mistaken for something else. This is because new strains of virus have evolved during the last 50 years which mimic measles and cause a similar sort of rash.

If your child develops such a rash or a related skin disorder, and there are no accompanying symptoms which clearly indicate the diagnosis, it is wise to consult a practitioner of natural or orthodox medicine. Skin problems are rarely a threat to life, but they affect appearance and may cause scarring. This could well have a significant effect on your child's confidence and social outlook.

Injuries and trauma

Also included in this section of the book are problems caused by the knocks, falls, burns, scratches and scrapes of accidental injuries. Many of these affect the skin and the tissues immediately beneath, and many of them can be treated by natural medicines – in combination with orthodox medical measures as necessary.

If you suspect your child has suffered a serious injury, such as a broken bone, then do not hesitate to summon the emergency services at the first possible opportunity. Following such urgent action, it is worthwhile using herbal remedies and other natural medicines as first-aid measures to ease pain and give comfort. When injured or in pain, most of us respond in a positive way to being given medicine or some other treatment. When your child sees you taking action, he or she will be put more at ease, knowing that help is at hand. Above all, remain calm and confident. Try not to transmit worry and anxiety to your child, since this may weaken and deflect his or her healing energies.

During the recovery period, natural therapies can also be used to promote healing. This applies especially to mothers and babies who have undergone a difficult childbirth (page 183).

SKIN RASHES

Skin rashes are common in childhood. In some cases there are other symptoms that indicate one of the children's infectious diseases (page 122). However, in many cases the rash is difficult to diagnose, and it is usually advisable to obtain a practitioner's opinion.

Causes and factors In natural medicine, rashes are considered to be caused by poisons in the body. In the past, rashes were seen in the later stages of feverish diseases, and they were much feared. Nowadays, these fevers are rarely seen, and most rashes result from expulsion of poisons, often associated with "latent heat" (page 26).

The poisons come from a variety of sources. As explained more fully on page 126, every child is born with some accumulated poison, and it is beneficial to rid the body of it during the disease of measles. In children immunized against measles, mumps and rubella (german measles), the normal way for these poisons to be expelled is blocked. As a result, rashes without fever are more common. They come and go without obvious cause up to the age of about 14, and may linger for months.

Physical causes of rashes include the accumulation of latent heat, too much meat or sugar, excessive amounts of fruit juice, and a food allergy.

Emotional causes are more likely in children over seven years of age. Your child may have not yet learned to communicate his or her feelings, or may be under intense pressure at school.

General care

For any rash, always consider your child's diet. Ensure that he or she eats plenty of fresh natural foods and avoids red meat, spicy or fatty foods, sugar, fruit juice, and foods with preservatives and colorings. Bear in mind the possibility of an allergic reaction.

Consider also the emotional factors behind the rash, and see if anything can be done to alleviate them. Make sure your child has enough sleep (page 20) and plenty of physical exercise.

TREATMENT FOR SKIN RASHES

The most effective therapy is usually homoeopathy, but the treatment is relatively complex and not easy to carry out at home, so it is advisable to consult a practitioner.

Herbs

Note: See page 40 for dosages and cautions for herbs.
• Echinacea (*Echinacea purpurea*).

• Burdock (*Arctium lappa*), especially to clear a rash left after a severe attack of chickenpox.

Homoeopathy

Note: See page 54 for dosages and cautions for homoeopathic remedies.
• When the rash shows blisters like a nettle sting – Urtica urens.

• When the rash is very itchy – Sulphur may help.
• When the rash is red and burning – Ars. alb.

Bach flower remedies

Note: See page 66 for information on Bach remedies. Consult each remedy's indications for your child's individual case.

ECZEMA AND CRADLE CAP

The red, sore-looking skin rash of eczema is one of the commonest of childhood complaints. Orthodox medicine can do relatively little to cure it, the best being to alleviate the symptoms with external application of creams and ointments (such as those containing cortisone and other "steroids"). In contrast, natural medicines are often successful in promoting a permanent cure of the condition.

Cradle cap is the scaly, dirty-looking crust on the scalp which appears in some babies. Although it does not closely resemble eczema, and usually disappears as the baby grows, it has the same underlying cause as eczema.

Physical causes

In Chinese medicine, the cause of childhood eczema is simple – it is due to a malfunctioning digestive system. Before birth, a baby receives nourishment from the mother through the umbilical cord, so the baby's digestive system does not have to work. After birth, one of the biggest problems the baby faces is digesting food. Relative to size, a baby's food requirements are enormous, in order to provide for growth. This can lead to the "liver congestion" pattern of illness (page 23). In otherwise healthy children, poisons rise up to the skin's surface, causing eczema.

Emotional factors On the emotional plane, eczema arises from hidden feelings or the inability to communicate feelings and be understood. When a child is under stress, and feels something strongly but cannot express these feelings, this can affect the digestion and give rise to eczema. As noted on page 18, children under seven years do not normally restrain their feelings, and so this is not a common cause for eczema in babies – although it may be a contributing factor. It is, however, the major factor after seven years of age.

Eczema and asthma Eczema and asthma (page 104) are closely related – in Chinese medicine, the skin is said to be the "third lung". In children who have weak lungs, eczema may easily develop into asthma. On the physical level, poisons which cause eczema when "they rise" to the skin can also "go inwards" to the lungs. On the emotional level, the same restrained feelings which give rise to eczema can cause asthma.

Symptoms and types of eczema

There are three main types of eczema: wet, dry, and itching. They all originate from the liver congestion pattern of illness, the differences being due to the constitution of the individual child.

Eczema commonly occurs behind the ears, in the creases of the elbows and at the backs of the knees, but it can appear virtually anywhere on the body. It commonly develops first at three to six months old – a time of great stress to the baby's digestive system.

Wet eczema The affected patches of skin ooze when scratched, and in severe cases bubbles of fluid form under the surface. The imbalance in the digestive system leads to accumulation of water in the tissues and is often accompanied by loose stools or diarrhea.

Dry eczema The surface is dry, with branlike scales which come off when rubbed. Underneath, the skin is red and sometimes bleeding. In Chinese medicine, this change is believed to be due to mucus

174

accumulating under the skin. The digestive imbalance produces this accumulation of thick mucus in the tissues, and is
often due to an "echo" disease (page 25).

Itching eczema The skin is usually red and
itches intensely – the child wants to
scratch and scratch, until the surface is
broken and bleeding. In Chinese medicine, the skin irritation is considered to be
due to impurities and poisons under the
skin. Often the child is constipated.

Diet

It is important to find foods that suit your
baby or child. When the digestion is
functioning well, the eczema will disappear. The main points are as follows:

Breastfed babies Give your baby regular
feeds, and not too much at a time. If he or
she has a large appetite, you may have to
be strong-minded in stopping your baby
from overfeeding or too much demand
feeding. Try the same remedies as for the
"internal heat" or "hot" type of vomiting
(page 143).

Make sure that your baby is burped
(winded) properly after feeds, and that he
or she does not go to sleep immediately
after eating. And avoid foods yourself
which may cause your baby's eczema – in
particular cheese, cow's milk, roast
peanuts, red meats, greasy foods, or rich
and spicy foods.

Bottlefed babies Most babies with eczema
have difficulty digesting cow's milk. Consider a temporary change to goat's milk or
soya milk. If these are not available, make
cow's milk more digestible by simmering
it for 15 minutes with half an onion.
Commercial brands of easy-to-digest milk

formulas are available from pharmacies
and on prescription. Make sure your baby
is not overfed. Give regular bottles, and
not too much at one time.

Weaned babies and toddlers If your baby
drinks a lot of milk, change from cow's
milk to goat's or soya milk. Avoid cheese
and peanuts (including peanut butter).
And watch out for any other foods you
suspect may be causing the problem –
especially orange juice.

Follow the guidelines for weaning your
baby (page 31). Avoid prawns, shrimps
and shellfish. Serve regular meals, and
not too much food at each serving. Try to
prevent snacks, particularly sweets, bis-
cuits and chocolates.

For older children, it may help to mix
linseed oil in the food, about half a
teaspoon each day.

Be on your guard for food allergy or
intolerance. There may be something in
your child's diet which is causing the
eczema. Check that there are no artificial
colorings, flavorings or preservatives
present. Typical foods which may cause an
allergic reaction are eggs, chicken, honey
and mucus-producing foods (page 36). To
find out if your child has an allergy,
remove the suspected food for a week –
introduce a diet of rice and carrots, and
note any effects.

General care and recovery

Do not apply cortisone cream (the orthodox medical treatment) unless the eczema
is very serious. Cortisone treats the symptoms effectively, but it makes the skin
more sensitive, and it pushes the poisons
back into the body. The suppressed
poisons may weaken the lungs and make
the child more susceptible to asthma. Do

175

not be worried by the appearance of the eczema. It may look unpleasant, but a problem which is only skin-deep is rarely a serious threat to health.

Beware of soap powders and detergents used for washing nappies and clothes, which may irritate your child's skin.

Recovery A common reaction to all treatments is that the eczema worsens before it gets better. So do not be discouraged! Usually, any change after the treatment is a change for the better. A baby may be irritable for a few days after treatment starts, and there may be some flatulence

and several rather bad-smelling nappies as the decomposed food and poisons are expelled. As treatment progresses, you should see a change in mood. Rough, violent children usually become calmer and more pleasant. Quiet, docile types, on the other hand, become more vigorous and assertive. This may cause initial disruption, but eventually such children become more enjoyable, being more positive and less of a "doormat".

If no changes at all occur after a week of treatment, this indicates that the remedies are not effective in your child's particular case, so select alternatives.

TREATMENT FOR ECZEMA AND CRADLE CAP

Since eczema is always related to digestion, it is essential to pay attention to your child's diet (page 175). Only then can other types of therapies help.

Herbs

Note: See page 40 for dosages and cautions for herbs.
- Give 20 drops of a tincture consisting of 3 parts Burdock (*Arctium lappa*), 3 parts Butternut (*Juglans cinerea*) and 1 part Black root (*Leptandra virginica*). Take 3 times daily. Half dose for under 3 years old, quarter dose for under 1 year old.
- Other herbs which may help are Nettle (*Urtica urens*), Sarsparilla (*Smilax officinalis*), Dandelion (*Taraxacum vulgare*) or Dock (*Rumex crispus*).

Bach remedies

Note: See page 66 for information on Bach remedies.

These are helpful for all babies and children. There is no specific remedy. Each child should be considered as an individual.

External treatments

The following remedies, applied directly to the affected skin, are available from many pharmacies and natural medicine suppliers. Always follow the instructions on the package.
- For dry skin – orthodox moisturizing creams.
- For dry skin and to soothe heat and soreness – Marigold (*Calendula*) cream.
- To relieve itching – Urtica

lotion or ointment.
- For heat and soreness – Plantain (*Plantago*) ointment.
- To relieve pain and itching – Bach Flower Rescue remedy ointment.
- For cradle cap – Olive oil rubbed into the scalp, left on overnight and washed out next morning.
- Add a 5mls teaspoon of "baby oil" or 1 cup of Chamomile tea (*Anthemis nobilis*) to the bath water, to relieve itching. Or 2-3 drops of Bach Rescue remedy in the bath water should relieve pain and itching.

BOILS

Boils are raised, round, infected spots on the skin. They start at about five millimeters (less than half an inch) in diameter. In mild cases they grow only a little larger, while in severe cases the swelling and redness may extend for up to five centimeters (two inches) across.

At first a boil is merely a raised patch of skin. As time goes on it turns a deep red or purple color, becomes swollen and painful, and then a white or yellowish "head" appears in the middle where the pus collects. Usually head formation is a turning point. If the boil is lanced (see details on page 178) so that the pus can flow out, healing starts.

Causes and factors

Most boils are due to infection by staphylococcal bacteria. The infection is localized (restricted to the area of the boil), and the body reacts by fighting the bacteria with the white cells of its immune system. Many white cells and bacteria die in the process, forming pus.

In natural medicine, it is believed that boils cannot occur unless the balance of the body is disturbed, allowing the bacteria to thrive. This imbalance is often characterized by poor fat metabolism, which leads to a greasy or dirty skin, and for this reason the condition is often known as "impure blood".

Physical factors Boils arise when more rich foods are eaten than can be transformed properly inside the body. A lot of rich food can be utilized if plenty of exercise is taken, but if your child lives an indoor or sedentary life, then the excess proteins and fats cannot be digested properly and are likely to lead to boils. Peanuts, eggs, chicken and dark meats are particularly to be avoided, while fresh vegetables are

---

THE USE OF ANTIBIOTICS

Orthodox medical treatment may involve antibiotics. These have a striking effect on boils, making them disappear in a day or two. But although this approach produces quick results, it is not the best in the long term – except when the child's health is seriously threatened. Antibiotic drugs do not solve the underlying problem. Instead, they simply suppress or even compound it (page 82).

---

encouraged. If your child will not eat fresh fruits and vegetables, vitamin and mineral supplements may help.

Mental and emotional factors Boils are more likely to occur when too much mental effort is combined with lack of attention to the physical body and not enough time for play. If a child does not get sufficient sleep (page 20), he or she may become irritable and angry – emotions characteristically associated with boils.

General care, diet and recovery

Ensure your child has enough rest and time to play, and encourage plenty of physical exercise rather than too much concentrated mental activity.

Avoid eggs, dark meats, chicken and peanuts. Provide plenty of fresh vegetables; if these are in short supply, vitamin and mineral supplements can be given and may be of assistance.

Recovery Besides helping to cure the boils, the internal remedies should make the child more cheerful and lively, and able to tackle problems more effectively. This may take several days, or even weeks in stubborn cases. If boils recur regularly, you have probably not yet found the root of the problem. It may help to seek the advice of a practitioner of natural medicine, who will examine your child physically, and also form an impression of your child's personality and of your family's general lifestyle. In very rare cases, frequently recurring boils indicate a more deep-rooted medical problem such as diabetes, which is causing the bodily imbalance. If you suspect this, it is wise to consult an orthodox medical practitioner.

TREATMENT FOR BOILS

External treatments

- Apply a poultice to the boil. An established remedy is China clay (Kaolin), but Marshmallow leaves or root (*Althea officinalis*), Comfrey (*Symphytum officinalis*), and Burdock leaves or root (*Arctium lappa*), also make excellent poultices.

China clay comes in moist form, but the herbs are prepared by moistening the dried herb and mashing it gently in warm water. This preparation is placed on a gauze pad and applied to the boil. It calms the pain and "draws out" the boil to a head.

Change the poultice 2-3 times daily – more frequently if there is much discharge – until the pain eases and the boil has gone down.

Herbs

Note: See page 40 for dosages and cautions for herbs.

Take the herbs internally in the standard way. For each one, give the child 50mgs 2 times daily. Half dosage under 3 years of age.

- When there is phlegm, and a yellow coat on the tongue – try Echinacea (*Echinacea purpurea*).
- When there is a watery discharge from the nose or loose stools – add Tormentil (*Potentilla tormentilla*).
- When there is constipation, and the child is lethargic and irritable – add Licorice (*Glycyrrhiza glabra*).
- Elecampane (*Inula helenium*) may also be helpful.

Homoeopathy

Note: See page 54 for dosages and cautions for homoeopathic remedies.

Give each remedy 3 times daily.
- In the initial stages, when the skin is red, swollen and itchy, and the glands are swollen – Rhus tox.
- As the boil turns purple and forms a head, and especially if the child feels hot and is generally irritable, miserable and selfish – Sulphur.
- When the boil has turned purple and there is a burning, stinging pain from the site and the area around – Tar. arv.

Tissue salts

Note: See page 64 for information on tissue salts.
- Nat. sulph. 3 times daily.

Lancing a boil

When the head forms, a boil is often at its most painful, due to the pressure of the pus collecting under the surface. This can be relieved by piercing, or lancing, the skin to allow pus to escape. For small boils this can be done safely in the home.

Use a fine, sharp needle that has been sterilized by passing the point slowly through a match flame. Gently pierce the skin with the cooled needle. Mop up the pus over a few minutes, and dress the boil with a clean covering.

For large, "angry"-looking boils, it is wise to consult a practitioner of orthodox or natural medicine for advice on lancing.

INJURIES AND TRAUMA

Cuts, grazes, bites and stings

Minor cuts and grazes can be dealt with at home, but for more serious ones, take your child straight to an orthodox medical doctor or emergency center. Orthodox medicine is especially good at treating such injuries. However, natural medicines can help to reduce pain and permanent damage, and accelerate healing. If a wound or sting becomes infected, with yellow or green pus and an increase in swelling, tenderness and pain, orthodox medical treatment is by antibiotic drugs. There are natural alternatives which are usually effective (see below).

NATURAL MEDICINES FOR EMERGENCIES

Ointments	Uses
Calendula	Antiseptic, cooling, may be applied safely to wounds and first degree burns
Green ointment	Antiseptic, cooling, healing (page 184), detoxifying, antirheumatic, may be applied safely to wounds, first degree burns, bruises, insect bites, sprains
Hypericum	Relieves pain, especially effective for pain from superficial nerves as in grazes or fingers shut in the door
Sage	Antiseptic, assists in formation of healing scar tissue

Tincture	Uses
Arnica	For external application to reduce swellings

Homoeopathy	Uses
Arnica	May be taken internally for all bruises and swellings from injury
Ledum	Taken internally to reduce the pain from being pierced by a sharp object
Staphisagria	Relieves the pain of jagged, lacerated wounds
Hypericum	Relieves the pain of grazes and assists healing
Ferr. phos.	Assists recovery if much blood or body fluid has been lost

TREATMENT FOR CUTS AND GRAZES

- If there is much bleeding, stop the flow of blood by pressure over the wound.
- Clean the wound. Remove all foreign objects and dirt, and apply a natural antiseptic ointment such as Calendula or wash in antiseptic water.
- If there is much pain, as in a graze – apply Hypericum ointment.
- If there is a lot of bleeding or the cut is deep – put powdered Sage (*Salvia officinalis*) on the wound. This helps to stop the blood flow and assists scab formation.
- Cover the wound with a sterile dressing (such as an adhesive plaster).

- Check the wound and replace the dressing daily.
- Administer natural remedies to reduce shock and promote healing – such as Arnica or Bach Rescue remedy.
- If the wound is from a sharp pointed instrument such as a needle, give homoeopathic Ledum.

Infected (septic) wounds

- Echinacea (*Echinacea purpurea*). Give either as tablets, 50mgs 3 times daily for children (half dosage for babies), or as a tea. This reduces pus formation.

- An alternative to Echinacea is homoeopathic Hep. sulph. 3 times daily.
- Apply a thin film of Garlic paste to the wound for 20-30 minutes, 3 times daily (no longer, because garlic oil may burn the flesh). Garlic is a natural antibiotic and promotes tissue repair when applied externally.
- An alternative to Garlic is Papaya, which should be crushed into a paste, and may be kept on the wound in a thin layer for 2-3 hours at a time.

TREATMENT FOR BITES AND STINGS

The pain from a bite or sting can be considerably reduced by quick application of an antidote. Follow this with a natural ointment such as Green ointment (page 184).

Antidotes and ointment

- Bee stings are acidic and can be neutralized by an alkali such as bicarbonate of soda ("bicarb").
- Wasp stings, being alkaline, are neutralized by an acid such as vinegar or lemon juice. (Remember this as Bees for Bicarbonate of soda, and Wasps for "Winegar".)

- Irritation and itching from insect bites can be considerably reduced by quickly applying Green ointment (page 184). This is particularly so for mosquito and horsefly bites.

Homoeopathy

Note: See page 54 for doses and cautions for homoeopathic remedies.

Choose the remedy according to how the child reacts. Give 30X potency, if available, 3 times daily.
- When the affected part goes cold and is either numb or very sensitive to touch –

administer Ledum 30X.
- If pain shoots up the limb from the bite – Hypericum 30X.
- If there is a stinging pain and rapid swelling around the site – Apis 30X.
- If the part turns red and feels burning hot – Cantharis 30X.
- If the part goes blue and burning hot – Tar. cub. 30X.

Bruises, sprains and broken bones

Natural remedies can relieve much of the discomfort and suffering which accompany these injuries. In mild cases, treatment may be given at home. Serious injuries should receive attention from an orthodox medical doctor or emergency center with natural remedies being administered as part of first aid. In the case of a head injury, treat as for a bruise – even if there are no signs of bruising. Natural remedies can considerably reduce the likelihood of concussion. After a head injury, quickly take your child to a hospital or medical center for a check-up.

TREATMENTS FOR BRUISES, SPRAINS AND BROKEN BONES

Bruises

- Apply either Green ointment (page 184) or Arnica tincture externally.
- Give homoeopathic Arnica internally.

These remedies should considerably reduce swelling and pain. If there is deep bruising, they bring the bruises to the surface and so speed healing.

Sprains

Note: See page 54 for dosages and cautions for homoeopathic remedies.
- Treat bruising as above.
- Then, if there is swelling around the sprain – apply Green ointment or Arnica tincture.
- Give homoeopathic Rhus tox. hourly for 6 hours, then reduce the dose to 3 times daily for 2 weeks.
- If the joint near the injury becomes swollen and painful on the slightest movement – homoeopathic Bryonia 30X, 3 times daily, until the swelling subsides.

- If the injury is deep and near a bone – homoeopathic Ruta 3 times daily for 3 weeks.
- If the sprain is still not relieved – homoeopathic Hypericum 3 times daily for 2 weeks.
- If the sprain persists, or your child remains in pain or uncomfortable, consult a practitioner of natural medicine.

Broken bones

Broken bones require emergency medical attention.
- Before professional help is available, pain and swelling can be considerably reduced by administering homoeopathic Arnica or the Bach Rescue remedy.
- After the bone has been set – Comfrey (*Symphytum officinalis*) as a tea. Infuse 1 heaped 5mls teaspoon of herb in a mug of water, and give to the child 3 times daily. (The old name for comfrey is "knit-bone".)
- Homoeopathic remedies include Calc. phos. and Ruta.

Other therapies

- Acupuncture is especially effective for sprains.
- Acupuncture and hand healing can be helpful for bones that are slow to mend.

Caution

Some children seem hardly affected by small bones which are broken, such as in the wrist or foot. However it is important to obtain medical advice in such cases. If the bones mend and knit together out of alignment, this may cause deformity, aching and other problems later in life. If in doubt, always consult a medical practitioner.

181

Burns and scalds (includes sunburn)

Burns are caused by dry heat, such as electricity, flames or chemicals. Scalds are caused by moist heat – usually boiling liquids or steam. The effect of burns and scalds are similar, as are the treatments.

In a first degree burn, damage is superficial, limited to the outer layer of skin, and marked by redness, warmth and tenderness, and sometimes blistering. Although initially painful, these burns are rarely dangerous unless they cover a relatively large area.

Sunburn (see opposite) is a first degree burn, which may be accompanied by swelling and fever. Natural medicines can considerably reduce these reactions. However, sunburn is more easily prevented, by the usual measures such as graduated exposure, avoiding exposure around midday when the sun's rays are strongest, and using a sunscreen lotion.

In a second degree burn, the damage extends deeper, affecting the lower skin layers, and causing blisters. Third degree burns affect all the skin layers and expose raw, seared tissue beneath.

FIRST AID AND TREATMENT FOR BURNS AND SCALDS

Urgent actions

• Quickly remove clothing saturated in boiling water or corrosive chemicals. If the clothes are smouldering, but are not burnt, remove them carefully. Leave burnt clothing in place, as this forms a protective layer against the skin, reducing the risk of fluid loss and infection.
• Remove any restricting items such as watches, bracelets, bangles, rings, belts or shoes, in case of swelling.
• For mild (first degree) burns – immediately plunge the affected area into cold water, or spray with a cold shower, or keep under running cold water, or apply an ice pack, for at least 10 minutes. This reduces the heat, pain and inflammation, and prevents the burn's effects and damage from going

any deeper into the tissues.
• Leave blisters intact, to reduce the risk of infection.
• Cover the burn with a sterile dressing or clean cloth. A clean, dry sheet may be used if a proper dressing is not available.
• For second and third degree burns – summon urgent medical aid. DO NOT IMMERSE THE BURN IN WATER. Treat for shock, giving the Bach Rescue remedy.

Herbs

Note: See page 40 for dosages and cautions for herbs.
• If the skin is unbroken – apply Aloe vera gel or a natural burn ointment such as Weleda ointment or Green ointment (page 184). This inhibits inflammation and should bring relief.

• If the skin is broken – apply Calendula (*Calendula officinalis*) ointment, from a tube rather than a jar, to reduce risk of cross-infection. Calendula (Marigold) is both cooling and antiseptic.

Homoeopathy

Note: See page 54 for doses and cautions for homoeopathic remedies.
The remedies can be used for all burns and may be combined with orthodox treatment.
• For burning pain, inflammation and blistering – Cantharis 3X or 6X, hourly.
• For deeper burns that destroy the skin, causing blisters and burning pains – Kali bich. 3X or 6X 2-hourly.
• For weeping and suppuration after burns – Hep. sulph. every 4 hours.

SUNBURN

Natural medicines can ease the mild kinds of burns caused by over-exposure to the sun.

- For pain and burning – apply Calendula and Hypericum ointments.
- To relieve pain – cut a tomato in two and gently apply to the site.
- For pain and burning – homoeopathic Causticum 6X.
- For swelling and fever – homoeopathic Apis. mel. 6X taken internally.

Orthodox surgery

If your baby or child undergoes orthodox medical surgery, natural medicines given both before and after the operation can assist in strengthening the body and dispelling the effects of the trauma. Homoeopathy is the principle home therapy in this situation. Of the other natural treatments, acupuncture and healing are also effective if given before and afterwards. The effect is to bring vitality to the part of the body that is operated on, so that it can better withstand the trauma, and the healing process takes place more quickly. In China, the use of acupuncture after surgery reduces recuperation time by up to one-half, and also lessens complications.

Difficult or premature childbirth

If your child was born prematurely, or if you and your baby went through a difficult birth, then it is likely that you will both be in a state of shock.

Once the immediate problem of survival is dealt with, it is advisable to contact a practitioner of natural medicine as soon as possible – for both mother and child. Therapies of particular help in this situation are homoeopathy, acupuncture, cranial osteopathy (for the baby) and also the Bach remedies.

TREATMENT FOR SURGERY OR DIFFICULT CHILDBIRTH

Homoeopathy

Note: See page 54 for dosages and cautions for homoeopathic remedies.
- Before surgery – Arnica 3 times daily for 2 days before the operation.
- After surgery – Arnica every 2 hours for the first 12 hours, then 3 times daily for at least 2 weeks.
- If Arnica is used, it is unlikely that wounds will turn septic. If they do, give homoeopathic Hypericum.
- After a difficult or premature birth, as a simple first aid measure – Arnica, 3 times daily for both mother and child.

Bach remedies

Note: See page 66 for information on Bach remedies.
- Bach Rescue remedy helps to diminish the trauma of an operation and aids recovery after a difficult birth. Give 3 times daily for a week.
- Other Bach remedies may also help any mental or emotional problems. See the indications for each remedy, for further details.

THE HOME NATURAL MEDICINE CHEST

Most households have a cupboard some-where for pills, ointments and similar items. If you become interested in natural medicines, it is worthwhile building up a basic stock of commonly-used remedies.

As explained on page 10, most people find that they are instinctively drawn to one type of natural therapy, such as herbs, or homoeopathy. The basic medicine chest provides a good starting point from which you can explore your use of natural medicines and their effects on your family. Then, as you progress, you can stock more of the types of remedies with which you feel comfortable. Remember that therapeutic massages may also be used with the natural remedies, or with orthodox medicines.

The medicine chest should be in a convenient place and readily accessible, even in the middle of the night, but it should be inaccessible to children.

When ill, most of us respond to something being done. Be calm, confident and encouraging as you give the remedy to your child.

GREEN OINTMENT

This traditional remedy is based on Green or Elder-leaf oil (*Sambucus nigra*), once widely available from pharmacists as "Oleum viride". Today you will probably have to make both it and Hypericum oil (another ingredient of Green ointment) at home. However, it is well worth the effort.

Press about 150-200 grams (about 10oz) of freshly-picked Elder leaves into a clean glass jar, as tightly as possible. Add about 500mls (0.75pt) of pure olive oil, to cover the leaves. Secure the top and leave to stand for about four weeks.

Then press out the oil, using either a muslin or nylon "forcing bag", or a fruit press. Both of these items are available at general stores or shops, and are helpful in preparing various herbal tinctures and syrups.

At the same time, prepare Hypericum oil from the flowers and leaves of St John's Wort (*Hypericum perfoliatum*), as for Elder oil.

To make the Green ointment, you will need:
- 25mls (0.75oz) of oil of Elder-leaf,
- 25mls (0.75oz) of oil of Hypericum,

- 8 grams (0.75oz) of beeswax,
- 20 drops of oil of Eucalyptus, and
- 3 drops of oil of Wintergreen.

These last three ingredients are available at good pharmacists or herbalists. Put the Elder-leaf oil, Hypericum oil and beeswax into a heatproof glass jar and immerse in boiling water until the beeswax melts. Add the Eucalyptus and Wintergreen oils, stir, cover at once (to keep the volatile oils) and allow to cool.

BASIC MEDICINE CHEST

Herbs

- Dried, powered Sage (*Salvia officinalis*) for wounds.
- Mother tincture of Arnica (*Arnica montana*).
- Green ointment.

Homoeopathic remedies

- Ars. alb., Arnica and Rhus tox., all at 6X potency.
- Chamomilla 3X teething granules, paste or a similar preparation.

Bach remedy

- The Rescue remedy.
  Also useful are cotton-wool balls, adhesive plasters, small forceps and similar equipment.

FURTHER NATURAL MEDICINES

Further herbs

If you are more inclined to use herbal remedies, stock the following as mother tinctures in 25mls dropper bottles:
- Black root (*Leptandra virginica*).
- Butternut (*Juglans cinerea*).
- Catmint (*Nepeta cataria*).
- Gentian (*Gentiana lutea*).
- Golden seal (*Hydrastis canadensis*).
- Licorice (*Glycyrrhiza glabra*).
- Lobelia (*Lobelia inflata*)
- Motherwort (*Leonurus cardiaca*).

In addition, keep supplies of these herbal syrups, often obtainable ready-made from health food stores and natural medicine suppliers:
- Elderflower and Peppermint.
- Horehound and Aniseed.
- Wild cherry.
- A general cough mixture such as Coltsfoot and Hyssop.
  Useful herbal pills include:
- Those containing Valerian (*Valeriana officinalis*) for sleeping problems.
- Echinacea (*Echinacea purpurea*) for spots and boils.

Suitable dried herbs, which should be replaced yearly, are:
- Chamomile (*Anthemis nobilis*) as the whole plant.
- Sage (*Salvia officinalis*) in seed form.
- Fennel (*Foeniculum vulgaris*) in seed form.
- Lime (*Tilia*) flowers.

Further homoeopathic remedies

If you are just beginning with homoeopathy, obtain a stock of the 12 tissue salts, which are closely related to the homoeopathic series of remedies (page 64).

As you progress, collect the following remedies at 6X potency:
- Aconite.
- Belladonna.
- Bryonia.
- Calc. carb.
- Carbo veg.
- Gelsemium.
- Ferr. phos.
- Merc. sol.
- Nat. mur.
- Nux vomica.
- Pulsatilla.
- Silica.
- Sulphur.
  (Ferr. phos., Nat. mur. and Silica are also tissue salts.)

Bach remedies

If there is one set of remedies that the author would advise above all others, for simple and safe home use, it is the Bach remedies.

185

RESOURCES

Further reading

Natural medicines and complementary therapies have become increasingly popular in recent years. As a consequence, many books and booklets have been published on these subjects. The following selected titles deal with specific therapies, such as herbs or homoeopathy, in greater depth – although most apply to adults and do not focus on children's remedies. Some titles are regularly revised and updated, so try to obtain the most recent edition. Consult a bookseller specializing in health and natural medicine publications, or ask your local practitioner of natural medicine for advice.

Herbs

● *Culpeper's Complete Herbal*, Nicholas Culpeper (editions by various publishers)
● *The Herb Book*, John Lust, Bantam Books
● *The Illustrated Herbal Handbook*, Juliette de Baracli Levy, Faber & Faber
● *A Modern Herbal*, Mrs Grieve, Penguin Books
● *The New Age Herbalist*, ed. Richard Mabey, Collier/Macmillan

Homoeopathy

● *Everybody's Guide to Homoeopathic Medicines*, Dr M Panos & J Heimlich
● *Homoeopathic Medicine: A Doctor's Guide to Remedies for Common Ailments*, Dr Trevor Smith
● *Homoeopathy: The Family Handbook*, Unwin Hyman
● *Pocket Manual of Materia Medica with Repertory*, Boericke (editions by various publishers)

Bach remedies

● *Bach Flower Therapy, Theory and Practice*, M Scheffer, Thorsons
● *Dictionary of Bach Flower Remedies*, T Hyne-Jones, CW Daniel Publishers
● *The Twelve Healers*, Dr E Bach, CW Daniel Publishers

186

Useful addresses

There are many stockists of natural medicines, including health food and whole food shops, and some pharmacies (chemist's shops). Look in your area business telephone directory, or ask your local practitioner of natural medicine for advice, or consult one of the organizations listed below. Numerous stockists operate a mail order service – write to them direct for further details.

To contact a practitioner of natural medicine, write to the appropriate organization as listed below for further advice. Some societies hold lists of qualified practitioners, or they will refer you to the relevant address.

Organizations and societies

• American Association of Naturopathic Physicians, Post Office Box 20386, Seattle, Washington 98102. Phone 206-323-7610
• American Holistic Medical Association and Foundation, 2002 Eastlake Avenue East, Seattle, Washington 98102. Phone 206-322-6842. (Write for details of their regular magazine)
• International Foundation for Homeopathy, 2366 Eastlake Avenue East, Suite 301, Seattle, Washington 98102. Phone 206-324-8230
• Ellon (Bach USA) Inc., PO Box 320, Woodmere, NY 11598

In addition, the following publish or review books on natural and holistic therapies:
• Eastland Press, 611 Post Avenue, Suite 3, Seattle, Washington 98104. Phone 206-587-6013
• Redwing Reviews, Redwing Book Co, 44 Linden Street, Brookline, Ma 02146. Phone 617-738-4664

INDEX

The main page reference for each major entry is printed in **bold** type. Page references to illustrations are in *italics*.

Acknowledgements

The author would like to thank: the doctors at the Nanjing College of Traditional Chinese Medicine, who were his teachers; Miss Chow Kwan Yun, for valuable advice and many new insights into homoeopathy; and Nichola Guest, for her help in many ways.

Gaia Books would like to thank: Jo and Francis Lofthouse, Sam and Joshua Nall, Alan and Martin Parker, Lucilla Scott, Anna Zalewska and Hazel Beecher for patiently modelling for the illustrations; Michele Staple, Libby Hoseason, Rosanne Hooper and Philippa Underwood for editorial assistance; Jane Parker for the index.

Photographic credits

Pages 9, 39, 122 Anthea Sieveking/Network; page 13 Ian West/Bubbles; page 19 Michael Boys/Susan Griggs Agency; page 30 Camilla Jessel; page 81 Loisjoy Thurston/Bubbles; pages 132, 160 Sandra Lousada/Susan Griggs Agency; page 134 Shona Wood.

Approximate equivalents

One drop = 0.04mls (page 42)
One teacup = 8fl ozs = 250mls (page 40)
One tablespoon = 15mls
One teaspoon = 5mls (page 40)
One wineglass = 2fl ozs = 100mls (page 41)